THE CROSS
& THE
CONSTITUTION

"Allan Erickson speaks for millions of people of faith in a forceful, clear, and thoughtful voice. In the end, I may not agree with all his conclusions and commentary, but they are dependably provocative and persuasive."

—Michael Medved, bestselling author of *The 10 Big Lies about America* and nationally syndicated talk radio host

"We have known Allan Erickson for over ten years and admire him not only as a writer but a speaker too. He is a man of faith with strong moral convictions; a patriot who loves his country and a husband and father who loves his family. His writing style is much like how he speaks. He is insightful, poignant, and touching. He is not afraid to tackle subjects he is well informed on. We always look forward to reading his articles and sharing them with our friends and family. We are very excited about the prospect of an upcoming book."

—Craig and Carol Vetter
Vetter Corporation, Carmel, CA
www.craigvetter.com

"As someone who has known Allan Erickson for years and enjoyed his incisive writings, keen analytical mind and quick wit for almost as long, I was very pleased to hear that he has decided to write a book. Even before he took to the blogosphere and affiliated with various organizations, I was fortunate to partake of his offerings on the phone and in emails. Allan's take on the world around us is always enlightening and stimulating. He consistently takes apart the liberal argument and puts progressives in their place. He doesn't suffer fools easily, no matter what their political or social status might be. One doesn't have to observe his excellent logic and punditry long to see that there is clearly a strong spiritual and moral anchor guiding him."

—Bill Hemingway
CEO and Chairman (Retired),
Bellatrix Systems, Inc.
Lt. Col., USMC (Retired)

"I have known Allan for three years. I know that he is passionate about what he believes in. That passion carries over into all of his writings. I know from personal experience that he is a man who not only 'talks the talk,' but 'walks the walk.'"

—Scott Jones
Dundee, OR
Retired Police Officer
Father of a Purple Heart Marine

THE CROSS & THE CONSTITUTION

In the Age of Incoherence

ALLAN ERICKSON

The Cross and the Constitution
Copyright © 2011 by Allan Erickson. All rights reserved.

No part of this publication may be reproduced, stored in a retrieval system or transmitted in any way by any means, electronic, mechanical, photocopy, recording or otherwise without the prior permission of the author except as provided by USA copyright law.

All scripture quotations, unless otherwise indicated, are taken from the *Holy Bible, New International Version®*, "NIV." Copyright © 1973, 1978, 1984 by Biblica, Inc. Used by permission of Zondervan. All rights reserved worldwide. www.zondervan.com

Scripture quotations marked "MSG" are taken from *The Message*, Copyright © 1993, 1994, 1995, 1996, 2000, 2001, 2002. Used by permission of NavPress Publishing Group. All rights reserved.

The opinions expressed by the author are not necessarily those of Tate Publishing, LLC.

Published by Tate Publishing & Enterprises, LLC
127 E. Trade Center Terrace | Mustang, Oklahoma 73064 USA
1.888.361.9473 | www.tatepublishing.com

Tate Publishing is committed to excellence in the publishing industry. The company reflects the philosophy established by the founders, based on Psalm 68:11,
"The Lord gave the word and great was the company of those who published it."

Book design copyright © 2011 by Tate Publishing, LLC. All rights reserved.
Cover design by Kellie Vincent
Interior design by Sarah Kirchen
Photo by Nicholas Butler, Bella Photo Works, Orland, FL

Published in the United States of America

ISBN: 978-1-61346-487-8
1. Political Science / General
2. Political Science / Essays
11.11.03

There is one very special person
without whom I'd never have written a word.

Countless hours she handled the hundreds of details
involved in running a household, freeing me up to write.

She patiently kept life and limb together, as the writing and
the time involved meant sacrifice in several ways.

Always encouraging and willing to give me valued feedback,
she is as much the author.

So this first book is dedicated to my dear wife, Jodi.

ACKNOWLEDGMENTS

I cannot recall where I heard it or read it, but it is, in my opinion, the best definition of *humility:* "Believing that everything you are and everything you hope to be are gifts from God and other people."

Therefore, thank you, LORD, for the gifts and the people in my life, people who've inspired me and taught me and confronted me when I needed it: my dear folks; my precious kids; Nancy Matthias; Jim Simpson; Harris Sherline; Gil and Nan Moore; Kent Munro; Bob and Peg Chadwick; Bill and Katy Hemingway; Rev. Jim Watson; Craig and Carol Vetter; Rev. Dick Sartwell; Megan Palmer and the staff at Tate Publishing; Jay Jamieson, MD; Edwin Espana; Rev. Abraham Rababy; Rev. Kent Walton; Rev. Jeff Getsinger; Rev. Shaun McNay; Tito Molfino; Arlen Williams; David Crowe; Debbie Higgins; Randy E. King; the men at Saturday Morning Fellowship; the Quaker elders in Newberg; Michael Medved; Sally Vaci; Rev. Shawn Anderson; Roger and Betty Jamieson; Rev. Kevin Kopsa; Teresa Mancinelli; Lars Larson; Yamhill County Tea Party; Veritas School personnel, especially Bryan Lynch; cousin Pam; sister Cindy; the men at the Antelope, Oregon, retreat summer 2010; Gail Wickersham; Jay Martin; Jack Crabtree; Scott Jones, Garrett Jones; James Higgins; Marcus Glimpse; Derek Jones; Joe Crabtree; Rob Cornilles; Guy Glimpse; Jeff Jones; Ken Parker; and John Dick, KKMC.

"What the founders feared most has come to pass: we have created an enormously powerful federal government, now presiding over a desperately split and antagonistic population. Combine this reality with looming bankruptcy and unprecedented foreign threats, and we are found standing on the edge, staring into the abyss."

AE

TABLE OF CONTENTS

Introduction.................................... 17

A Prediction.................................... 19

Post Ground Zero Angst: Life and Work,
Fear and the Future 20

The Oyster...................................... 27

The Storm after the Storm 30

Letter from Uncle Sam 34

No Peace, No Honor, No Strategy................. 38

The Mass Psychology of Surrender 44

Asking Charlie Gibson a Few Questions 47

Bill Maher: Man of Faith 52

Ariana Huffington: War Profiteer 54

Pastors Becoming Political Activists:
Intentionally Provoking the IRS 58

Nine Terrifying Words 61

Will We Prefer the Calm of Despotism?................ 65

Anybody Notice We're Broke?...................... 69

Our Folly Will Be Clear to Everyone.................. 72

Why Are LGBT People So Hacked with Christians?....... 76

Theophobia and Persecution....................... 82

Savaging of Sarah Palin........................... 89

Submit to the Government in All Things?.............. 93

What Obama Is Doing No Mystery,
Welcome One World Government.................... 99

Abortionist Dr. George Tiller Killed................. 104

The Three-Page Bible............................ 109

The Parable of the Town Hall...................... 112

Dark Days for the Republic........................ 115

War on Terror or "Overseas Contingencies"............ 119

Obama's War on Fox and Half the Country............ 123

The Blessings of Liberty or the Curse of the Collective?...... 128

Thought Is now a Crime.......................... 137

Lethal Naïveté or Willful Stupidity: Fort Hood Shooter....... 139

Tea Party People and Paranoid Politicians.............. 144

The Leadership Vacuum:
Adapt, Migrate, or Become Extinct.................. 147

US Taxpayers Funding Terrorism: The Ties that Blind........ 151

Fort Hood Killer: Facts and Fantasy................. 156

Khalid Sheikh Mohammad Plays Obama.............. 160

Real Greatness: A Visit to the Reagan Ranch........... 165

Destroyer of Worlds: Global Warming Tyrants Run Amok   171

The Truth about Homosexuality and Christianity 174

Onward Christian Soldiers: The Manhattan Declaration. 177

Meeting Saul Alinsky on the Backside of History. 179

Khalid Sheikh Mohammed Puts America and Israel on Trial 185

Thomas Jefferson Loved Christ 187

Ben Franklin Is Praying for Us 189

The Age of Incoherence 192

Prez Says Motor City Unbomber "Isolated Extremist". 197

Limbaugh: Teddy Bear Gladiator. 200

The Last Best Hope of Man on Earth 203

The Election of Scott Brown:
"These Have No Ears". 207

War for Oil and the US Marine Corps. 211

POTUS Attacks SCOTUS, Harms Rest of US. 214

The War on Christianity I 216

The War on Christianity II. 221

The War on Christianity III 226

Do You Wonder What Is Happening in America Today? 229

Cheney Versus Obama-Biden—War or Contingency?. 232

Iraq, Bush, "Torture," and the War on Terrorism. 242

Give me Liberty or Give me My Check:
That Is the Question 252

From the Abundance of the Heart, the Mouth speaks. 254

Good-Bye America: Land of the "Me," Home of the Knave. 258

Full Stern Ahead: Workers Unite (or Else) 261

Obama Stimulus: Fraud, Corruption, Favoritism, Waste 264

Islamization of the West:
"Israel Is Fighting for All of Us." 267

Obama "Corrupt," Says Gingrich 271

America on the Brink: Liberty or Death. 274

Thou Shalt Not Speak Ill 278

Disinformation and National Decline 281

Money, Power, and Freedom:
Food for Thought for the Right and the Left 287

With Friends Like America, Israel's Enemies Flourish 291

Islam Is Not a Religion of Peace:
We Are At War with Sharia. 294

Party of the Rich too Big to Fail 298

Hugo Chávez: State Sponsor of Terrorism, Not on the List   300

Syrian Missiles to Hezbollah: New War in Middle East?. 303

It's about Trust, Stupid. 305

They're All in Bed Together: Nighty Night, America 310

Exploiting Illegal Immigration: The Essence of Sedition 313

President Victim 318

Is Obama a fascist? 324

Reverend Graham:
Obama Administration Disenfranchises Christians 330

The New Inquisition and the Assault on Liberty 335

Bum Rushing Limbaugh 342

Friend of the World, Enemy of God:
the Church in America 346

Memorial Day Memories. 353

Obamacare:
Add Senior Citizens to Endangered Species List 355

The Power of Positive Politics. 358

Governance by Bayonet. 361

Depths of Moral and Financial Bankruptcy 363

Barack's Big Bluff: Playing Poker with the American People 366

Why Do They Say Obama Is Anti-American?. 369

The People Versus the Powerful 374

Christians: We Are to Blame! 376

Tuesday Is Not about Different
Opinions on the Issues. 378

Fact-Driven Voters Confront
Arrogance-Driven Administration. 383

Election Observations. 388

Sharia Law Is No Big Deal 392

Throwing Israel to the Wolves. 395

Powerful Dems Tell Obama not to Seek Re-Election 398

Giving Thanks for Our Men and Women in Uniform 401

New World Order: Many Are the Plans of Man 404

Man unto Himself:
The Death of Common Sense 407

The Low Point for Liberalism: Self-Ridicule 412

The Corpse that Is Liberalism. 416

Islam Versus Christianity:
The Stark Hypocrisy of the Left 420

Marine Loses Leg, Returns to Combat 424

"Progressives" Say Obama Found Wanting 427

The Perfect Law that Gives Freedom 431

Reagan: Courageous, Consistent, Compassionate, Courteous 434

A Weiner Named Anthony 439

This Column Is racist 443

Iran Declares War on Israel, Again 448

Revised Declaration of Independence for 2011 451

Death of Osama: Cause Célèbre? 457

Pinball President 461

Krugman, the anti-American Left, and 9/11 463

Afterword 466

Epilogue 468

INTRODUCTION

Several years ago I just started writing. It was the only way I could fight back. September 11 changed everything for everyone.

My oldest son, Ian, came to me, saying he wanted to join the Marine Corps. I so admired his sense of duty, his courage, his willingness to serve; it sparked something in me. His brothers, Sean and Luke, and sister, Eva, are following suit in their own ways. Their devotion to country motivated me to do what I could to protect and defend the Constitution. Something just took over, and in thinking it over, it seemed obvious we were making a huge mistake as a nation by turning our backs on the two things which have served us best: the Cross and the Constitution, working together to create the greatest force for good ever known.

Many of us at home with sons in Iraq listened to President Bush being abused and felt the call to step up and get involved.

I watched as my kids were jolted out of their childhoods. Allana was spared because she was born later. Ian, Sean, Eva, and Luke, however, witnessed the events of 9/11 and the storms afterward. It was traumatic, of course. Their generation bears the mark of that trauma.

Watching them struggle to adjust and hearing the old voices from the 1960s condemn our president and our military caused something in me to snap. I wanted back in the fight. I wanted to do something to try and impact the future for my kids' sake. So I started to write.

I was also motivated by a re-energized sense of patriotism and faith. It seemed to me the 9/11 attacks were directed at the heart of my country and my faith, and the attacks by radical leftists were similar in nature. So I began pounding the keyboard, trying to make sense of things, and working to fight back in the best way I could, all in an effort to persuade others to get into the fight as well.

As the forces of anti-Americanism became more and more institutionalized with the rise of Barack Obama, my motivation became passion. I started seeking a wider audience. A friend, someone I've never met in person, Nancy Matthis, set up a blog for me. (Thanks, Nancy at Americandaughter.com!) Then another friend I've yet to meet in person, James Simpson, urged me to write for Examiner.com. (Thanks, Jim at DC Independent Examiner.com!)

I've written a column every few days for years. This book is a collection of some of those efforts, arranged chronologically. (This book is not intended to be read cover-to-cover. Let the table of contents be your guide.) I hope you find them useful as you join in the fight to achieve the greatest good for the greatest number. God bless the good old USA.

A PREDICTION

Excerpt from editorial posted September 30, 2008

(If elected) Mr. Obama will experience the same meat grinder all presidents face.

He will be confronted daily with no-win situations, a series of catch-22 circumstances, forced to make damned-if-you-do-damned-if-you-don't decisions. Despite all his good intentions, he will be vilified, first from one sector then the next. He will look at the same intelligence Bush reads every day, and he will soon realize the options are few.

The real problem is Obama has never made an executive decision. He has no experience guiding him. His advisors will drive him crazy with hundreds of conflicting recommendations.

This will force him to rely on his political philosophy and his instincts. His political philosophy is rooted in expediency, moral relativism, and radicalism, which are inherently anchorless. He has made it clear he believes Scripture is not a good guide to public policy. He appeals to the Founders then ignores them. Without a set of core values, a person is made to drift with the winds of political fortune, which invariably translates into chaos, and weakness and serial crises. There will be no legislative consensus or coherence, à la Jimmy Carter.

Consequently, Obama will be forced to run on instinct. Exclusive reliance on instinct always means a focus on sheer survival, the antithesis of leadership.

At that point the meat grinder will accelerate.

POST GROUND ZERO ANGST: LIFE AND WORK, FEAR AND THE FUTURE

March 8, 2002

On Sept. 11, 2001, our world was turned upside down, and inside out. Several weeks after the events in New York, Pennsylvania, and Washington, D.C., the horrific images replay in our minds, grief remains, overcome incrementally by glimmers of hope, and pangs of fear, itself prodded by the prospect of more terrorist attacks, economic upheaval, and a sense of national vulnerability, despite the successful war against the Taliban.

In our personal lives, Sept. 11 set off smaller Sept. 11s. Once dormant or simmering personal and professional issues have been exacerbated and exaggerated. Marriage conflicts and family difficulties, financial hardships, meaning of life issues, and the full range of general reassessments have been forged in our lives by the blast furnace of international hatred and acts of unspeakable, incomprehensible violence. People are looking for answers, for meaning. Many are turning to God.

We work and attend to the basic responsibilities of life, now played out under the threat of biological and nuclear warfare and the likelihood of escalating conflict at home and abroad. With one eye on a hopeful future, we proceed with the other looking over one shoulder: encouraged by our leaders to be vigilant, watchful and cautious on the one hand, and on the other we are advised to lead normal lives. And even in the face of the new threats made real by 9/11, for however long, we enjoy a new unity of spirit and purpose: the dawning of a new patriotism? Still, many ask: how do we live normally when everything has become abnormal?

If ever we needed heroic leaders, it is now. We need people with the mantle of Churchill, Lincoln, Anwar El Sadat, Reagan, Thatcher, or Golda Meir. Thankfully we have many such people at the helm at home, and at the heads of state in the coalition. But we need more. We need to be heroic on the local level, becoming leaders with a new vision, committed to effective navigation in a sea of change and uncertainty. Our president has said the most patriotic things we can do are resume normal life, work hard, contribute to economic recovery, and tend to our families while we keep a sharp eye out for unusual activity. Like the Hebrews long ago, we are called to rebuild the temple with one hand, holding a sword in the other.

What does all this mean in the day-to-day, in our working lives, in business, and what are the challenges business leaders, owners, and managers face as they seek to become more effective leaders?

This writer does not pretend to have original answers or suggestions. However many contemporary writers and leaders have put out a series of articles recently that make real headway in assessing organizational problems, and recommending solutions applicable to a wide range of situations in the workplace and elsewhere. The American organization—political, social, spiritual—has been failing in many areas for years. If September 11 prompts us to solve our problems, something great will emerge from the rubble.

One excellent starting point is considering the following quote from business and management writers Warren Bennis and Burt Wanus, considered best in class thinking these things through: "The problem with many organizations, and especially ones that are failing, is that they tend to be over-managed and under-led." (Sounds vaguely like the federal government.)

What of organizations in crisis and the affect of management on success or failure?

Crisis tends to drive people one of three directions: we either move courageously into the chaos, becoming agents of order and hope, or we run away, or we try desperately to control and manipulate events in hopes of influencing outcomes. The first is leadership. The second is simply flight. The last is management.

Leaders motivate people with a brilliant torch of inspiration fueled by integrity, vision, courage, and charisma. Cowards flee. Managers often resort to thumbscrews, bayonets, and cattle prods. Is it all so black and white? I think so. It's the distinction between compulsion and inspiration, between freedom and slavery, democracy and communism/fascism, capitalism and socialism, grace and legalism.

People who volunteer, responding to the call of a true leader, cannot be defeated. People who submit grudgingly under the pressure of management to conform eventually sabotage the community. In crisis—where true character is revealed—we must look for leaders, follow them, and ignore the managers, that is, if we are interested in the long view, because managers tend to be near-sighted, quick-fix types, while leaders impact centuries.

Jerry Useem, writing in the November 12 edition of Fortune, puts it simply and brilliantly: "After years of losing ground to its dowdy cousin, Management, Leadership is back. Bosses inherit subordinates. Leaders earn followers."

I would add: leaders act, managers react. (Certainly, managers are needed, necessary and crucial to a well-oiled machine, but management should be subservient to leaders, and so should accounting, human resources and legal.)

Business, political, social, and spiritual leaders and writers today point to a pinnacle problem: fear. From the Harvard Business School to the Los Angeles Times, the boardroom to the loading dock, from sociology departments to churches, mosques and synagogues, fear is the 800-pound gorilla in the national living room.

In our little corner of the world—technical, sales, and management recruiting in the office products industry—fear is driving many companies to freeze hiring. Fear is causing job seekers to table plans for career development especially if taking a promotion involves relocation. Some would assert it's prudent to adopt a "wait and see" attitude. Others would agree with President Franklin Roosevelt: "The only thing we have to fear...is fear itself."

The antidote to fear is courage. Ralph Waldo Emerson said, "Do the thing you fear and the death of fear is certain." It takes courage to do the thing you fear. Winston Churchill reminded us that, "Without courage, all other virtues lose their meaning." All virtue is moral excellence. Moral excellence comes from God. Therefore the virtue of courage can only be appropriated, not conjured. The only way to do the thing you fear is to get God-gutsy. (True and good leadership is God-inspired, appropriated, inviting the cooperation of others. False and destructive leadership is driven by human wisdom and generally demands compliance. Followers need courage to distinguish between true/false-good/bad leadership, thereby confronting fear while embracing hope.) Massive business interest in things spiritual is a natural response to fear and a crying out for courage when we admit we are confronted with things too big for us.

In Fortune magazine, July 9, 2001, the cover story was: "God and Business—The Surprising Quest for Spiritual Renewal in the American Workplace," by Marc Gunther.

Why should it be surprising, this spiritual renewal, even in the business world? Perhaps the subhead is a function of pre versus post Sept. 11 perception?

God-given courage to grapple with fear is yielding spiritual and monetary dividends in the workplace. Here are select quotes from Gunther's article, offered up as food for thought:

- "...work from your soul." Jack Shea, Chicago-based scholar, health-care consultant and theologian.

- "When you ask how to bring God into your work it's by not getting caught up in making money or achieving power so that they become your gods." Jose Zeilstra, J.P. Morgan

- "Spirituality is in convergence with all the cutting-edge thinking in management and organizational behavior. It creates a higher-performing organization." Hamilton Beasley, George Washington University teacher, and former oil company exec.

- "...there is creative energy in work that is somehow tied to God's creative energy...perhaps we can use it to transform the workplace into something remarkable." Gregory F. A. Pearce, author of Spirituality@Work.

- "Are you willing to be a channel in the divine economy?" Rev. Dr. Thomas K. Tewell.

- "*Avodah,* a Hebrew word, means both *work* and *worship.*" David Miller, former IBM exec/investment banker, Avodah Institute.

- "I think a lot of what I do here at Greyston is my ministry." Julius Walls Jr., CEO of Greyston Bakery.

People who have been to the depths of despair most often emerge having discovered the pure value of a healthy spiritual walk applied to all aspects of life.

The paradoxes of the spiritual life—that we win by giving up, that we are victors by surrendering, that we lead best as servants, that the last shall become first—are lost on a mind convinced that humanism is the only rational god on earth.

Despair can help us understand our need for God, or it can drive us to make the enormous error of focusing on self-will, self-protection, and self-determination, the pillars of humanism. If Sept.

11 teaches us anything, it is that we are not sufficient, we are all vulnerable, and we need something much greater that ourselves. After all, if coping effectively means having all the facts and the processing power to interpret those facts, I'm lost: I have neither the database nor the intelligence to grapple and cope at the highest levels.

To provide insights for those of you in particular who tend to break out in hives when you hear the words "spirituality" or "God," here are some of the highest contributions true leaders provide, especially in crisis, and a list of guiding principles or leadership guideposts (Fortune, Nov. 12, 2001 pages 128–132) that appear to have been field-tested in a secular sense (and of course, not surprisingly, there are many crossovers to "spiritual" principles):

- Stand up and be seen: leaders must be excessively visible
- Embrace brutal optimism: emotions are contagious, be cooler than cool
- Stick to the facts: speak straightforwardly or not at all
- The bottom line comes second: the first thing is for people to know they are valued, secure and cared about
- Find a story: use forward-looking narratives to inspire (EX: Abraham Lincoln, 1861- The Union stands for liberty, secession would destroy the Union, therefore secession threatens liberty.)

Other ideas with merit from contemporary business leaders in the Post Ground Zero era (from the article *"Beyond Business as Usual, Managing Fear and Uncertainty," Harvard Business School, Management Update, October* 2001, by Loren Gary):

- Create a predictable rhythm so distraught employees can sign up and support strategies and face challenges (Bennis).
- Beware the rush to judgment and action (Bennis).

- Provide an unvarnished description of the situation, credible reasons for hope, and a shared understanding that forges a sense of community among employees (Bennis).
- The adaptive leader's task is to involve everyone in figuring out what the real problems are—-and to keep everyone engaged while they collaboratively discover solutions. (Ronald A. Heifetz, Center for Public Leadership, John F. Kennedy School of Government, Harvard.)
- Provide a context in which all interested parties, the leader included, can create a vision, mission, or purpose they can collectively uphold (Robert Kegan, psychologist and professor, Harvard Graduate School of Education).
- Recognize your people! Exit interviews reveal that 70% of people who resign, leave because of a lack of recognition, a failure by management to express genuine appreciation for the contributions of employees (Kimberly Rath, managing director of Talent+, an HR consulting firm in Lincoln, Nebraska).

Summary: create, provide, involve, collectively uphold, express appreciation, be encouraging, face facts, ooze optimism, paint word pictures to inspire, be accountable by being visible.

Ultimately, if we are brutally honest, the world and its challenges are too big for us in our own strength. Therefore, eventually, we must admit our need for, and ask for, power much greater than our own, to survive, and thrive.

THE OYSTER

October 1, 2005

The pinnacle of creation was an oyster. The oyster was placed in a perfect environment with everything required for sustainability. But a woeful thing occurred. The Creator loved the oyster and warned him not to stray from the perfect environment, but the oyster didn't listen. He wandered into a dangerous place where a speck of sand invaded his soft, inner tissues, a speck placed there by an enemy of the Creator, an enemy full of hate and destruction. The speck began ripping at the tender inward parts, tearing away at the oyster's most sensitive places, causing enormous pain and threatening death.

So the oyster began secreting a substance to cover the speck, to take off its rough edges, all in an effort to save itself. The oyster, thinking himself clever, thought the problem of the speck was solved, and the oyster, assuming self-sufficiency, marveled at its own creative powers, placing great value on the resulting pearl. Yet the problem of the speck remained. Although the speck had become a pearl, it nonetheless continued to exist, threatening to choke the oyster the larger it grew, causing the oyster chronic stomach problems.

Now the Creator had a different solution to the problem of the speck. The Creator promised to remove it altogether, not just cover it up. There was a condition placed by the Creator, however. The oyster had to cooperate. The Creator, in the name of love, refused to force any oyster against its will. The Creator told the oyster it had to choose to voluntarily allow the Creator to remove the speck. This required the oyster to let go of its sense of power and self-sufficiency. The Creator's solution required the oyster to completely submit to the Creator's power but to do so willingly, even happily.

Some oysters gladly bought into the Creator's plan. They reasoned with the Creator that indeed a partial solution was no solution at all. They agreed with the Creator the problem of the speck could only be solved by complete removal, and they willingly allowed the Creator to remove the speck. These oysters realized they had no use for self-manufactured pearls, seeing what the Creator offered was far superior. These oysters returned happily to the original position, but it was not yet a perfect environment with everything required for sustainability. Whenever they acquired another speck, they simply went to the Creator, asking it be removed. The Creator promised to re-create the perfect environment and destroy the enemy.

Other oysters resisted, however. Some went so far as to repudiate the Creator, even denying his existence. These oysters reveled in their pearl making, concluding it was far better to rely on their own resources than accept the Creator's solution, seeing it as no solution at all, even calling it slavery. For the oysters refusing the Creator, the problem only got worse because once the oysters starting making pearls, seeing them as the most valuable objects in existence, they could not stop.

The larger the pearls grew, the harder it was for the oysters to function. Eventually, these oysters could not completely close their shells. In this state, more specks invaded the oysters, causing the need for more secretion. An ever-increasing struggle for survival ensued. They began attacking each other in their frustration and pain. They even began attacking those oysters that had gone to the Creator asking for help, calling on urchins to attack those protected oysters.

Still the Creator reached out to the rebellious oysters, inviting them to accept his healing solution, but they refused. They formed committees and discussion groups and action plans, all in an effort to solve the problem of more and more specks ripping at their tender places. They thought more pearl production would be the answer, but, as they saw, this approach only aggravated the problem.

One group concluded the solution was to remove all the sand from their environment, but that proved impossible even though they tried for centuries through voluntary communal effort, efforts that routinely turned into tyranny because they could never sustain volunteerism, these oysters being steeped in selfishness.

Another group simply accepted shorter lives, choosing to use painkillers of various kinds. Still another group advocated for a complete change of location in a desperate attempt to escape all sand in the universe.

And another group angrily denied sand was the problem, blaming the Creator instead, insisting they'd work out the solution sooner or later. These oysters grew increasingly mean and grouchy, and they eventually died, cursing the sand, the pearls, themselves, and the Creator.

All along the Creator continued inviting the rebellious oysters to accept his solution, grieving over their pain and their stubborn resistance. He warned the wandering oysters that one day he would create a whole new environment, a place especially reserved for the oysters that submitted to his plan and happily cooperated, a new environment not available to oysters who insisted on holding on to their pearls and their selfish ways.

And one day it happened.

All the oysters accepting the Creator's plan went to live with him forever in a perfect place with no sand and no pearls.

All the oysters rejecting the Creator went to live in a dark place full of sand where no pearl and no painkiller offered relief anymore, forever.

And the Creator carried the pain of the speck forevermore.

Additional resource: Google "Incredible Prophecies: Do They Prove God Exists? Part Two. If Specific Prophecies Were Fulfilled by the Messiah, Does the Science of Probability Consider This Proof There Is a God?"

THE STORM AFTER THE STORM

September 5, 2005
American journalism has become more and more a conduit for seething rage, hysteria, and sensationalism, all embraced for the sake of ratings and profits. Of course, this has been going on for years, but it is reaching new heights of arrogance and presumption. In the wake of Katrina, 150 mph winds blowing through various media organizations are sending storm surges and floods of condemnation in the wrong direction for the wrong reasons, making a bad situation worse.

For months and months, witness the total lack of any good news coming out of Iraq (there is plenty to report) and now we see the same negative reporting out of New Orleans. And the two are being cleverly and inappropriately linked. An ABC interviewer tried to corner the president, asking a loaded question (a way to make a statement without regard to the interviewee's response). She "asked" if being overextended in Iraq (assumption) we now are without adequate resources to respond to Katrina. The president confidently replied Americans will win the war on terror and help the people in the Gulf States.

Last week it was infuriating to watch ABC's coverage, all of it essentially laying blame on this administration, calling Bush to task for lack of funding for levees, lack of pre-disaster planning, failure to achieve command and control after the storm, failure to save people rapidly enough or supply food, water, medical care. NBC and CBS have joined the blame game, piling on with ghoulish glee.

Never mind that concerted efforts have saved thousands of lives and evacuated tens of thousands more; never mind that a colossal disaster overwhelmed everyone and the response has been enormous and is ongoing. Never mind that rescue workers could use a little encouragement in the face of such tremendous devastation and need. Never mind that people long ago decided to build New Orleans in a hole surrounded by a river, a lake and an ocean, right in the center of hurricane country. Never mind that the levee issue dates back decades.

Instead of reporting facts and being of some use in this crisis, most media outlets appear to believe it's more important to find fault and cast aspersions, all of them leading to President Bush of course. The pundits expect miracles and want us to believe all the world's woes can be laid at the threshold of the White House. According to the bulk of news and "analysis" coming out of the Gulf States, no one is doing anything right.

Some have even tried playing the race card, implying there is intentional neglect because so many victims are black. What is so astounding is so many seem to believe this bilge.

And the drumbeat of blame continues on into the night with voices raised against the oil companies, and the governor of Mississippi, a Republican. Of course the governor of Louisiana and the mayor of New Orleans get a pass. Guess which political party they belong to? Is it true local officials offered blanket evacuation for everyone regardless of economic status prior to the hurricane hitting the coast? Who was responsible to be first responders? Who was responsible to evacuate people, the state and city, or the feds?

RFK Jr. went so far as to say the failure to address global warming caused Katrina, and that of course is completely the fault of this president. RFK Jr. apparently believes hurricanes didn't occur before

2000, and this president could have stopped global warming if he wanted to.

It is mind numbing how ABC commentators and reporters and anchors assume they know more about the dimensions of this disaster than the experts on the ground. They fly in, get a few sound bites and some B roll, and go on air, rapidly condemning the very people attempting to provide aid under the most difficult circumstances.

Throughout last week, so-called journalists on Air America could be heard doing much the same, assuming they know more than state, local, and federal officials, casting blanket condemnations in every direction, rather than focusing energy on fundraising and relief efforts themselves. Hysterical. Hypocritical. One Air America talker actually called the president a wolf in sheep's clothing, saying he is an agent of Satan. No kidding. Another Air America voice of reason charged the president is actually glad the hurricane is killing so many in blue states, thus lessening his political opposition. This lunacy ranks up there with the accusation the president knew about the 9/11 conspiracy ahead of time, but let it happen so as to give him license to invade Iraq. Still, people give these voices credence, and our major media outlets lend credibility by providing access, repeatedly.

I'm sickened by the viciousness these so-called journalists spew 24/7, without regard for any sense of common courtesy, critical thinking, or due consideration. It serves no one's interests in the face of this horrific disaster to be running around like so many Chicken Littles trying to gain political traction on the backs of so many suffering people in these stricken Gulf States.

Again, like their "coverage" of Iraq, they tell not one positive story, they report no good news about progress being made. The entire slant is on the downside, and who is to blame: always the blame game. Imagine trying to access 90,000 square miles of devastation to help victims of this storm. Roads were closed by debris. Subsequent flooding made access to many areas impossible on the surface, forcing rescue efforts via helicopters, plucking people one at a time. And then we heard about gangs firing upon rescue helicopters. Unbelievable.

Instead of serving the public interest by providing news and information in a supportive and positive fashion, so as to give those poor people some hope, direction, and encouragement, they do the opposite and inflame an already tough situation, to the detriment of all.

They should be ashamed, but I fear they are beyond accountability, because they have forsaken all sense of propriety, leaving humility behind in their mad dash to break "news" and bash our President. It is simply disgraceful. It is especially despicable when you consider what they call journalism is in reality a circus aimed at generating ratings to reap profits, all while promoting a Leftist political agenda under the guise of objectivity.

The media-orchestrated storm after the storm is causing great damage as well. However, in the wake of this storm, don't expect any relief from government or anyone else.

LETTER FROM UNCLE SAM

Feb. 15, 2006

Dear Islamo-fascists:

You know who you are, and so do I. Let me introduce myself. I'm Uncle Sam, otherwise known in your circles as the Great Satan.

You will no doubt be surprised to learn I've been used by the Most High to frustrate Satan many times.

I'm writing in the interests of fairness. When the other shoe drops, I don't want you to say you were never warned.

For many years now you have called for the complete destruction of America and Israel and our respective ways of life. You see, I take this personally, because I'm deeply in love with America and Israel.

For all her faults America has always provided people with the best hope of life, liberty, and the pursuit of happiness, and not only a hope, a reality.

You should understand clear lessons from history as you plot our demise. It is my hope these lessons will encourage you to invest your time and energy in building your own societies, rather than foaming at the mouth over the perceived deficiencies on our side of the pond.

Early on, when we were only a few, living in a wilderness surrounded by lethal dangers, we built a nation, by hand. King George wanted to take it away from us. He commanded the world's super military power at the time. We handed him his cucumber sandwich on a platter, then slapped him silly, and ran him out of town. That "divine right" jazz doesn't play too well in the colonies. Remember that.

Driving the lobster backs off cost us a lot, in blood and treasure, but for us, the cost of liberty and justice is never too high. Remember that.

The British came back for another licking a short time later, and we sent them packing, again. (Today, the dear Brits are among our best friends. How many times have you completely reconciled with an enemy? Oh, that's right, you have no "former" enemies: you just keep adding to the list.)

Only a few years later we discovered we had become our own worst enemy.

We were forced to repent of the sin of slavery.

Our passion for liberty and justice was again costly. The family feud turned to Civil War, brother against brother, and 600,000 died during those four years. Many thought America was committing suicide. Few thought we would survive. We not only survived, we thrived, despite a shameful reconstruction period leaving blacks in circumstances not far removed from slavery. So for the next 140 years we struggled to make things right, and we continue to work toward the highest goals of full justice and liberty. We do not give up easily. Remember that.

We do the right thing not because some thug threatens us with a gun or a roadside bomb. We do the right thing because we've been taught (and we believe) life is all about forgiveness and fairness and tolerance and healing and reconciliation and moving onward and upward. Too bad you don't get that yet.

Back to more lessons from history.

Before and after the Civil War, the Spanish and the Mexicans and others got the idea we were ripe for the plucking, but they learned it's not profitable to provoke Lady Liberty.

After this, the Kaiser found out the Yanks were coming, and the European family feud was finally settled thanks to the Shining City on a Hill.

In short order the Fuehrer and the Emperor thought they'd take over the world, and they very nearly pulled it off. They didn't expect the Allies, inspired by a bunch of U.S. farm boys and city slickers and Rosie riveters, would stand in their way and bring them to their knees.

After WWII we hoped we had finally secured the peace.

We went on to rebuild Europe and Japan and other countries, again reconciling with former enemies, even helping them. We worked hard at home simultaneously to secure a promising future for our children. Almost immediately however we were confronted by another drooling tyrant, the Soviet Empire.

And so for forty years we fought them around the world, sometimes in Hot Wars, but always in the Cold War. I don't need to tell you how we disappointed Russian ambitions, and as in WWII, we liberated millions of oppressed people in the process.

We didn't go looking for these fights during the last 230 years. We didn't seek this one with you. But the result will be the same. We've faced worse than you, and you deserve no better than was delivered our former adversaries. After you there will be another enemy of freedom lined up to challenge the forces of goodness, but they'll get what they deserve as well. Remember that.

We've taken it on the chin from you chaps for forty years. We won't take it anymore.

Unlike your honorable ancestors riding the deserts of Africa, real warriors and the finest horsemen the world has ever seen, you hide behind women and children, believing you can overcome us psychologically. Justice demands murderers like you pay the price, eventually. And you think using WMD will deliver victory. Nuts.

Now that you've provoked the entire European community, helping us prove our point about your nature, for the entire world to see, the Western powers may be forced to use the big hammer should you continue your murderous ways. Since you show no signs of relenting (indeed you escalate) it is likely you'll kiss the big hammer sooner rather than later.

Yet our strength does not reside in the big hammer.

Do you know where our real strength resides? I'll tell you.

We love the God of love, and since He loves the little guy, we also love the little guy. You, on the other hand, murder the little guy.

This is precisely why, in the end, we will prevail, and you will suffer.

Don't say you were never warned.

Sincerely,

Uncle Sam

PS: All this goes for you too Hugo, and you too, Mr. Il.

NO PEACE, NO HONOR, NO STRATEGY

Nov. 14, 2006

Anti-War Activist John Murtha told Anti-American Katie Couric last night he felt vindicated by the election. Murtha, Pelosi's lap dog for years, will become her henchman in the House. "Strategic Redeployment" is their Nixon-speak for "Humiliating Defeat, Demoralize the Troops, Screw the Iraqis."

Ah, nation-building. Ah, strengthening alliances. Murtha was asked if ditching the Iraqis to fend for themselves would invite a worse situation. He casually dismissed the possibility, saying things couldn't be worse. How wrong can anyone be?

Having won the election by talking conservative, true liberal colors now bleed blue through the thin veneer of campaign primping and posturing, none of it speaking to the real heart of the matter: the lethal, global Islamic threat to Western civilization, and the impotent, disorganized response from Europe and the U.S.

Given the Murtha mindset, we can expect more impotence and disorganization. Murtha said last night we are wasting money in Iraq, money we should use for education, prescription drugs and healthcare, as if there is no Islamic threat, as if our priority should be domestic policy. President Bush may have been in denial about aspects of the developing situation in Iraq, but it would appear Murtha and Pelosi are in denial concerning reality itself.

Dear fellow Americans, we are in a fight to the death with an enemy playing without rules, a vicious opponent pledged to eradicate us by any means. Can we at least agree on two things: 1) let's stop majoring on the minors, and 2) let's formulate an intelligent strategy for victory and thus survival, based on a realistic policy toward Islamic fascism, a policy recognizing there is no room for negotiation simply because their aim is to destroy us?

It has been said a problem well stated is half solved, so let's look hard at the problem. In addition to our woeful lack of understanding of Islam and the real threat we face, our strategy in Iraq has been flawed, and it is time to face it, and change it.

American Daughter.com published today the excellent remarks of Dr. Mitchell M. Zais, Brigadier General, U.S. Army (Ret.), contained in his Newberry College convocation address, delivered November 9. It is the kind of thoughtful analysis we have needed, void of self-serving partisan bias and cheap shots so characteristic of the national dialogue these last few years. Zais's essential point—-

> "Our strategy in Iraq has been: fight the war on the cheap; ask the ground forces to perform missions that are more suitably performed by other branches of the American government; inconvenience the American people as little as possible, and continue to fund the Air Force and Navy at the same levels that they have been funded at for the last 30 years while shortchanging the Army and Marines who are doing all of the fighting."

If these are flaws, and it appears obvious they are and have been, then will Baker/Hamilton advise the president to (?):

- increase troop levels and spending on the Iraqi operation
- reassign ground troops to kill or arrest terrorists, taking areas and holding them, letting the Iraqis conduct other law enforcement

- bring the mainstream of Americans into the center of the struggle by educating them about the real nature of this threat, and calling upon them to shoulder the burden along with the troops
- realign funding to square with real needs in the field

Sounds like Colin Powell and others were right about strategy and troop levels needed to secure Iraq, thus building the bulwark against terror we think effective at confronting it long term.

Zais makes another excellent point, we have relied on technology, hoping for a fast-food kind of convenience war, an In 'n Out hit and leave approach. Our thinking and our expectations are all fouled up. We don't know our enemy. Zais continues:

> Technologists have a hard time comprehending the motivations of a suicide bomber or a mother who celebrates the death of her son in such a way. It's difficult for them to understand that to overcome centuries of ethnic hatred and murder it will take more than one generation. It's hard for them to accept that for young men with little education, no wives or children, and few job prospects, war against the West is the only thing that gives meaning to their lives. But *war on the ground is not conducted with technology*. It is fought by 25-year-old sergeants leading 19-year-old soldiers carrying rifles, in a dangerous and alien environment, where you can't tell combatants from noncombatants, Shiites from Sunnis, or suicide bombers from freedom seeking Iraqis. This means war on the street is neither antiseptic nor surgical. It's dirty, complicated, and fraught with confusion and error.

So instead of supporting the brave sergeants and soldiers we've sent into hell, we castigate them in the press, arrest them, indict them, presume guilt, jail them, condemn them and convict and sentence them. Sound like a strategy for victory to you?

We all have to get our hands dirty. One of the reasons we failed for forty years to deal with terrorism effectively is we relied on technology in our intelligence gathering operations. Human resource (spies) infiltrating enemy groups were reduced to near oblivion, other than on the silver screen, taking a backseat to sensors and drones and cameras and satellites and microphones. Ultimately, we paid for that mistake on 9/11. In like kind, we are paying militarily for putting too much hope on technology, and too little confidence in, and support of, the flesh and blood warrior most skilled and effective in taking down fanatics.

One such warrior is Paul Rieckhoff, Founder and Executive Director, Iraq & Afghanistan Veterans of America (largest such group), and author of *Chasing Ghosts,* Penguin, 2006. He served with the Army in Iraq, and he confirms much of what Zais is saying, especially when it comes to revamping strategy based on sound policy, and deploying tactics accordingly. He also emphasizes the absolute necessity for supporting our military people, in large measure by bringing the mass of Americans into the war, something the Dems will never do simply because they refuse to acknowledge the threat, fear losing votes, decline fighting back, as if self-defense is a sin. American leadership has failed to engage the majority of civilians in active support and personal involvement in the war effort.

Let's face it folks, if you don't have a relative in uniform, you've really not had your head in the game.

Two Marines joined Rieckhoff on the Charlie Rose program recently, confirming much of what Zais is saying. Vets are speaking out, and we should listen to them. Unlike the Kerry-speak of days gone by, these are real warriors speaking from a patriotic heart bent on victory. The people on the ground, the ones doing all the bleeding and dying, often have much to teach the civilian commanders far from the fray.

The more vets we have speaking out about how best to defend the country, the better.

We also need to hear from more people with deep experience in the Middle East, people who speak Arabic, individuals who know the Islamic mind. Interestingly, the President met with Baker and Hamilton and others yesterday, but we didn't see anyone at the table with these kinds of credentials. (One fear is the Baker/Hamilton-Iraq Study Group tends to view U.S. support of Israel as negotiable, a possible way to lessen Islamic hatred of the West.)

In WWII, with a fledgling intelligence capability, we broke the Japanese codes, and infiltrated Nazi communications networks, outwitting them and defeating them by fighting smart and fighting hard, using human assets, ours and theirs. We are fighting hard thanks to our men and women in uniform, but our leaders have not done enough to help us fight smart in too many ways.

If the federal authorities don't allow our military and intelligence experts to intercept, interrogate, incarcerate, and in some cases, incinerate, then at some point, simply to survive, a President will have to institute marshal law, and then listen for the howl about civil/judicial rights. Why let it go that far if we don't have to?

Most Americans don't know what is going on. The media is doing a terrible job of telling the whole story. Most politicians are self-serving blabber mouths ill-equipped to meet the challenges of the day, incapable or unwilling to step out and speak plainly.

We the People must now step up and move this country forward to face our enemies—-foreign and domestic—- with a cold stare and a steel hand.

The alternative is bowing to Allah, or having your head severed, Mr. Murtha... as if you'll even be around on that day. This excerpt from a Cal Thomas column, "The biggest winners," Nov. 4, 2006, Townhall.com, is prophetic:

> In an effort to take Iraq off the table as an issue in the 2008 presidential campaign, the Bush administration adopts most of the provisions of the Iraq Study Group. In a modern version of the Paris Peace Talks, which allowed the United States to have

"peace with honor" and withdraw from Vietnam (resulting in the deaths, imprisonment and "re-education" of unknown numbers of Vietnamese who wanted to be free), the administration then orders a "redeployment" of forces after "negotiations" with Syria and Iran (recommended by Blair). This allows just enough time for American troops to leave before al-Qaeda murders the elected leadership and takes over Iraq.

Meanwhile in the United States, mosques and Islamic schools paid for by the extremist Wahhabi sect, multiply like fast-food franchises. Terrorists are imported and recruited from prisons. Al-Qaeda announces that weapons of mass destruction have been placed in key American and European cities. They demand that the United States withdraw its protection of Israel. If we refuse, they threaten to detonate their weapons, killing millions of people. What president, or prime minister, will reject that demand? After capitulating on the installment plan, who will have the political or moral capital (or military capacity) to stop Armageddon?

Tough question. Do we have tough answers, or do we remain in a position of no peace, no honor, no strategy?

THE MASS PSYCHOLOGY OF SURRENDER

April 12, 2007

The U.S. military has worked miracles in Iraq, but to listen to the apparent American majority, Iraq is a mess, and therefore, we must leave sooner rather than later.

Today's bombing of the Iraqi parliament, rather than provoke our outrage, only fuels the voices of defeat and retreat. Instead of condemning murderous terrorists, we turn on our own president. Have we gone completely mad?

Never mind honor, our own security interests, our promises to the Iraqis, our standing in the world, or the fallout from surrendering to murderers. It's a mess, so let's run away. This seems the clarion call of most Americans, if we are to believe CBS, NBC, ABC, CNN, and the rest.

Has the American eagle morphed into a mangy chicken?

If it's true, then the majority of Americans, led by people like Hillary Clinton, Nancy Pelosi, Harry Reid, Barack Obama, and Ted Kennedy have become slovenly cowards unworthy of the liberty handed them by the blood of real patriots.

If this is true, Moslem extremists are right about us: we don't have the balls to resist them over the long haul. We've become a bunch of timid couch potatoes, so focused on self-indulgence, we've lost the impulse even to self-defense.

And if all this is true, ultimate defeat is a foregone conclusion. Our moral and spiritual weakness dooms us. Have we really become so weakened by this mass psychology of surrender we can no longer muster the gumption to even take a stand for goodness?

At a recent meeting, MoveOn.org members picked Sen. Barack Obama (Ill.) as the candidate who "would be best able to lead the country out of Iraq."

How does one embrace "leadership" focused on surrender and defeat? What kind of "leadership" advances such an agenda? If Iraq is the front on the war on terror, how can it be we've made it a priority to withdraw from the front lines, unless of course we've decided simply to hand over the keys and lay down? Never mind Iraq, let's just surrender in the entire war on terror and have done with it.

The American people made a serious mistake capitulating to the forces of surrender last November, voting Pelosi and her minions into power. Today, she decries extending the terms of military service in Iraq for three months, following her cordial meeting with a mass murderer in Damascus, completely contradicting the President, and our Constitution. Patriots who've volunteered extend their service for three months, which is woeful in her estimation, but the very people funding the murder of our brave soldiers, she embraces in Syria.

Is anyone paying attention? Does anyone recognize the traitors among us?

Lest we forget, we invaded Iraq for a number of reasons, based in part on the old adage, 'the best defense is a strong offense.' Saddam was a threat. Everyone agreed, including the limp-wristed Euro-appeasers. Iraq violated every cease-fire agreement from the Gulf War, stymied the U.N. at every turn, denied weapons inspectors, and told the world to go to hell for years and years. Invasion was a legal resumption of hostilities, not pre-emption, voted on by Congress giving the President war powers and authority to invade.

Saddam supported terrorism in a hundred ways. Even the *NY Times* acknowledged he was developing nukes (sorry Joe and Valerie of Plame fame). Overriding all these considerations, it was decided we must establish a battle line in the terrorists' own backyard, an offensive move designed to protect American civilians.

It's worked. Any terror attacks since 9/11 on American soil? Do we thank the president and his team for protecting us? Hell no. We ridicule and condemn and malign and slander. What a bunch of ungrateful little weasels we've become.

And what do we hear today, flying full in the face of all truth, all factual information?

"No WMD. Bush lied, people died. No war for oil." Sophomoric, one-dimensional whining punctuated by willful ignorance, and sloth.

We don't need al Qaeda with WMD to destroy us: we are doing a good job of it ourselves.

The Founders are spinning in their graves.

ASKING CHARLIE GIBSON A FEW QUESTIONS

September 14, 2008

"The Public has a right to know."

This has long been the justification reporters use to interview people, dig through files and records, and "cover" the news. They are right. The public does have a right to know in this democratic republic. Too bad so many reporters don't care to cover the news any more. They would rather be part of the news, even make the news, and enjoy the celebrity that comes of it.

Hey! It's more fun and there's more money in it compared to that dreary craft practiced by grizzled old reporters who love the truth more than fame, and accuracy more than money.

Since the public does have a right to know, we would like to ask a question or two of Charlie Gibson, please.

Going into the interview with you, Sarah Palin had experienced unprecedented smears and personal attacks from the massive media.

Suspecting you would join the mob (and you did not disappoint), was she right to exercise a little "anticipatory self-defense?"

Your performance, and the performance of many of your colleagues, settles the question of media bias in favor of the Left, once and for all.

When you asked her to define the Bush Doctrine, she suspected you were setting her up. So she asked for clarification. Instead of giving her clarification, you were condescending, and evasive. So, she gave you an answer from 30,000 feet but you insisted the focus be at much lower elevation, just Pre-Emption. And you practically clucked with disdain, in so many words, telling us she is ignorant on the subject.

You showed your hand Charlie.

It was disappointing to witness your prejudicial attitude toward Palin. It was obvious you had already decided she was unqualified to be either Vice President, or President. Your "interview" was actually an exercise in confirming your prejudicial assessments.

In the old days our journalism professors taught us to work hard to be fair, accurate, non-judgmental, balanced and thorough. They taught us if we concentrated on these areas in our reporting, we would do the best job of approaching objectivity, which, they insisted, was our duty, if we gave a rip about serving the public interest.

Charlie, your approach to Palin didn't even try to achieve the appearance of objectivity.

Had you done your job, ABC viewers would have learned much more about the real Sarah Palin.

Instead you tried to force them to accept the Sarah Palin you perceive.

The distinction is important.

On the one hand, real journalism is a truth-quest exercised as a public service, and a vital service in this democratic republic.

What we got from you was propaganda.

Instead of wasting airtime you could simply have scrolled the following on the screen for your viewers:

"Charlie Gibson met with Sarah Palin for a long conversation in Alaska this week. As Charlie rightly suspected, Gov. Palin is unqualified to be Vice President, much less President, because she doesn't know what Charlie knows about the Bush Doctrine, foreign policy, energy, the economy, abortion, women, separation of church and state, and so on."

It seemed to a lot us in the viewing audience you didn't give us our money's worth, Charlie.

We are the ones who purchase the products and services your network peddles, so your bosses can pay your $8 million salary. We are the people who made you number one in the ratings. Surely we should get more for our money than a smear job dressed up like something approaching serious journalism.

When do we get to see the interview with Joe Biden as you grill him for not paying his CPA $15,000 for the last twenty years, only settling up when the story threatened to go public? When do we get to see you ask Joe about his son and lobbyists and influence peddling in DC? When do we get to see you ask Joe about his vote against the Gulf War, his vote for the Iraq war and his vote against the Surge, and what that tells us about his vast foreign policy acumen? When do we get to see you ask about his racist remarks about people from India in Delaware working in convenience stores? When do we get to see you press him about how his Catholicism informs his public policy positions, and why the Church doesn't think he should take communion?

For that matter, Charlie, when will we get to see you grimace over your spectacles as you stare down Obama and ask him why he said the fifty-seven states of America, and why he recommended the Security Council handle Georgia since the Russians have veto power on the Security Council? When will you ask Obama to explain why the following people/organizations endorse him: Castro, Chavez, Ahmadinejad, Hamas, Hezbollah, MoveOn.org, the Communist Party, and Bill Ayers? When will we find out more about the Chicago Machine, what Obama actually did as a community organizer, more about his accomplishments as a senator in Illinois and DC, and why after 143 days as a U.S. Senator he announced he was running for President? When will you ask him what would have happened had we followed his advice and pulled out of Iraq in 2006? When will we hear about how Obama's faith in abortion on demand leads him to support infanticide? When will we see you ask serious questions about how Rev. Wright influenced Obama's politics for twenty years? When will we see you grill Obama about his associations with people like Bill Ayers and Rashid Khalidi? When will you demand the L.A. Times release the video of Obama and Khalidi raising money for terrorists?

On the day we get to see these interviews and hear you ask these questions we might begin to believe you are a real journalist interested in fairness, accuracy, balance, thoroughness and objectivity.

As to the Bush Doctrine, one last question.

Do you know, that in addition to the question of Pre-Emption, the Bush Doctrine also includes these elements:

- taking the offensive in the war on Islamic terrorism,
- fighting them overseas so they don't attack our families here,
- establishing battle lines in Iraq to draw them in and concentrate their forces to dispatch them more efficiently, thus saving many lives and many years of effort,
- democratization in Iraq and Afghanistan as a non-military means of defeating the enemy, and as a stabilizing influence regionally,
- treating state sponsors of terror as the terrorists they are,
- drawing a hard line against murderers and murderer states and imposing sanctions until they agree to join the civilized world,
- gathering nations in coordinated resistance to nuclear aggression threatened by N. Korea and Iran,

- case-by-case analysis of how to fight and defeat Al Qaeda wherever they are found hiding behind women and children,
- strong support of Israel,
- efforts to convince other countries, such as Indonesia, to join us in the fight against Islamic murderers,
- improved global intelligence gathering to identify terrorists, track their movements, discover their plans, identify their means of support, take out their leaders, disrupt their tactics and strategies, thus preventing attacks,
- massive aid to Africa and activities designed to dissuade Muslims from embracing extremism,
- efforts to get the Europeans to support the war against terror,
- diplomatic efforts to get NATO more involved in Afghanistan ... just to name a few.

Was Sarah Palin right to ask you for clarification, Charlie?

Oh, and by the way, feral adolescents like Bill Maher and Keith Olbermann believe you did a marvelous job.

We can agree with Bill and Keith in this respect: you did a great job of representing what much of journalism has become in this country—-an attack machine serving Leftist interests, a machine directed by powerful ownership forces unconcerned about journalism in "the public interest."

It has become almost impossible to differentiate Saturday Night Live from ABC News and the rest.

That's the joke.

You have prostituted yourselves for celebrity.

You do not serve the public interest, you serve yourselves, and the corporate interests that use you to sell Buicks.

BILL MAHER: MAN OF FAITH

October 6, 2008

Although he doesn't know it, Bill Maher is a man of faith.

He has faith his audience will sustain him no matter what comes out of his mouth on Friday nights.

He has faith his money and his prominence guarantee female companionship.

He has faith his brain stem will continue to regulate his metabolism, blood flow, respiration, and brain function.

He has faith Time Warner and HBO will protect him from legitimate criticism and that the FCC is too busy trying to regulate the Internet to bother with his slanderous and profane remarks.

He has faith Todd Palin is not vindictive.

Bill has faith people will forget his idiotic remarks about the 9/11 hijackers.

Bill Maher has faith there is no God, and if it turns out there is, well, Bill has faith he won't be held accountable.

He has faith when he dies, that is all there is to it; there is no hell. This measured against the words of Christ in Mark 8:36 (NIV): "What good is it for a man to gain the whole world, yet forfeit his soul?"

Bill Maher prefers placing faith in human wisdom and his own intelligence, suggesting it is intelligent to wage war on people of faith, roughly 90 percent of the world's population. That's hardly intelligent, and it's not a function of faith. It's just foolishness.

The faith of Bill Maher remains self-centered, antagonistic to a sense of community, the idea of people working for the greatest good for the greatest number. Yet he wants us to believe he cares about community.

Recommendation: rather than waste time watching Maher's *Religulous*, rent or buy *An American Carol*, and have a lot of fun, or get *Fireproof* or *Courageous*, and be challenged to be a better person, even as you are masterfully entertained.

ARIANA HUFFINGTON: WAR PROFITEER

October 13, 2008

Arianna Huffington needs to chill. Her seething slander and heartless denunciations are beyond ridiculous. Her attacks against the mainstream media for hiring certain people are simply laughable.

Concerning Tony Snow, may he rest in peace, she writes on HuffPo, April 28, 2008, that he lied to us, consistently, saying he promoted " … some pre-packaged PR pitch cooked up in the White House to keep us in the dark. This was always Snow's specialty—along with a glib dismissiveness (sic) that made him the poster child for the Bush administration's brand of Callous Conservatism."

Now there's credibility Arianna style. You really don't need help to remain in the dark, girl. Most people will tell you Tony Snow was one of the finest human beings who ever lived.

Well, read on, because it has been made Kristol clear by Arianna Huffington: American politics is not, and cannot be, an exercise in reasoned debate engaged by contending patriotic parties working to acquire legitimate majorities.

No. Those who disagree with Arianna and friends (Soros, MoveOn, Daily Kos, Obama) are the "enemies of … reality." Of course, to embrace this lunacy, one must agree only Arianna has a grip on reality, which is, needless to say, unreal.

Arianna readily admits, as far as the left is concerned, politics is war: the right is the enemy, an enemy to be destroyed not debated.

She celebrates this kind of warfare on her propagandist blog, ignoring her own hyper-partisanship, at the same time accusing the MSM (the MSM!) of bias rightward. Yes, we all know how the massive media only serves the interests of conservative Christians and Republicans!

The author of *Pigs at the Trough* appears totally disinterested in the pigs at Fannie and Freddie, yet she seeks our vote of confidence with a book entitled: *Right Is Wrong: How the Lunatic Fringe Hijacked America, Shredded the Constitution, and Made Us All Less Safe.*

Presumably the "lunatic fringe" encompasses the Americans who put GWB in the White House twice, but let's not quibble. Arianna has already demonstrated a chronic aversion to facts. (And don't the facts have something to do with honesty, truth, and... reality?)

Arianna declares, "... make no mistake, (Karl) Rove, (Bill) Kristol, and (Tony) Snow are the enemies—of honesty, truth, facts, reality, and the public's right to know. Anything."

Certainly, Americans are a contentious lot. We've been buttin' heads since 1776. However, for Arianna, a once-devoted conservative, to insist politics is warfare belies her ignorance concerning values we once held dear, values that have tended to bind us together rather than rip us apart. Obviously she prefers ripping.

And if binding together in these perilous times provides the tipping point to survival, Arianna's worldview tends to hand our future to our real enemies. In other words, demonizing Americans who disagree with her is not only sophomoric; it actively works against the greatest good for the greatest number.

The founders set up a system of government where competing points of view could be heard, debated, and evaluated such that compromise and consensus might yield positive decision making. All this, it was expected, would be conducted in the context of honor, fair play, and mutual respect, the assumption being everyone at the table sought what was best for the country.

Arianna and like-minded people prefer we divide into warring camps. They prefer savage politics and reject the politics of good will. While she points the boney finger of accusation—denigrating good men by going so low as calling them the enemies of truth—she simultaneously ignores serial crimes in her own camp and excoriates a massive media sympathetic to her cause.

In war, all that matters is winning. Some people fight according to the rules. Others decide that winning is so important the rules don't matter. This is what Saul Alinsky taught Barack Obama, and this is what Arianna embraces.

So in war, without rules, ACORN, Ayers, Rezko, Jeremiah Wright, and Farrakhan are of no concern to Arianna and her allies. These are mere distractions unless the MSM picks up the scent.

Dick Morris, writing today, indicates those associations will be of interest to most Americans if the markets stabilize and financial chaos no longer occupies the front page:

> As ACORN gets raided by the FBI, it will hurt Obama. He was general counsel to its Illinois affiliate, and Obama channeled millions to the radical group when he got control over the money William Ayers got from the Annenberg Foundation. All of these ties are damning for Obama and will reinforce the doubts that Wright first put in our minds. They will lead people to question Obama's values and his fitness for the presidency. A man whose spiritual adviser is Wright, whose financial backer is Tony Rezko, and whose first major employer was William Ayers might not be a good choice for president. But for these associations to loom large enough in our consciousness to impact our vote, the market has to settle down so we can hear the campaign over its din.

Will voters turn and consider the glaring warning lights on Obama's dashboard?

Not if Arianna and her cohorts have their way.

Dominating media, education, entertainment, and politics for fifty years, the left has learned how to manipulate, confuse, and distract the public. And the left knows if you appeal to selfishness, you have an advantage right out of the gate. Most people are motivated by selfishness, and so the left preys upon that destructive impulse. Hence, the left tutored people away from self-reliance and hard work, urging them to insist on government largess, appealing to selfishness, all in the name of benevolence, of course, behind the slogan of hope and change.

Arianna, leading the Obama charge, will have you believe it is their "right" to rule this country because anyone who disagrees with them is the enemy of "honesty, truth, facts, and reality."

Historically, leftist domination always translates into tyranny, always.

Thus Arianna and friends trend tyrannical, waging war against our fundamental strengths: mutual respect, fairness, love of country, and a tradition of preferring patriotism to ideology.

Fueled by an almost hysterical devotion to ideology bordering on psychosis, Arianna cannot even extend mercy to the deceased, slandering Tony Snow—by all accounts one of the most decent, honest, and respected figures ever to grace American public life.

Misinformation accomplished Arianna. Your blog is a battle-axe in the war you obviously relish and profit from.

PASTORS BECOMING POLITICAL ACTIVISTS: INTENTIONALLY PROVOKING THE IRS

October 16, 2008

Did you know most Christian pastors do not have full freedom of speech rights in America, thanks to former President Lyndon Johnson and Congress?

It's true. At least that is what pastors have been led to believe.

Churches are tax exempt as charitable organizations. According to IRS rules, however, churches can have tax exemption stripped if churches endorse a candidate. These rules were put in place in 1954 by Congress approving an amendment submitted by then Sen. Lyndon Johnson. Nonprofits are supposedly prohibited from political activism as well, but obviously, in the case of organizations like ACORN and Obama's Public Allies, the law is selectively enforced.

Why did Johnson seek to prohibit churches and nonprofits from political activities? Certain pastors in Texas opposed him. He sought to silence them. Interesting: the accelerated liberal trend to silence opposition voices. What of the free exercise clause?

And so pastors have been cowed for years, silenced by threats from the federal government right here in America.

But all that is changing.

Now comes word that a tiny cadre of three dozen or so activist pastors, working in conjunction with the Arizona-based religious rights legal firm known as the Alliance Defense Fund, are not only exercising their constitutional rights but also stand ready to challenge a 1954 amendment to the tax code that says nonprofit, tax-exempt entities may not "participate in or intervene in...any political campaign on behalf of any candidate for public office."

"Christian Pastors Stand Up," by Doug Patton
Human Events, Oct. 1, 2008

Yesterday words got feet in Arkansas.

In a predominantly black church in a city known for its past racial strife, Bishop Robert Smith is taking sides. His targets: Democratic presidential nominee Barack Obama and federal restrictions barring Smith's endorsement of Republican John McCain. At the end of a recent sermon on abortion and gay marriage, Smith told about 50 worshippers at his Word of Outreach Christian Center, "I will be voting for John McCain and Sarah Palin."

Pastor challenges IRS Policy,
Oct. 15, 2008,
Arkansas Online.com

Bishop Robert Smith is being joined by many others. WorldNetDaily.com reports June 20, 2008:

Gus Booth, a pastor in Warroad, Minn., preached from the pulpit, "If you are a Christian, you cannot support a candidate like Barack Obama," knowing that he was violating federal tax code and jeopardizing his church's tax-exempt status by speaking against a specific candidate.

Of course, it is worth noting liberal and radical pastors have long enjoyed both tax exemption and full freedom to endorse any candidate they like without sanction.

Jeremiah Wright, Father Pfleger, and Reverend Meeks are notable examples. When was the last time anyone reminded Jesse Jackson or Al Sharpton about IRS rules?

Note: for clarification on the legalities of politics from the pulpit, consult this 2004 article by Mat Staver of Liberty Counsel: *"Pastors, Churches and Politics: What May Pastors and Churches Do?"* It is a comprehensive guide to your freedoms under law, even in the face of IRS rules.

NINE TERRIFYING WORDS

October 17, 2008

People dispute this, but many say Winston Churchill once stated the following: "If you are not liberal in youth, you have no heart, and if you are not conservative in later life, you have no head."

I followed the pattern. As a college student, and for years afterward, I was liberal, very liberal, in my entire worldview, not just politically.

I recall a newspaper editor of mine years ago describing his journey from liberal to conservative, explaining that the realities and difficulties of life eventually confront and contradict liberal presuppositions, chief among them, the idea that sheer human wisdom will overcome human wickedness if we build and maintain correct and benevolent political and economic structures required to dispel injustice and poverty.

Of course the trouble is agreeing on what the "correct" structures are, and agreeing how to maintain those structures. However the larger issue involves the reliability of sheer human wisdom. Cutting to the bottom line: has human wisdom ever delivered us from human wickedness, ever?

Liberals routinely urge us to rely on human wisdom manifest in government for salvation. The trouble with liberalism is the core philosophy: human wisdom is reliable when expressed through bureaucracy. Since when?

Ever been to a V.A. Hospital?

Sure, roads get built, at huge cost overruns.

Has the $50B a year Energy Department created by Jimmy Carter produced one dime's worth of independence from foreign oil? What has the $25B a year Education Department ever done for you, other than provide declining test scores and soaring dropout rates? How about government-sponsored family planning giving us 50 million abortions, STD epidemics, teen pregnancy, promiscuity, much of this impacting negatively the very building block of society, the nuclear family.

Examples of government incompetence and waste are monumental. About the only government-run outfit of merit is the Post Office, but they clear the place with an AK periodically.

Our military is brilliant, but even there, line troops joke about SNAFU.

And then, the most glaring recent example of liberalism run amok—Fannie Mae, Freddie Mac—a massive fraud by government trying to engineer outcomes, yielding economic destruction, leaving the poor worse off than before.

Ronald Reagan was absolutely correct proclaiming: "The nine most terrifying words in the English language are: 'I'm from the government and I'm here to help.'"

I'm reading his diaries. Very insightful. In 1982 he said unless we reform Social Security, Medicare, and Medicaid, those programs will overwhelm the federal budget to the detriment of all other spending priorities. Here we are today, and those programs consume 45 percent of the budget. With Boomers now retiring and submitting claims, the system will collapse in less fifteen years.

The only practical solution is generating more government revenue through economic growth stimulated by tax cuts, open markets, and renewed productivity, coupled with drastic cuts in federal spending, the Republican platform.

Instead, Democrats insist on increasing taxes and increasing spending, all in the name of relying on human wisdom and government. Trouble is, this platform will only accelerate economic decline, hastening collapse. Some people think that is the idea, for once the collapse occurs, a new socialist utopia can be constructed on top of the rubble.

Let's remember, our country was born out of a deep suspicion of government, a deep resentment felt toward oppressive bureaucracy, and a violent rejection of the idea government was the answer, coupled with a hunger for freedom. Thanks to an ever-expanding federal government populated by politicians who no longer represent the people, we face much the same situation as did the Founding Fathers. This is no longer a government by, for and of the people as Lincoln proclaimed. It is a government by, for and of liberals, and the "new" structures they are building to "dispel injustice and poverty," are simply more government domination, and control, especially control of the economy.

We were in a huge debt situation before the crash and the $1.5 trillion bailout, before many banks were 'nationalized.' Politicians have put us in hock up to our ear lobes. We are slaves to debt and government. Think of the control government will have over your life once government controls your health care, cradle to grave.

The Founders would be astonished and ashamed to see people who call themselves Americans willingly allow government shackles to destroy the original achievements of the Revolution.

In 1972 I voted for Shirley Chisholm. Back then I was a liberal, and she was a champion of the underdog. She was also a champion of open government. She hated the back room dealing in Washington. She also scolded voters, saying Americans get the government they deserve, and if we don't like what's going on, we have the power to change it. She got my vote because she had guts and spoke plainly.

The question is, will Americans vote freedom Nov. 4 and return to the principles that launched our great Republic, or will we meekly walk into the prison cell and close the door, content to be housed and fed, no longer a free and vibrant people?

The Founders knew something about human wickedness and the power of power to corrupt. This is precisely why they designed a system of checks and balances so that the three branches of government would be restrained. The idea was to avoid too much power centering in one place so as to corrupt the entire government.

The assumption is Barack Obama will be our next president, he will preside over a heavily liberalized Legislature, and he will appoint liberal Justices, creating a heavily liberalized judiciary. If this happens, too much partisan power will dominate the three branches, and checks and balances will be drastically diminished, perhaps rendered impotent.

So here is a reason to vote McCain: preservation of the system of checks and balances.

Here is a positive reason to vote McCain: if you understand the preservation of freedom requires hard choices that often run contrary to self interest (a matter of the head, not the heart), then you also understand we must stand with Lincoln, Churchill and Reagan, and vote to preserve traditional Americanism.

And besides, in a world more dangerous than ever, does it make sense to gamble on an unknown quantity when you have a known and reliable alternative?

Leftists academics and media types said Reagan was unqualified, ignorant, reactionary, stupid, uninformed and out of touch, but Reagan's presidency is now seen as one of the most successful in history, simply because he had faith in traditional American values, promoted them, and confronted evil.

I could be wrong, but I suspect Shirley Chisholm would be mighty proud of Sarah Palin. I am absolutely positive Reagan is applauding Palin.

WILL WE PREFER THE CALM OF DESPOTISM?

October 21, 2008

Our second president said this at the end of his life, speaking directly to us, here and now:

> Posterity, you will never know how much it cost the present generation to preserve your freedom. I hope you will make good use of it. If you do not, I shall repent in heaven that ever I took half the pains to preserve it.
>
> President John Adams

Much has been written about the two Americas: rich and poor, red and blue, right and left, traditional and post-modern, religious and agnostic.

Given politics driven by different ideas about our purpose, it can be said we have divided into two increasingly warlike camps. These camps have been locked in struggle for the soul of the country for at least sixty years.

One camp—considered New Age—is populated by people born in the post-WWII era. They were raised in the 1950s, came of age in the 60s, then launched a new vision of America, something dramatically different from what had gone before, a counter culture, in short, a systematic repudiation and contradiction of every element of traditionalism premised upon the notion America is inherently evil—

racist, sexist, imperialistic, jingoistic. It is supposed, in this camp, these ills can only be cured by a purging of all things Judeo-Christian and free market and military, and government is the logical agent to exact this purging. This camp—what this writer calls Americans In Name Only (AINO)—has worked hard to successfully conquer and control government, education, media, entertainment, and publishing. Consequently, tax dollars fund legal advocacy groups that tear down the Ten Commandments, insist the Boy Scouts allow homosexual leaders, force gay marriage through judicial activism, deny rights to people in the womb, codify assisted suicide, and employ the arm of law enforcement to stifle free speech and enforce new codes of politically correct behavior. Ultimately, conformity and control are the tools used to build the new "consensus," by force, if necessary. Some might say it is King George in a different robe, bearing the likeness of Karl Marx. These AINOs are the driving force behind the Obama candidacy, with the help of foreign powers.

The other camp—considered old hat—are people born somewhere before and during WWII, raised in various times of struggle and depravation, coming of age even today in the hearts and minds of ten year olds. Sadly, members of that greatest generation are dying off rapidly, their torchbearers now minority voices dominated by media, Malibu, and Manhattan.

This second camp we call traditionalists. How do we define traditional Americanism in this pluralistic society? One might be tempted to gaze on Norman Rockwell paintings in a kind of nostalgic exercise to capture a sense of traditionalism, risking hyper romanticism. Another might embrace the 1940s or the 1830s or 1776 to find strands of traditionalism. Yet traditional Americanism is not a place or a painting or a period of time. Traditional Americanism lives in a set of simple ideas and essential virtues: liberty, equal opportunity, justice, goodness, charity, hope, promise, community, volunteerism, fidelity, honor, faith, prudence, restraint, service, economy, individualism, self-reliance, family, and courage. Revisionists will scream objections, but the truth is our moral lifeblood has always flowed from Judeo-Christian traditions not from an embrace of AINO universalism.

Based on their understanding of the laws of nature and the presence of the Creator, the founders struggled to birth our country, first by shedding blood to throw off the domination of England, then by sweat and tears to form the government, followed by more sweat and tears and sometimes blood, arguing what emphasis to place: strong central government or states' rights; isolationist foreign policy or expansionist engagement; government setting the pace in promoting social change versus change from the bottom up by the people informing government as they worked it out for themselves. The dynamics shifted here and there, back and forth, and continue today. The miracle of this experiment conducted by free and independent people is just that, a miracle.

Like all things, this miracle has a life span and will be replaced by something else, something less, as the miracle worker is displaced.

What the founders feared most has come to pass: we have created an enormously powerful federal government, now presiding over a desperately split and antagonistic population. Combine this reality with looming bankruptcy and unprecedented foreign threats, and we are found standing on the edge, staring into the abyss.

We have traveled far afield from our roots. And if the polls are correct, we insist on traveling further. At a time when proven traditional Americanism should wisely inform our proceedings to affect our salvation, like stubborn children we appear insistent on an alternative path, one that suggests implementing methods already shown to be failures: larger government, more taxation, government-prescribed social engineering, central control of the economy, attempts to appease enemies, weakened national defense, erosion of family and morality. Will we actually sell our birthright for a bowl of stew and healthcare?

Do we really think it wise and enlightened to place faith in government instead of our proven track record walking in the traditions of our fathers? Did not our revolution contradict the idea government is the solution, either monarchy or democracy? Have we fallen so far as to demonize a good woman like Sarah Palin and exalt a person like Barack Obama, a man who won't even take a stand for the civil rights of babies who survive abortion?

By putting Senator Obama in the White House, we will be saying we have crossed over from being primarily a country of traditionalists, to Americans in name only. We will have placed our feet on a new threshold. The path beyond is grimly lit. Yet one thing is certain: we will, in doing this, squander the liberty purchased and sustained by so many for so long. We will, in doing this, say to our Creator, "You are no longer the centerpiece of this republic but merely a side show, and a tenuous one at that." Do modern ears cringe at the strident words from a giant of Americanism?

> They that can give up essential liberty to obtain a little temporary safety deserve neither liberty nor safety.
>
> Benjamin Franklin
> *An Historical Review of Pennsylvania, from its origin, etc.*, 1759.

Are we then making good use of this great freedom by handing it over to those who would destroy it? Are we deserving of liberty if we refuse to protect and defend it?

Our third president, Thomas Jefferson, said, "Experience hath shewn, that even under the best forms [of government] those entrusted with power have, in time, and by slow operations, perverted it into tyranny." And, "Timid men prefer the calm of despotism to the tempestuous sea of liberty."

Timid people fail to preserve freedom and, rather, accept the calm of despotism by electing Barack Obama. Therefore, to recapture liberty, there will be tempestuous seas ahead or a passing away of the miracle forever.

ANYBODY NOTICE WE'RE BROKE?

October 28, 2008
Problem:

> Medicare is under water by $30 trillion dollars, Social Security by $5.7 trillion, and that's just considering a 75-year horizon.
>
> David Walker, former Comptroller General, former Democrat

For your information: Medicare and Social Security make up 45 percent of the federal budget.

Solution: "Clearly you want to minimize tax burdens in order to maximize economic growth, maximize disposable income, and maximize investment, productivity, innovation, to maintain our competitive advantage," declares David Walker.

The last thing we do is follow Obama's plan: raise taxes, increase federal spending, cut defense, extend benefits and amnesty to illegal aliens, ignore border security, allow the UN to tax Americans, launch government funded healthcare, restrict trade.

The problem is going to get much worse very quickly with boomers filing for benefits in the face of a shrinking workforce.

Measures we can take to solve the problem: freeze spending on all but essential services; stabilize the housing market (protect families' homes); encourage long-term investment in the stock market with tax breaks; cut taxes for everyone (which has always stimulated the economy and actually increased revenue to the treasury); go through the federal budget line by line to reduce spending and cut ineffective/wasteful programs; increase trade; support small business and corporations so they expand and create jobs; tax reform making it simpler and more equitable*, real energy independence and development of domestic sources of petroleum so we can transition to cleaner alternatives; and use nuclear and clean coal to get there as well.

(*In reality we already have income redistribution. The top 25 percent of income earners pay 86 percent of the income taxes, and the lower 40 percent of income earners pay nothing at all. We are already soaking the rich, the very people best positioned to invest and grow the economy and create jobs. Dumb.)

We are seeing wealthy Americans move resources offshore and away from Obama's IRS. The Obama effect is already being seen in the markets as well.

As to defense as a percentage of the overall budget, get a load of this: again, David Walker.

1965: 43% of the federal budget spent on defense
2005: 20% of federal budget spent on defense

Who in his right mind suggests cutting defense and hamstringing our military and intelligence agencies in a time of unprecedented threats worldwide?

Recommendations from David Walker:

1. Re-impose budget controls both in terms of taxes and spending

2. Increase transparency in terms of long-term costs projected

3. Must reform entitlement programs (cut and reorganize, not expand)

4. Must re-engineer the base of mandatory and discretionary spending

5. "Clearly you want to minimize tax burdens in order to maximize economic growth, maximize disposable income, and maximize investment, productivity, innovation, to maintain our competitive advantage," declares David Walker. (JFK understood this and agrees with McCain by the way.)

6. "There are lots of numbers and they are all big and bad. This is about values and people." Public officials have a responsibility to leave the country better positioned for the future. This has been our tradition.

"The baby boomer generation may be the first in our history to break that tradition," says Walker, calling it immoral.

This is about our kids and grand kids.

In short, we have to tighten our belts dramatically and become hyper-disciplined concerning government spending, yet Obama wants to take us in the opposite direction, insisting on an orgy of new spending, and this will bankrupt us and destroy our economy.

OUR FOLLY WILL BE CLEAR TO EVERYONE

November 6, 2008

It may be President-Elect Obama will govern broadly and effectively. That remains to be seen.

What we see today is the left insisting those who opposed Obama are narrow-minded, right-winged Christian bigots, racists, homophobes, sexists, and imperialists (as seen on HuffingtonPost.com or MSNBC). Of course, their irrational and continuous hatred of George W. Bush fuels resentment just as it launched Obama's presidential ambitions, and it cannot be denied he exploited those resentments, however misguided, doing so brilliantly.

Honest people who raise legitimate concerns about an Obama presidency based on valid political philosophy and issue-orientation should not be vilified simply for having an opinion, but this seems the popular past time of leftists, ironically contradicting their exclusive claims to kindness and diversity. Remember Saul Alinsky's Rules for Radicals: in the place of logical debate, it is better to demonize the opposition and ridicule it.

How intolerant the left! How unkind they are to anyone who holds a divergent point of view. What is it called when one group refuses the right of conscience to another? The savaging of Sarah Palin condemns them.

Christians are, by definition, narrow minded according to the left, but what can be more narrow minded than the bigoted hatred expressed by the left against the most diverse community on earth? Christians embrace an enormous range of people from all nations, all walks of life, all creeds and colors, all political orientations, and all corners of the world, all agreeing Christ is God, God is love, and serving God promotes goodness.

Why is Barack Obama's Christianity palatable but not Pat Robertson's? The points of departure involve issues like gay marriage and abortion and freedom. Now who is narrow minded? And the left behind Obama is a force for unity?

Mr. Obama is obviously intelligent, charismatic, capable, learned, and articulate.

However, there are two things he will never accomplish: he will never change the nature of man or the will of God.

Once the euphoria of the moment passes, people will realize the world is dangerous not because of Christians, not because of America, or George W. Bush, but because of despotism, lunatic terrorists, and leftist control freaks hell bent on imposing their amoral secularism on everyone.

Perhaps at that time people will once again consider the claims of Christ and embrace the truth, rejecting the universalism being peddled by Mr. Obama and the Democrats, concluding in the end there are no political solutions ultimately.

Feeling good for the moment is one thing. Being right for eternity is *the thing*.

Why is the world seemingly orgasmic over the election of Barack Obama?

People have been sold a bill of goods. Ask most Obama supporters why they support him, and generally it boils down to, "He makes people feel good."

It will be very sad when they wake up in a few weeks or months to realize GWB is not the enemy and America is not the enemy, but rather the devil, working through human beings, is the enemy, and Mr. Obama can no more deliver them from the devil or the ravages of human nature than can GWB or anyone else.

The world is cheering because they think the election of Mr. Obama means deliverance from fear and an ushering in of a new age of peace and prosperity. It will not happen. Remember, the Word talks about what it will look like in the last days, about judgment, disobedient people, false prophets, and vain imaginations.

> *But mark this: There will be terrible times in the last days. People will be lovers of themselves, lovers of money, boastful, proud, abusive, disobedient to their parents, ungrateful, unholy, without love, unforgiving, slanderous, without self-control, brutal, not lovers of the good, treacherous, rash, conceited, lovers of pleasure rather than lovers of God—having a form of godliness but denying its power.* Have nothing to do with them. They are the kind who worm their way into homes and gain control over weak-willed women, who are loaded down with sins and are swayed by all kinds of evil desires, *always learning but never able to acknowledge the truth.* Just as Jannes and Jambres opposed Moses, so also these men oppose the truth—men of depraved minds, who, as far as the faith is concerned, are rejected. But they will not get very far because, as in the case of those men, their folly will be clear to everyone."
>
> 2 Timothy 3:1–9 (emphasis added)

Our country is being overwhelmed by wickedness. In this light, Isaiah 57 is especially applicable.

America will be judged because of greed in high places and immorality. And indeed, the world is being judged for these and many sins. We compound our offense by placing faith in a mere man and ignoring the warnings from heaven.

Calling Mr. Obama a false prophet may be stretching it, but when he says he is a Christian but also says universalism is "required" as a basis for democracy and insists abortion is a constitutional right, it is legitimate to raise the issue of consistency and fidelity.

Many people of good will wish Mr. Obama the best, but there are those who have lived long enough to see the facts of life played out over and over, remaining convinced there is no pie in the sky, also remaining optimistic and hopeful, not succumbing to cynicism.

Ultimately, as the Word says, let God be God and every man a liar. By godly faith we rise. By human wisdom we fall. When will we learn? The truth will stand regardless of elections, popular trends, or the passions of the day, and, in time, our "folly will be clear to everyone."

WHY ARE LGBT PEOPLE SO HACKED WITH CHRISTIANS?

November 14, 2008
Perhaps secular ears will hear...

Not long ago a gay couple in West Hollywood hung Sarah Palin in effigy. That image will loom large in the minds of the Palin children for many years, perhaps for a lifetime.

In recent days at demonstrations in Palm Springs we've seen gay protestors knock a cross out of the hands of a grandmother, stomp all over it, and scream in her face. She is filing charges.

We've seen homosexual protestors invade church services Sunday morning and rail against people, shouting threats. We've seen what appears to be Anthrax mailed to LDS churches. We have seen protests throughout southern California and threats of more violence and demonstrations. And we have heard LGBT leaders call blacks ignorant bigots for voting in favor of Proposition Eight in California.

All this is no way to build consensus, invite understanding, or forward the cause of mutual respect.

It appears we are incapable of engaging a rational discussion when it comes to the topic of homosexuality. Many of us in the traditional faith community want to challenge those in the LGBT community to consider: perhaps Christians are not hate-filled homophobes but instead rational people with a legitimate point of view. Why are you so intolerant of our point of view? Why do you give yourselves permission to do violence against us? Maybe gay marriage is unhealthy for everyone. Regardless, don't people have a right to an opinion? Do they not have the right to vote their conscience on issues central to the organization of society?

The answer is no if we listen to contemporary gay activists.

For those more moderate in approach and sensibility, please try to understand where Christians are coming from. Quell the emotion for a time and try to come at this with hardcore objectivity and rational inquiry.

Our belief is God is very clear in his Word.

People have the freedom to accept his Word or not. Neither God nor man is forcing anyone to do, or not do, something or other. Is that plausible to you? We are simply following the dictates of our conscience. Do we have the freedom to do so? Do we have the right to do so?

What does God's Word say about homosexual behaviors and gay marriage?

Here are the most often cited passages from both Old and New Testaments. Please read carefully.

> Do not lie with a man as one lies with a woman; that is detestable.
>
> Leviticus 18:22

> If a man lies with a man as one lies with a woman, both of them have done what is detestable. They must be put to death; their blood will be on their own heads.
>
> Leviticus 20:13

Keep in mind laws in Leviticus were laid down for the Jews at a specific time for specific reasons. Obviously as Christians we do not believe people should be put to death today. We live under an entirely new covenant and dispensation, one governed by grace and mercy and love, not the law. However, God does not change his mind about the nature of sin or move from calling something detestable to calling it blessed or sanctioned. This should be obvious.

> Because of this, God gave them over to shameful lusts. Even their women exchanged natural relations for unnatural ones. In the same way the men also abandoned natural relations with women and were inflamed with lust for one another. Men committed indecent acts with other men, and received in themselves the due penalty for their perversion.
>
> Romans 1:26–27

> Do you not know that the wicked will not inherit the kingdom of God? Do not be deceived: Neither the sexually immoral nor idolaters nor adulterers nor male prostitutes nor homosexual offenders nor thieves nor the greedy nor drunkards nor slanderers nor swindlers will inherit the kingdom of God.
>
> 1 Corinthians 6:9–10

> …knowing this: that the law is not made for a righteous person, but for the lawless and insubordinate, for the ungodly and for sinners, for the unholy and profane, for murderers of fathers and murderers of mothers, for manslayers, for fornicators, for sodomites, for kidnappers, for liars, for perjurers, and if there is any other thing that is contrary to sound doctrine…
>
> 1 Timothy 1:9–10

Let's remember the Word also says all have fallen short of the Glory of God, all are sinners, and no one does good, not one.

As Christians, we simply believe Christ and his Word, and the Word is obviously very clear. Demanding we act in ways contrary to what we believe is to attempt to force us to deny our Lord and deny conscience. Is that so hard to understand? Does our devotion make us homophobes by default? Of course not. Nor is it appropriate for members of the LGBT community to attack us, as we've seen in recent days in the wake of the passage of Proposition Eight in California.

No doubt gays will come back, saying, "You are asking us to deny our conscience telling us homosexuality is sin." Well, somebody is wrong, and somebody is right. Logic alone disallows both parties claiming truth. Perhaps the following will help explain our point of view further.

I've had gay friends as far back as 1972. One old friend, who is long gone, once told me gay activism was entirely misguided. He said there was no point declaring war on the larger society. (Gays comprise 3–4 percent of the population.) He said it would only cause endless turmoil for no good reason. I think he was right. It is understood that flying under the radar is anathema to many people in the homosexual world, but this is where my friend concluded the matter for himself. The fact he was a college professor may carry weight with some people.

It pains me to think homosexual friends are headed for judgment. What is the most loving thing I can do? Accommodate their sin as they stumble into hell or try to dissuade them from following a destructive and unhealthy lifestyle that ultimately leads to eternal separation from God? The answer is obvious. If I ignore the sin of a brother and let him fall, die, and go to hell, one of two things must be true: either I do not love that brother, or I do not believe sin will visit these consequences.

If my brother's house is on fire, do I stand on the sidewalk and wish him well and walk away, or do I rush in to save him?

It is not an act of love to silently standby and pat people on the back while they destroy themselves.

And it is not discrimination to speak the truth in love.

We have always held to the idea of community standards of morality as defined by the majority. Several states voted against gay marriage this last go around. Is there any respect for voters out there? So far, all states have voted against gay marriage except one. If the people in that state want to codify gay marriage, so be it.

Why must the LGBT community insist the majority submit to their vision of marriage? There is a distinct tyrannical flavor to it.

Otherwise, it is astounding to hear so-called pastors ignore God's Word, accommodate sin—which is killing people—and bow to tyrants.

Lord, help us.

As always, the Lord of love shows the way.

When the religious hypocrites threw the adulterous woman at Jesus' feet, challenging him to give the order to stone her to death, the Master waited for a teachable moment, challenged the sinners to cast the first stone, loved the woman, and told her to "sin no more." He restored her, not by accommodating her sin, not by looking the other way, but by protecting her and leading her into the light, by his grace.

With Christ as our example we must "go and do likewise." We should neither condemn sinners nor codify sin into law, all the while recognizing we too are all sinners, saved only by grace, and that, "not of ourselves, lest anyone should boast" (Eph. 2:9).

Pastors who prefer accommodation to salvation lean to their own understanding, lead people to destruction, and dishonor the Lord, all in the same breath.

> Trust in the Lord with all your heart and lean not on your own understanding; in all your ways acknowledge him, and he will make your paths straight.
>
> Proverbs 3: 5,6

We can no sooner force gay people to be straight that we can force Christians to be atheists. God never forces anyone to do anything. He simply invites people to enter his rest and enjoy a loving relationship with him, thereby allowing the Holy Spirit to conform us to

Christ, the personification of Truth. Entering this loving relationship allows a person to enjoy the essence of true freedom.

Christians should be able to take a stand for our beliefs, and we should be able to do so in this country without being assaulted. Any objective examination of the record shows Christians do not assault members of the LGBT community.

Hopefully members of the LGBT community will try to understand Christian beliefs and confront this ludicrous idea Christians are somehow filled with hate and out to get them. It's a lie from the pit of hell, and, somehow people know this, but they let the lie goad them to violence nonetheless.

We continue to pray for peaceful resolution, asking for an end to hostilities and an embrace of understanding, even an understanding unto salvation. Most Christians I know are willing to live and let live but cannot, as a matter of conscience, sanction gay marriage. It appears more and more LGBT people are not willing to live and let live but are pleased to fight and fight some more.

If that is the case, we are in for a long fight.

THEOPHOBIA AND PERSECUTION

November 20, 2008

Not long ago I attended a presentation by high school students. They were introduced as the cream of the crop. They gave verbal presentations concerning the knowledge they had acquired studying our democratic republic. After the formal presentations, there was a question-and-answer period. One question posed, "Do rights come from God or government?"

The students agreed: Americans' rights come from government.

We hear a lot about rights these days and not much about responsibility. We hear various groups clamoring for their "rights," routinely calling on government to provide these "rights." (My teachers and my folks told me the only rights I had were to life, liberty, and the pursuit of happiness, and from there it was up to me.)

Homosexuals demand the right to marriage. Many people claim rights to abortion, healthcare, a college education, a job, secure retirement, and, according to some, everyone has a right to believe and act according to the dictates of his/her own conscience exclusively. Indeed, one of the published humanist principles is personal autonomy is a higher good than responsibility to your neighbor or obedience to fixed moral duties. (Translation: do your own thing so long as it's not hurtful. The trouble with self-indulgence is it always hurtful.) Selfishness is praised in humanism, justified with the attitude doing one's own thing is fine so long as others are not hurt. The trouble is selfishness and the inevitable addiction to self-indulgence always hurts others, and frequently destroys the indulgent one. Selfishness is synonymous with sin.

In our post-modern, secularized world, selfishness becomes a civil right because supposedly everyone has innumerable rights endowed by government, a growing list in fact—more rights than we can fund!

Except Christians. People today actually call for diminishing the rights of Christians. Some have suggested we not be allowed to vote. Not kidding. Why? Well, that is simple if you understand that Christians are intolerant homophobes, bigots, racists, and fanatics. So naturally we are increasingly targeted for ostracism and worse. We are a menace to society. All that love-your-neighbor stuff is very harmful, don't you know.

We hear endlessly about homophobia. The word resounds twenty-four-seven and seems to have for years.

In the interest of equal time, let's talk about theophobia for a while!

By *theophobia* I do not mean the "fear of God." Biblical "fear of God" means the due respect and reverence one appropriately feels toward the King of the universe, and such good feelings are said to be "the beginning of wisdom," reference Proverbs 1:7 and Psalm 103:13. (Please look it up.)

However, a healthy fear of the one who has "the power to throw you into hell" is quite the motivator as well, reference Luke 12:4,5.

What I mean by *theophobia* here is the irrational and prejudicial fear of all things religious, particularly Christianity, and especially the conservative kind.

Considering this definition, is it right to designate theophobic people like Christopher Hitchens, Bill Maher, Michelle Goldberg, Richard Dawkins, and Chris Hedges? All tell us religious people are irrational, even deranged, especially Christians, and conservative Christians are the worst because we promote a new nationalism, which always leads to fascism. (They are quick to dismiss the argument patriotism preserves liberty, the very opposite of fascism.)

"Scholar" Juan Cole, University of Michigan professor, went so far recently to say fundamentalist Islam and traditional Christianity are the same: we are all theocrats! Now how is that for academic prowess, deep perception, and articulation of nuanced understanding?

Not long ago Cole's kin—Rosie O'Donnell, Robert Reich, and Bill Moyers—all claimed traditional Christians (all those wild-eyed Jesus lovers opposed to gay marriage and abortion), yeah, all those anti-intellectual knuckle-draggers, well, they are no different than the Taliban, seething masses of morons hell-bent on establishing theocracy. (And here we've had four hundred years to get there, and we've still failed!)

Who wouldn't fear theocrats? How many of us would eagerly board a plane for an extended stay in Iran?

Ironically, those attacking Christianity and Christians with the accusation we seek theocracy fail to understand, or refuse to acknowledge, that it has been Christians throughout history standing in the way of all kinds of tyrants. After all, let's remember it was Christians who brought Rome to her knees and ended gladiators slaughtering one another in the arena, Christians who stood in the way of Islamic aggression down through the centuries, Christians who challenged the feudal system, the exclusivity of the Roman Church, the divine right of kings and the notion any man could own another. Furthermore, lest we forget, it was a band of Christian colonists who wrote the First Amendment, so let's not have any more of this bilge about Christians being the agents of despotism. It's always been a lie from the pit of hell.

Given the drumbeat about horrible Christians for years, there are growing numbers of people who actually hate Christians, content to ignore their own bigotry on the road to persecution. So far the persecution has only amounted to a few physical assaults here and there, such as the grandmother confronted by gay activists in Palm Springs on November 13, 2008. They screamed at her, roughed her up, and knocked the cross out of her hands then stomped on it.

Kids are routinely hammered in school for any expression of Christ's love. You don't have to go far to find endless examples of how secular political correctness gives teachers and students permission to confront and denigrate Christian students from kindergarten through college.

As the anti-Christ sentiment escalates, one wonders how long it will be before we see in America what we've seen for years overseas: violent persecution, torture, and murder. Vitriol always precedes outright violence. Thugs have to work themselves up to it you see. As the anti-Christ rhetoric booms across the land, is it unthinkable it could ever lead to killing? Are such thoughts plain paranoid?

If theophobia is coming to our shores, what does it look like overseas, and what can we learn from observing the treatment of Christians in other countries? You have to go looking because it's not roundly reported, is it? It has been called the most ignored news story in decades: the global persecution, torture, and killing of Christians.

Remember, it all starts with verbal violence.

This WorldNetDaily report Feb. 18, 2002 illuminates the point, as do the incidents following:

> Christian persecution sounds like something from the distant past—conjuring up images of the early followers of Jesus being thrown to the lions, and various apostles being crucified or otherwise martyred for their faith. (All but John died violent deaths.) In reality, more Christians have died for their beliefs in the last century than in all other past centuries combined.
>
> The Islamic world is a hostile place for Christians: In Saudi Arabia, for instance, Christianity is illegal, and conversion from Islam is punishable by death. In Pakistan, the death penalty is prescribed for anyone who "blasphemes" Islam—something that occurs automatically during Christian evangelism. In Egypt and elsewhere, Christian girls have acid thrown in their face by Islamic extremists if they refuse to convert to Islam, or are raped, or worse. At best, in the more enlightened Islamic societies,

Christians (as well as Jews) are second-class citizens, have a special tax imposed upon them, and do not share the rights of Muslims.

The communist world is no better. According to recent reports from groups monitoring religious persecution, the Chinese government is cracking down as never before on "underground" Christians—those who do not join the "official" Chinese churches. The Committee for Investigation on Persecution of Religion in China published what it said were official documents—implicating top-level Chinese leaders—that outline a campaign that includes torture to stamp out independent worship. Researchers said that in "house churches" (those not sanctioned by the totalitarian government) in 20 provinces, 129 people had been killed recently, 23,686 arrested and 4,014 sentenced to "re-education."

A Christian aid worker, a woman not involved in evangelism, a British citizen, was gunned down recently in Afghanistan. She was targeted for assassination by Muslim leaders solely for her Christian faith. She was there helping the disabled.

"Female *aid worker shot* dead in *Afghanistan*,"
The Telegraph, Oct 20, 2008

Iraq: Two Christian Sisters Killed

On Nov. 12, two sisters were killed and their mother wounded by a gang of Islamic extremists in the al-Qahira section of Mosul, Iraq, according to VOM contacts. The gunmen shot one of the sisters as she was waiting for a bus outside their home. They then stormed into the home, killed the other sister and injured their mother. A bomb placed by the assailants at the entrance of the house detonated as police arrived on the scene, injuring several officers.

Voice of the Martyrs, Nov. 12, 2008

The situation for Iraqi Christians has been intolerable for years: "Between 1991 and 2002, 300,000 of them migrated out of the country" (ChristiansofIraq.com).

Hundreds of thousands of Iraqis have been displaced since the 2003 invasion, and many thousands have been slaughtered by Muslim extremists.

And it all goes unreported, though there are efforts to identify and confront the atrocities. However, thanks to the work of David Barrett and Todd Johnson, found in the report "World Christian Trends," William Carey Library, 2001, we learn:

> The persecution of Christians, especially in Islamic and communist countries, gained a much higher profile beginning in early 1996. It is estimated more followers of Christ have died for their faith in the 20th century than in all the 19 previous centuries combined. In his Focus on the Family Newsletter, James Dobson wrote, "More than an estimated 160,000 believers were martyred in 1996, and countless others were subjected to unimaginable horrors. And the persecution appears to be escalating exponentially."

Other notable aspects of the Barrett/Johnson study:

Total number of Christian matyred through the year 2000: 70 million

Those most responsible for killing Christians between AD 33–2000:

State ruling power	55,871,000
Atheists (overlap with above)	31,689,000
Muslims	9,121,000

Any wonder Christians are a little leery of government, especially atheists in charge of government?

All this comes as no surprise to serious Christians. After all, the LORD told us flat out we would be hated for loving him and for following him, and he says the time will come when people will believe they are doing God a favor killing us (John 16:2). In killing Jews and Christians, Muslims believe they are doing God a favor—*now that's a theocracy worthy of attention.*

We don't have government domination in the United States because Americans believe our rights come from God—at least that's what the Declaration says. By taking God out of the arrangement, government inevitably replaces God, and then people are made subservient to government, a prescription for tyranny.

Elementary, high school, and college students throughout the country are being systematically indoctrinated, contrary to the Declaration, taught to embrace government as god.

How is this for a stunning realization: your tax dollars wasted on a massive scale used to corrupt youth leading to the destruction of America?

All of it because Christians have allowed themselves to be cowed by secular humanists, atheists, and theophobes.

Bill Ayers is grinning in the dark.

Al Qaeda doesn't have to lift a finger.

SAVAGING OF SARAH PALIN

December 17, 2008

> ... *out of the overflow of the heart, the mouth speaks.*
>
> Matthew 12:34

One of the people reacting to an earlier post here accused me of hyperbole when I said the vitriol leveled at Sarah Palin these last three months amounts to shameful barbarism, a blot on the national character. Hyperbole. So, just for the sake of illustration, here is a partial list of the things said and done, *keeping in mind, all the allegations are untrue, much of it conjured up by Obama operatives:*

- Professor Juan Cole, Middle East Studies, University of Michigan, wrote an article comparing Palin's Christianity and political philosophy to fundamentalist Islam, essentially saying Palin is a theocrat, no different than the Taliban. Now there's scholarship for you.
- Larry Flynt and the porn movie he produced starring a Palin look alike
- The strip show featuring Palin look alikes

- The gay men in West Hollywood that hung Palin in effigy during Halloween (nice memory for the Palin children)

Other accusations/slander and libel:
- she claimed Trig was her son but it was actually her daughter's
- she had an affair with her husband's business partner
- she used her public office to engage a personal vendetta
- she is a liar, a moron, an ignoramus and a theocrat
- her husband has sex with his daughters
- she cut funds for unwed teenage mothers
- she tried to censor books at the Wasilla library
- she moved to legislate the teaching of creationism in Alaskan schools
- she hates gay people
- she is a racist
- she is a horrible mother for running for VP when she has all those kids
- she took $500k from the RNC for clothes
- she is an idiot for having a child so late in life
- she thinks Africa is a country
- she thinks she knows about foreign policy because she can see Russia from her house
- she doesn't know what the Bush doctrine is
- she can't discuss SCOTUS decisions
- her church is a lunatic asylum that supports African witch doctors
- her fellow church goers speak in tongues and worship with snakes

- she endorses murdering wolves from helicopters
- she doesn't care about polar bears
- she's a war monger
- she promotes abstinence but her daughter got pregnant out of wedlock so that makes her a hypocrite
- her hair is dumb
- her wardrobe is antiquated
- she is a dominatrix
- her only qualification to run for VP is she hasn't had an abortion

- she is not a feminist, she is not even a woman
- Sandra Bernhardt wanted her gang raped
- Madonna wanted to slap her, shouting "Sarah F—king Palin" at concerts
- many celebrities and political leaders said they hate her and wished her ill
- Rep. Rangel called her disabled
- Whoopee Goldberg called her "very dangerous"
- Bill Maher referred to her as a M.I.L.F. and claimed Trig was fathered by John Edwards, just to be funny of course, ha, ha.

So is it any wonder somebody poured gas all around Palin's church and torched the place last week?

Consider: James Chapter 3: 5–10 (from The Message)

⁵ A word out of your mouth may seem of no account, but it can accomplish nearly anything–or destroy it! ⁶ A careless or wrongly placed word out of your mouth can do that. By our speech we can ruin the world, turn harmony to chaos, throw mud on a

reputation, send the whole world up in smoke and go up in smoke with it, smoke right from the pit of hell. [7] This is scary: You can tame a tiger, [8] but you can't tame a tongue–it's never been done. The tongue runs wild, a wanton killer. [9] With our tongues we bless God our Father; with the same tongues we curse the very men and women he made in his image. [10] Curses and blessings out of the same mouth!

Jesus proclaims in Matthew 15:11: "What goes into a man's mouth does not make him 'unclean,' but what comes out of his mouth, that is what makes him 'unclean.'"

And in Matthew 12:34 he says: "You brood of vipers, how can you who are evil say anything good? For out of the overflow of the heart the mouth speaks."

Finally, as to Judgment, Matthew 12:36: "But I tell you that men will have to give account on the day of judgment for every careless word they have spoken."

Judgment will include weak-kneed Christians who have joined in the savaging.

Something is terribly wrong with a society that stands by casually witnessing the lynching of a good, decent, accomplished, and godly woman.

SUBMIT TO THE GOVERNMENT IN ALL THINGS?

March 30, 2009
Today's dilemma for people of conscience

If we face the truth squarely, asking what has allowed so much evil to overwhelm our country, surely we must admit the silence of good people has contributed enormously.

Our pastor—God bless him—is a man of faith and honor, someone to respect and uphold in prayer. Sunday, his sermon raised compelling questions about faith, submission to authority and obedience to the counsel of Scripture.

Part of his sermon referenced Romans 13:1: "Everyone must submit himself to the governing authorities, for there is no authority except that which God has established."

The passage goes on to explain that anyone who rebels against the government is rebelling against what God has established, bringing judgment upon themselves. Obedience to government authority is therefore consequential, and a matter of conscience.

Our pastor pointed out that Paul wrote these words while imprisoned for two years, suffering serious mistreatment at the hands of government. He pointed out that Believers must wrestle with these things, allowing the weight of Scripture to inform our thinking and our behavior. He also said that for him, it was a straightforward matter: obey the government, pay your taxes and support your President, your reasonable service.

I'm wrestling. I find myself suffering severe cognitive dissonance: contradictory thoughts fighting for prominence in my mind and my soul.

I hear the Lord's voice telling me all Scripture is God-breathed, render to Caesar, store up treasure in heaven.

I also hear the news: the government is using tax dollars to fund abortion overseas; it promotes Planned Parenthood; Congress is working to destroy all limits on abortion passed by state legislatures; the government promotes homosexuality; there is a proposal to force doctors to perform abortions even if they object as a matter of conscience; the powerful in government support partial birth abortion and our President has supported the practice of allowing babies to die if they survive an abortion; the number two person in the Justice Department has a long track record of defending child pornography; and, AIG and CITI bailout money (our tax dollars) is being channeled to Sharia compliant organizations which fund terrorism.

How does one uphold Scripture and, at the same time, submit to government, allowing tax money to be spent in such ways?

One might say one's civic and spiritual duty is to pay taxes and let God judge, for He will repay, and He will judge.

Another will say, "No! I will not pay taxes, I will not fund the murder of innocent babies, I will not participate in atrocities and grievous sin being practiced by my government!"

Further along in Romans 13 we are admonished to pay taxes, followed immediately by passages reminding us about the commandments, including "do not murder."

This is a dilemma. For those of us who consider abortion murder, paying taxes to this government amounts to subsidizing murder, it amounts to participating in murder. It is a grave matter of conscience.

What will American pastors do if the government makes it a hate crime to preach against the sin of homosexuality? Will they submit to the government or to God?

The American people have made it clear on many occasions we do not want tax money funding abortion, we believe doctors should be allowed to follow the dictates of conscience, we believe it is wrong to discriminate against homosexuals just as we believe same-sex marriage is wrong, we do not support partial birth abortion, and we strongly object to government bailouts, especially when that money finds its way into the hands of terrorists.

Does the federal government respect our wishes and like a good public servant respond to the wishes of the people? No! This government dictates and manipulates and decrees by executive order, insisting many of us ignore the deepest points of conviction and conscience. Like King George, this government imposes it's will indiscriminately: a tyrant by definition.

Is this then a point of no return?

Are there more compelling Scriptural requirements of a Believer at such time as government becomes overwhelmingly evil?

Certainly, Corrie ten Boom was not a scriptural 'rebel' for hiding Jews from the Nazis.

Dr. Martin Luther King, Jr. was not a 'rebel' for exercising his right to redress grievances.

Abolitionists who helped slaves to freedom, and Christians who fought child labor, were they 'rebels' for addressing the great evils of their day?

Was Henry David Thoreau a 'rebel' for refusing to pay taxes in protest of the Mexican-American War and slavery?

Were the Founding Fathers 'rebels' in a scriptural sense for Declaring Independence and throwing off the tyranny of Great Britain?

A first-rate book on this subject comes from Tom Minnery at Focus on the Family titled "Why You Can't Stay Silent, a Biblical Mandate to Shape Our Culture," Tyndale publishers, 2001. Billy Graham is quoted on page 51:

Christianity grew because its adherents were not silent. They said, "We cannot but speak the things we have seen and heard," a reference to the message of evangelism. Nor did they stop with expressing the great faith they had found. They stormed against the evils of their day until the very foundations of decadent Rome began to crumble. Is the church doing that today?

Billy Graham spoke those words in 1962, at the beginning of the Civil Rights movement, a movement the evangelical church ignored in large part. The Reverend Dr. Martin Luther King Jr. carried the water virtually alone. Think of the healing we might have accelerated in this country had the church "stormed against the great evils" of racism and discrimination fifty years ago.

Think of the opportunities we miss today by being likewise complacent and self-serving.

Baptist Pastor Greg Dixon wrote a column April 14, 2001, titled "Rethinking Romans 13," published by WorldNetDaily.com. It is well worth reading.

Pastor Dixon was arrested and his church was seized by the government because he refused to comply with government taxation policies involving the status of church workers. Here are some poignant excerpts from Pastor Dixon's column:

> In recent years, Christians have interpreted Romans 13 as a command for unlimited submission to government by God. Many proponents of this belief have sat passively by, in the soft pews of their place of worship, while evil has triumphed in most areas of family and church life. In our pacifistic smugness, many have allowed government to become god without even knowing.
>
> The opponents of unlimited submission to government are deemed as rebellious, anarchist and disobedient. However, there is no practical, historical or biblical consistency in the shallow agreements of these simpletons.
>
> In July of 1774, our forefathers met in Fairfax County, Va., and considered ways of forcing Great Britain to redress American

grievances. George Washington and George Mason were the instrumental agents in drafting what has come to be known as the "Fairfax Resolves."

[Resolve #6] "Resolved that Taxation and Representation are in their nature inseparable; that the right of withholding, or of giving and granting their own money is the only effectual security to a free people, against the encroachments of Despotism and Tyranny; and that whenever they yield to one they fall prey to the other."

In simple terms, the Resolves offered George III two obvious choices. One was to fulfill his covenant obligations and be the king and ruler to the American Colonies that he had agreed to be or, second, to prepare for war. George III was asked to reflect upon the fact, that if he did not keep his end of the covenant, there could "be but one appeal."

Last—and most important—it is not biblical. Daniel disobeyed Darius and went to the lions' den. The three Hebrew children broke the law for not bowing. The parents hid baby Moses from Pharaoh. Rahab lied to protect the Hebrew spies. The Apostles went to prison for preaching Christ in the authority of Heaven. Paul and his followers in Acts 17 did contrary to all the decrees of Caesar in order to make Jesus the King. Even Jesus lived in direct opposition of the political religious leaders of his day and went to the cross for us.

…we have a practical, historical and biblical mandate to fervently disobey any unconstitutional laws and all government officials who cease to be good ministers of Jesus Christ. God almighty is the only power that deserves unlimited obedience.

Most assuredly, no one is suggesting armed insurrection, or the withholding of taxes for casual reasons, to simply rob the government, the motivation rooted in truly selfish and rebellious impulse.

However, people of conscience, Christian or no, must allow the weight of the conscience to work and inform both belief and behavior.

If it is true this government has now become a glaring agent of immorality, acting contrary to the moral sense of the community, and indeed contrary to the clear laws of God, then all people of conscience must seriously consider which is the greater sin: supporting such a government, or refusing to do so, in full knowledge of the consequences.

I for one see the Master in the temple with a whip, and choose to follow.

WHAT OBAMA IS DOING NO MYSTERY, WELCOME ONE WORLD GOVERNMENT

May 9, 2009

Millions of Americans have been scratching their heads in recent months, asking, "What on earth is going on?"

Why the blitzkrieg to radically transform our country on practically every front?

Why one crisis after another?

Why is the government taking financial irresponsibility to new heights?

Why is this new government seemingly unconcerned about terrorism or our lethal enemies?

Why the push for gun control, expansion of abortion, control of the Internet, violations of civil rights, denigration of the Constitution, centralization of power?

Why is Christianity being attacked on every front?

Some assert Obama hates America. They say he wants to refashion America, transforming the country into a Euro-socialist state. But that was largely accomplished long ago, before Obama rose to power.

Some people think this president and his allies simply want America to modernize and more fully engage the rest of the world in more benevolent and positive ways, despite the fact America has led the march to modernity and is probably more engaged globally than most nation states.

Other people believe Obama is a plant, a tool, a man groomed from an early age to upend capitalism and help create an egalitarian utopia.

Well, it would appear Mr. Obama is a tool, all right, but only one in the shed.

If you read about the idea of an "open society" as put forward by George Soros, you get some sense of where Obama is taking us, but one doubts if either Obama or Soros fully realize the gamble they're insisting we take.

The collectivist impulse the Honorable Janice Rogers Brown has decried is only a part of the story.

The *impulse to achieve security and control*, even at the expense of liberty, appears the overriding motivation.

No doubt the traumas inflicted on humankind by twentieth-century world wars and attending atrocities have driven many thinkers, educators, and politicians to insist global problems can only be solved by global government. The rapidity of change, advances in technology and communications, nuclear proliferation, environmental degradation, and escalations of violence have combined to create a world that, they say, is unsustainable, a world on the brink of apocalypse.

All one need do is listen to the hyperbole broadcast by Al Gore to get the picture: unless humankind intervenes with global cooperation, we are doomed.

Terrorized by the prophets of world's end, masses of people anoint this or the other messiah, desperately crying out for "peace and safety" in fear of "sudden destruction."

Undoubtedly the forces pushing for global governance envision a benevolent community of man under a system of human-defined fairness, supposedly altruistic, and sufficiently powerful to crush all troublemakers, those who would trample the utopian dream. It isn't that the utopians hate America so much. Rather, America stands in their way. Christian America takes a stand for right versus wrong: she advances a clear moral agenda and protects and defends those values than hinder utopia. Therefore, America must give way. After all, you cannot create an egalitarian utopia if people insist on national sovereignty. You must destroy national identities to form global federalism, and, besides, nationalism causes wars and promotes tyranny, right? (Or so the argument goes.)

You can't achieve utopia if you have a bunch of religious fanatics claiming their rights come from God. For a global government to be installed, there must be consensus that rights come from government. Consequently, the religious fanatics must change or migrate or become extinct.

Therefore, these outdated ideas in the Constitution must be "directly confronted" and "turned upside down."

Get a load of this declaration by James MacGregor Burns in his 1984 book *The Power to Lead:*

> The framers of the U.S. Constitution have simply been too shrewd for us. They have outwitted us. They designed separate institutions that cannot be unified by mechanical linkages, frail bridges, tinkering. If we are to 'turn the Founders upside down'—-we must directly confront the constitutional structure they erected.

It is not hard to see that Burns, like many others including President Wilson, agree with Obama that America must be "fundamentally transformed" in order to advance global governance, our salvation.

It is no accident, therefore, that everyone connected to the Obama administration is cut from the same cloth: one world government advocates, or, as the new term describes it, "trans-nationalism."

Everything is viewed through a trans-national lens, and all policies direct the establishment of a global government.

After all, what person in his/her right mind would object to a hands-across-the-sea approach to international peace and understanding?

Secretary of State, Hillary Clinton, recently said that "ideology is so yesterday." What did she mean by that?

Well, in her mind, and in the minds of people like Bill Clinton, Barack Obama, most Democrats, and too many Republicans, it means the brave new world is not about socialism versus capitalism, creationism versus Darwinism, democracy versus communism, religion versus atheism, or the ruling class versus the third world. No. Hillary is right. It's not about ideology.

It's about *indisputable pragmatism*.

There is no other way you see.

Global federalism or one world government or trans-nationalism—whatever you call it—is our only salvation, according to the HRC and BHO and FDR and Woodrow Wilson.

And it has not been accomplished thus far by revolution. Instead their progress has been realized through infiltration, staged change, gradual paradigm shifts, and influence via education, the arts, media, entertainment, so-called journalism, and staged crises used to great advantage to convince people of this "indisputable pragmatism." It is so obvious it is beyond debate and discussion. It's Zen politics: it just is.

Al Gore, another tool, provides an excellent example to prove the point: the debate concerning man-made global warming is over, he says. (What a great crowbar in the advance of trans-nationalism.)

The establishment of world government—wholly dependent upon human intelligence and capability—relies solely on two frail presuppositions: the sufficiency of human wisdom and the expectation people will cooperate for the greater good, setting aside self-interest in support of the health of the collective.

History teaches over and over that people are selfish; they do not place self-interest in the back seat, and no amount of political pressure short of authoritarianism approaches the goal. Even the most extreme forms of authoritarianism fail to control and rightly direct the masses.

Secondly, history also teaches humans—existing as we do as combinations of angels and demons—cannot forsake an innate drive to be free. When the New World Order is threatened by freedom lovers, can there be any question who will prevail? Again, the only outcome must be tyranny.

And what kind of utopia exists thanks to the tyrant?

This, then, is the great gamble Soros and Obama force us to take—they ask us to bet on an inside straight; they suggest we ignore history and human nature and embrace one world government, knowing the odds are we will instead draw the tyranny card.

For when the dream of utopia is dashed, with democratic republicanism destroyed forever, the only card left is tyranny.

Security and control are illusions. Even tyrants eventually lose control, putting everyone's security at risk.

For two centuries America has stood for goodness. She has stood against the thug and the tyrant. She has disappointed their plans for world domination many times. For all her faults, she remains a beacon of hope and freedom.

If we surrender to the thugs promoting trans-nationalism and one world governing authority, the hope of the world dies with us.

ABORTIONIST DR. GEORGE TILLER KILLED

*The culture of death marches forward:
the murder of Tiller and the assault on truth*

June 1, 2009
Within hours of the shooting, the brain-damaged left started grinding out conspiracy theories, initiating the blame game.

Cristina Page, author of *How the Pro-Choice Movement Saved America* (quite a title, eh?), gives her opinion on HuffPo. She says pro-life "chatter" and "rhetoric" has increased in frequency and aggressiveness since Obama took office, concluding there is a pattern here: when pro-abortion presidents take power, pro-life people feel disenfranchised and they become violent. (But be sure to ignore the violence perpetrated against the unborn.)

Page notes there were no abortion-related acts of violence during the Bush administration, but during the Clinton years, violence against abortion providers increased markedly, and with the killing of Tiller, in her mind, there is a clear indication the pattern holds. Page's assertions are moronic. Correlation studies are not conclusive.

Of course she doesn't mention the fact most people do not support abortion on demand, especially if tax dollars support it, and this president has "frequently and aggressively" moved to fund abortion on demand with tax dollars, thus provoking the very pushback Page decries. Ever notice how a toddler never takes responsibility?

Therefore, if we want to play the blame game, using the "logic" of the left, isn't it just as plausible to blame Obama as anyone for Tiller's death?

Page goes so far as to assert the rhetoric of the pro-life movement is responsible for Tiller's death, making them murderers and terrorists. Make way for the thought police and the further erosion of free speech. Has it never occurred to Cristina Page it might make sense to blame the man who pulled the trigger?

Air America online, playing pretend journalism, employing stellar logic, claims Tiller's killer watched O'Reilly on TV, so it is "a fair question" to ask if O'Reilly is responsible for Tiller's death. Staying with the logic, Timothy McVeigh watched NBC coverage of Waco, so I guess Brokaw is responsible for the Oklahoma City bombing. Lately, people on the left have even likened Tea Party protestors to McVeigh, saying McVeigh is the logical founder of the anti-Obama movement.

Remember the left blaming Rush Limbaugh for Timothy McVeigh's crimes?

Shall we blame all actors for the death of Lincoln?

Everyone opposed to gay marriage is then responsible for the death of Matthew Shepard?

The age of incoherence strikes again.

Last October HuffPo writer Carol Burger killed her former lover Jessica Kalish by stabbing her 222 times with a screwdriver. Was that just a crime of passion, or is there a political angle somebody would like to cynically exploit even though gay-on-gay violence is routinely more vicious than run-of-the-mill murders?

Remember George Weber, the New York WABC newsman who was stabbed fifty times by a sixteen-year-old boy responding to an ad for rough sex? The left tried to blame Christians for that one too.

On the other side of the coin, anybody see anyone on the left shed a tear for Terry Schiavo? When Christians blamed the culture of death and a heartless judge for Terry's death, we were castigated as fundamentalists and fanatics.

When Rev. Fred Winters was gunned down in his Illinois church in March, did anyone on the right blame the anti-Christ rhetoric of the left for Winters' murder? (Not a word.) Did anyone on the left, including Obama, call the murder an outrage and send in the feds? (Didn't think so.)

With the murder of Tiller, keep in mind the "intelligence" report by DHS Secretary Napolitano warning of the dangers of rightwing extremists, anti-abortion protestors, gun owners, and returning military personnel.

AG Holder is sending US Marshalls, so the Tiller murder now has complete federal attention. No political motivations? Shouldn't the county sheriff there insist the feds stay out?

(Speaking of conspiracy theories: was this killer hired to hit Tiller to provide ammo for the left to shoot at the right? How is that for a "reasonable question," eh, Air America?)

The murder of Dr. Tiller plays nicely into the hands of those who seek the ultimate destruction of the conservative movement and traditional Americanism. That effort has always been fueled by emotionalism and propaganda demonizing conservatives. With Obama expressing "outrage," he leads the charge against all things conservative and traditional, using a tragic aberration as a springboard, classic propaganda.

Everything is political for these people, even a tragedy in a Kansas Lutheran church on a Sunday morning. Give the devil his due. He knows how to harden unbelievers and make believers look bad. The real war is spiritual. Notice how the leftist blogs are making Tiller a Christian saint.

Daily Kos is running stories glorifying Tiller, calling him a Christian, and condemning all pro-lifers, conservatives, and "other" Christians as being responsible for this murder. They reference "senseless acts of violence" like these over many years.

Legalized abortion has been around since 1973. Did Congress legalize abortion? No. The Supreme Court legalized the murder of babies by conjuring up a phony right to privacy argument, part of the tradition of interpreting the Constitution as a "living document." In the thirty-six years since, there have been three abortion doctors killed, not by anyone considered mainstream conservative or Christian, but by people obviously unbalanced.

Still, the likes of Daily Kos and Air America point to these incidents to indict millions of people of faith and conscience while they ignore the "senseless acts of violence" perpetrated against the millions of babies in the womb. Hypocrites.

Many prominent people are now stepping forward to make a hero out of Tiller, saying he courageously saved women's lives even under the constant threat of violence. What a crock. It would appear some people have such a seared conscience the dismembered bodies of infants do not elicit even the faintest sympathy. Those who reap profits by killing babies are made heroes. What world do we live in anymore?

Meanwhile, multiple murders perpetrated by Obama pal Bill Ayers and Weather Underground associates go virtually ignored. And many want to forget Obama voted numerous times to neglect babies who survive abortion so they die slowly, painfully, cast aside like trash, alone in the dark.

Few in leadership express "outrage" over the murder of two thousand, seven hundred unborn children daily in the United States.

Five babies killed every minute in America.

There is no justification for the murder of Dr. Tiller, just as there is no justification for the murder of babies in the womb. They have a right to life, liberty, and the pursuit of happiness like every other human being.

The God of love and mercy is furious about all murders. His judgment stands above all others.

For the record, Dr. Tiller's specialty was late-term abortions, or partial birth abortion, the killing of a full-term baby whose body has been delivered from the vaginal canal, but the head is still inside the mother's body. The doctor uses a pair of scissors, stabs the baby in the back of the neck, opens the scissors to expand the hole, giving access to the brain, which is then sucked out with a hose.

Anyone who defends this practice has lost conscience, just as anyone who cheers the murder of Dr. Tiller.

If you have the guts, sit down and search online for the video "Abortion: The Silent Scream Part 1 2 3 4 5 Complete Version." After viewing this video series, many abortionists take up other lines of work.

Obama said yesterday, "However profound our differences as Americans over difficult issues such as abortion, they cannot be resolved by heinous acts of violence." Such as the heinous acts of violent abortion funded by government, Mr. Obama?

Fifty million American babies murdered since 1973, and we call it a woman's right, merely a privacy issue, it's legal.

Holding to the logic, because Hitler made it legal to kill six million Jews, it was a German right to privacy?

Some people want other people out of the way for selfish reasons: that's the truth.

It all boils down to who has the power to decide who lives and who dies.

Allowing the state to exercise killing power outside the governance of due process while ignoring human rights is a moral outrage and a recipe for social disaster. The left would have us ignore the unborn and direct our rage at those seeking their protection.

And compounding the moral depravity and rush to destruction, the left insists on using this murder to gleefully skewer conservatives and Christians, another cynical power play in the blame game promoting a culture of death and the escalating culture war.

THE THREE-PAGE BIBLE

June 26, 2009
Okay, here is the straight story.

I'm God. The One True God. I have always existed. I'm King of the universe, I created everything, and in the beginning earth was just a wad of dirt. I formed it, formed you, created all the animals and plants and everything, and created a beautiful paradise for your ancient grandparents, Adam and Eve. For a short time I enjoyed such a wonderful, loving relationship with those two. I also created all the angels. I control everything from sub-atomic particles to an expanding, infinite universe, but I cannot control love. I've been working for many years communicating through chosen servants to tell you how much I love you. I always tell the truth. I always keep my word. Always. I am your eternal lover, and I am a jilted lover.

Creation is sustained by love, which makes sense, because I am Love. (I know this next bit will be a mind bender for you, but when I say I AM, I'm saying I am actually three persons in one being: Father, Son, and Holy Spirit. I know it doesn't compute. You'll just have to trust me on this, and everything else too by the way. That's what faith is all about.)

Some of the angels I created got prideful and decided they were going to take over. Their leader had led worship in my presence, but I was forced to throw them out, for the sake of love. Some of you say I should have destroyed evil by destroying Lucifer and the rebel angels, but you see, if you go around destroying everyone who opposes you, you destroy love in the process. Unless people love voluntarily there's no love at all. Lucifer was an angel, but when he led his rebellion, he became Satan. He lost all touch with love. He was the most beautiful angel, but, he became most ugly. Hell is his ultimate destination, a place he created for himself and for all who insist on following him. While I AM Love, I also hate evil. Evil is death. Love is life. I am sovereign. I call the shots. It's about justice.

Adam and Eve were happy in paradise. We enjoyed company in the cool of the evening. I only had one rule for them: don't eat from the tree of the knowledge of good and evil. That rule was there to protect them. (I only make rules to protect people. People have the option to disobey, to their own harm.) My commandments protect you from evil, from the influence of Satan. He loves to lead rebellions, and since I threw him out, all he wants to do is promote evil, and steal, kill and destroy. The rule not to eat from the tree was there to protect Adam and Eve, but they fell for the temptation of Satan, disobeyed, and threw the entire world into a death spiral. Giving the devil place has that effect.

It was heartbreaking, for all of us. My heart is still broken. After that, the whole world drifted away from me. I gave you the Ten Commandments so you could measure how far you had fallen and grasp the distance between us, understanding the nature of sin and evil. But I never left you, I never cut you off, and I always had a plan to save you from the enemy of your soul.

Did I know Satan would rebel, and that Adam and Eve would disobey? Of course. Remember, I know everything all the time everywhere. So why did I bother with Adam and Eve and the whole creation? I am eternally, infinitely creative and overflowing with love. I love and create and renew and love some more. It's my nature. Abundant life nourished by love is the center of my being. For me it was all worth it, even though I knew love would cost me dearly too. Lovers everywhere suffer rejection and ridicule. Love is a risk.

Anyway, after Adam and Eve disobeyed, the world fell into sin and death, which is what happens to everything apart from me, that's just the way it is. If you cut off a living thing from the source of nourishment, it dies. The human race went from bad to worse: killing, stealing, destroying, just like Satan. It would have been easier to just destroy the whole mess, but once again, love restrained me. However, there was a problem. I'm perfect. My justice is perfect. The whole human race had become murderous. Justice demanded the death penalty, but I just couldn't bring myself to do it, although the people in Noah's day had gone so far down, there was no hope of retrieving them, so I did give the earth a good scrubbing, allowing a remnant to survive to carry on. (There is great blessing at the end of the entire process. It will add up . Don't be afraid. Trust me.)

My perfect justice demanded the death penalty, but the love of the Holy Spirit called out to save people from sin and death, and it seemed hopeless to all the faithful angels, until they understood our long range plan as it unfolded. The Son is the key.

The Son stepped forward saying: "I'll go down and become one of them, fulfilling the law of love. I'll go and take their rightful penalty in my own body, fulfilling the law of justice. Then, for all who believe in me and accept my work on their behalf, a new Garden of Eden is available." And that is what happened. Satan was vanquished, evil destroyed, humanity saved, the laws of love and justice fulfilled. Today you have the same choice Adam and Eve had: serve Me or serve Satan. Trust me, there is no in between.

So now, we are working to get as many people back from Satan's cruel hands as possible, but we cannot force anyone, because that would violate the law of love. We love you and want you to come home. It's really as simple as that. If you believe on the LORD Jesus Christ, repent of your sin, and walk with Us, you will have the abundant life I've always wanted for you on earth, and the bliss of eternal life with Us in heaven.

Our perfect love casts out fear. And since Jesus took care of perfect justice, you are free, no longer under judgment, free to walk with me in the cool of the evening.

Don't waste any more time.

Come on home dear one.

THE PARABLE OF
THE TOWN HALL

August 20, 2009

In a small town in Oregon one Monday afternoon, assorted Americans gathered two hours before a planned town hall meeting with their congressman. The congressman, eager to hear from his constituents, had booked a meeting room at the local police station, a room capable of seating 126 people.

No one was allowed in prior to meeting time.

While about one thousand gathered outside in the heat, the congressman enjoyed cool drinks and air conditioning, the very same congressman who had recently voted in favor of economic stimulus spending without reading the legislation first.

One man outside in line decided to go into the lobby of the police station to ask why early arrivals could not be seated in the meeting room. He was told the congressman had ordered everyone outside, and, for security reasons, the police chief concurred. The man was further informed attendees would be granted access via a side door, not the main entrance.

Returning outside, the man noticed a large group already lined up outside the main entrance, so he went to the side door as advised.

Soon, the man was approached by a second man who said anyone opposed to Obamacare was a fool. Determining the first man was indeed opposed to Obamacare, the second man launched into a sermon about vile insurance companies, greedy doctors, corrupt Republicans, and filthy drug companies, essentially saying anyone opposed to Obamacare was a heartless criminal.

The first man, realizing one cannot reason with a turnip, remained silent for the most part, except to point out the federal government is already too powerful and inept, so granting it more power to mismanage healthcare is nonsense.

This inflamed the second man who began yelling such that his spittle flew in all directions.

Eventually a comrade of the spewers approached the first man, telling him he had to go to the back of the line. She said other people had arrived earlier than he, so he must go to the back of the line.

He asked her why.

She said it was a matter of fairness. One shouldn't cut in the line.

Informing her he had only followed instructions and that he was not responsible for others forming a line in the wrong place, he refused to move, amused by her insistence he move to accommodate people who had made a mistake, like asking one citizen to pay health insurance premiums for another who refused to take care of himself or demanding one citizen pay the mortgage of another.

Still, she insisted he move to the back.

He informed her, "Some people don't like being dictated to."

Miffed, she rejoined the spewers, whispering invective and pointing a boney finger.

Close by, two elderly women wearing Democrat buttons appeared weary from standing in the heat. Standing around them, the spewers did not seem to notice. Another man offered the women chairs and water. His placard read, 'Obamacare is a Nightmare.' The women thanked him for his kindness.

Eventually, various verbal skirmishes broke out at various places in the line, heated discussions that carried into the meeting room where the spewers cheered the Congressman and shouted down all opposition.

And the cloth-eared Congressman, playing both sides against the middle, kept his eye on re-election not far in the distance.

A week later in the local newspaper, the editor informed his readers the forces of hate had ruined the town hall meeting, and he didn't mean the spewers. Nor could he be bothered to attend the meeting or provide any news coverage fore or aft, choosing instead to "interview" the congressman and dutifully report whatever he had to say steno style.

Moral of the story: into every conservative's life, much spittle will fall. Stand your ground, be kind. And if you get fair treatment from the newspaperman, it means hell has indeed frozen over.

DARK DAYS FOR THE REPUBLIC

September 5, 2009
Civil war and revolution converge

You know what is not so funny? It's not so funny to look out and see powerful forces in the executive and legislative branches of government playing games with the lives of my wife and children. It isn't funny to realize the America they may inherit will not vaguely resemble the free and vibrant republic created by the founders or even come close to the America I fell in love with in the 1950s and 60s.

People used to talk about the counter culture as if it was a harmless fad, a passing fancy, the inevitable and short-lived expression of teenage angst given mass expression by technology and changing social structures. When pot gave way to cocaine and hippies made way for yuppies, people tended to think one era had ended and another had begun. Little did we realize the counter culture was only one of many bus stops along the way in the twentieth century, all of them strung out along a path designed to destroy the Judeo-Christian tradition, economic freedom, and our republican form government.

Early in the last century, anarchy was *la philosophie du jour*, and, since it is the nature of politics is to abhor a vacuum, anarchy had to give way to something, and what a something we got. Imagine the twentieth century without the world wars, genocide, and regional conflicts all sparked and sustained by the tyrannical regimes deriving from anarchy. Whether you note Chinese or Russian communism, soft socialism in continental Europe, or national socialism in Germany and other forms of fascism in Spain and Italy, all emanated from the mass appeal of anarchy rising from the war on traditionalism. Chaos invites the strongman.

The Founders were true intellectuals, classically trained, steeped in history, philosophy, the arts, sciences, humanities, and mathematics. They knew full well human government was self-corrupting. They knew from history, reason, and the laws of nature and God that, left to his own devices, man mucks things up in short order. Humans, therefore, needed a form of government that would protect them from government, from themselves, and from each other.

We are a murderous lot requiring restraint. And we are born to freedom. Too much freedom: anarchy. Too much restraint: despotism. Where, then, was the balance point?

The essential question before the founders at the convention: how do we craft a structure of government that provides essential functions but is self limiting and able to preempt the unending impulse of man to dominate man, whether in the form of monarchy or other authoritarian regime?

The brilliance of the founders revealed in the Constitution established a republic wherein the rule of law, modifying majority sentiment, is supervised by three co-equal, cross-checking branches of government, established to preserve liberty, ensure domestic tranquility, and protect the unalienable, God-given rights of the individual. The founders knew the Constitution must always be preserved, protected, and defended if Americans were to retain citizen authority to limit the size and power of the central government, that once that government grew beyond the limits imposed by the Constitution, the republic, and indeed liberty itself, would be in peril.

To replace the idea of God-given rights with the idea of man as his own god is to destroy the republic and with it liberty. Without the linkage between God and the rights of man, the rights of man become subject to the whims of man, and eventually they become alienable. So long as God protects our rights, government can never take them away, which is precisely what makes them unalienable. Hence the crucial linkage between God-given rights and the preservation of liberty.

Therefore, to disconnect God is to dismantle our republican structure according to the Constitution, an act of suicide.

And here we are today, on the thresh hold of drinking the Kool-Aid.

Many groups converging on the battlefield seek to destroy the republic and the Constitution and thereby destroy the traditional idea of America as defined by the founders' vision and genius. It does not matter if you call one group socialist, another communist, another anarchist, another neo-fascist, another statist, or another a democratic people's republic: all operate according to a collectivist notion of utopia driven by a reliance on human wisdom, that human wisdom 'rightly guided' and concentrated in a central government will plan and produce and provide and protect everyone's rights, including the 'right' to food, healthcare, housing, education, clothing, meaningful work, recreation, and retirement at the expense of liberty and all creative, productive elements in society.

And so we have the two competing visions for America today: the founders' vision versus the collectivist vision, freedom versus servitude, liberty versus conformity. Conservative America wants to protect, preserve, and defend the Constitution. Leftist America wants to turn the Constitution on its head. Thus, with a collectivist in the White House, the counter-culture revolution has arrived, and now we see a counter revolution emerging, citizen-waged, railing against the federal government while at the same time the competing visions of America square off in a kind of civil war.

You have to wonder about a president that stokes the fire and insists the nation bend to his will. Whether the battle is over First Amendment rights, Second Amendment rights, the right of private property, freedom of thought, conscience and movement, or on many other fronts involving states' rights, individual liberties and economic freedom, this president has made it crystal clear he wants more power, more control, and a free hand to force conformity.

This is no longer about fellow Americans working together to form a more perfect union. This is about large groups of occupiers waging war with traditionalists to radically transform our republic into a collective farm.

But there is another dimension to all this that is all the more ominous: the collectivists here want to join with collectivists worldwide to establish world government, world currency, and world justice. That may all sound very utopian, but as with all utopias, only the oligarchs benefit. Strong American sovereignty preserved and protected by a Constitutional and Republican form of government prevents global governance. Hence, for the collectivist with global ambitions (which is why global warming is so convenient), American sovereignty must die so that humankind can live.

Notice no one is advocating a global republic. No, the only means of achieving global governance is through the concentration of power in the hands of a few: oligarchy.

The rest of us are forced to embrace serfdom. And this is the progressivism they insist we welcome, endorse, and promote?

As for me and my house, we will fight for the Constitution, for the flag, and for the Republic for which it stands, one nation, under God, and by God, indivisible, impervious to the schemes of tyrants, for even a minority in God is a majority in the world.

WAR ON TERROR OR "OVERSEAS CONTINGENCIES"

September 12, 2009

Yesterday at a 9/11 memorial event, the president said we must renew our resolve to defeat al-Qaeda, which will likely sound strange to our military men and women in the field, people who volunteered with resolve, a resolve requiring no renewal, unless, of course, they've been demoralized during the last several months.

Mr. Obama promised yesterday to "do everything in our power to keep America safe." A few questions and thoughts come to mind in the context of these remarks and recent developments:

Mr. President, when you told us we should no longer say "war on terror" but rather encouraged us to say "human-caused catastrophe" or "overseas contingency operations," was that your way of renewing our resolve?

Was it renewing for you to bow to the king of Saudi Arabia?

Is it renewing and encouraging when you tell the world we did not live up to our values in the days following 9/11?

You seem to believe America was partly responsible for the 9/11 attacks because your pastor certainly believes that, as do many, many of your close associates and political allies. What a way to renew our resolve.

When you refuse to take responsibility and constantly blame Bush and Cheney for everything under the sun, suggesting they be investigated for war crimes, is that your way of providing leadership that renews and encourages resolve?

How does it strengthen our resolve when you persecute the very CIA personnel who've kept us safe for eight years?

Are you doing everything in your power to protect us by appointing Aunt Bea secretary of homeland security?

When you cut defense and weapons research and let Iraq drift into increasing violence, is that your way of renewing our resolve?

Where is the resolve when you tell the world we are wrong and sorry, over and over, groveling at the feet of murderers and dictators?

Please tell us how you are fulfilling your pledge and strengthening our resolve by closing Gitmo and releasing terrorists to kill again or how the troops are renewed by rules of engagement rendering them sitting ducks.

Exactly how do you plan on defeating Islamic terrorists when you cripple our intelligence-gathering capability and project weakness in the face of escalating attacks?

What is renewing about denying our Christian heritage and claiming we are an emerging Muslim nation, Mr. President? On many occasions you denigrate Christianity, reminding us of Jeremiah Wright, and you praise Islam, reminding us of Louis Farrakhan, and yet you expect us to rally to your call to renew our resolve?

Why should we believe you are doing everything in your power to keep us safe when you virtually ignore border security, and, instead of hunting terrorists, your surrogates accuse vets and certain citizens of being suspected terrorists?

Is it renewing to encourage controversies surrounding interrogation techniques, the release of classified documents and photographs, all for political purposes?

Since when is our faith in this government's ability to defend us built up by the likes of Harry Reid ("this war is lost") and Nancy

Pelosi ("the CIA lied to us"), two people you call friends and allies, two people you use as pawns in some kind of political game, distracting from the real work of providing our people real security?

When you appear to capitulate and appease in the face of lethal threats, over and over, whether it be by proposing negotiations without preconditions or submitting to demands for unilateral discussions, why should we believe you are really focused on America's best interests?

How is it renewing to watch you fumble the ball in Afghanistan where we prop up a corrupt regime and where our so-called ally Pakistan is no help in rooting out Taliban and other terror enclaves on either side of the border?

When our troops vote no confidence, how can we have confidence you know how to command the finest fighting force on earth?

When you appear weak in the face of Russia expansionist policies supportive of Iranian nuclear ambitions and weak in the face of Chavez, allying with Russia and Iran while Venezuela acquires nuclear weapons, how can we possibly renew our resolve given this kind of "leadership?"

Where is the resolve when we see you throw our ally Israel under the bus?

Why should we believe you really want to defeat terrorism when you send millions of dollars to terrorists in Gaza, or when you lift some sanctions on Syria, the first nation listed by our government as a state sponsor of terrorism?

How can we take you seriously when we learn your former green jobs czar believes 9/11 was an inside job, purposefully allowed to provide a pretext for war?

When you, and most of your appointees, express anti-American military sentiments, where is the resolve and renewal for us to applaud and support?

You allowed the continued persecution of the last Haditha defendant even though all Marines involved have been exonerated via the largest military investigation in history, and this is evidence of your standing to call for resolve and renewal?

Iran continually works to acquire a nuke, and they are heavily influencing Iraqi internal politics, yet you seem to ignore the situation and fall short in your support of Iranian demonstrators, and then you want us to accept your claim you are doing everything in your power to keep our kids safe?

After bowing to the Saudi king at the G20 summit, you go to the kingdom, you are treated like royalty, and you behave as if Abdullah is your sovereign in the very country that produced the 9/11 hijackers, and somehow we are supposed to ignore all this and believe you are our vigilant protector?

Your attorney general is soft on terrorists and Black Panthers but hard on American gun owners, and we are supposed to believe you guys are watchmen on the wall?

Well, given the facts, people are resolved to renew this republic by pledging to remove you from office in 2012 while building roadblocks to your ambitions in 2010.

About one million people in DC just called you a human-caused catastrophe, Mr. President, one deserving of a domestic contingency operation, namely, intense political opposition to thwart your grand designs and electoral opposition to defeat your machine and your philosophy for good. Thank you for renewing our resolve.

OBAMA'S WAR ON FOX AND HALF THE COUNTRY

October 22, 2009

On the one hand, we should celebrate the war between Fox News and the White House.

It is a good thing President Obama and company are angry with Fox. It means Fox is doing its job, you know, holding the executive branch accountable, like a real news organization.

Traditionally in America the fourth estate's role has been to challenge those in power, challenge the assumptions, examine the assertions, and check for accuracy, all the while carrying both sides of the story.

A real news organization serves the people, acting as a check on power by informing people so they can make good decisions at the polls.

The fact Fox is holding Obama's feet to the fire should cause rejoicing.

On the other hand, there are three bad news dimensions to all this: the rest of the media is content to lick Obama's boots; true to pattern Obama is glad to selfishly attack a private news organization (by the way, the most highly rated television news group in the nation), and the more Nero fiddles the higher the flames. (Remember who started the fire in the first place.)

Recall during the campaign Bill Maher telling Wolf Blitzer that CNN and HBO and the entire Time Warner organization were all working to get Obama elected. Maher's candor rocked Wolf but did not seem to faze anyone else, although the video on You Tube has been removed.

Speaking of the unfazed, Chris Matthews became the poster child for advocacy journalism with his leg tingle remark and his frank admission his central role is making sure Obama is successful. Some so-called journalists sellout cheap.

So long, adversarial press.

The White House obviously has many allies throughout the world of American "journalism," choosing now to wage war only on those who behave as real news agencies, those who actually serve the public interest.

Barack Obama is happy to fight a war on Fox, thereby working against the public interest. In so doing Obama shows himself amateurish, less than presidential.

Oh, that the commander in chief would fight the war on terror with as much energy and focus.

The truth is Barack Obama is becoming a most divisive president.

He preaches unity with his mouth, but with his hands, he sows division. Do not forget how he applied thug tactics during the campaign while denigrating Fox, insulting average Americans as gun-toting Bible thumpers, encouraging racial tensions as he always had through "community organizing," i.e., ACORN. Never forget how his machine took money from overseas. Remember how he raised an enormous war chest via the Internet with no way to track donors. Never forget the thug tactics used during the Texas caucuses, how law enforcement was used to suppress media criticism in Missouri, how free speech and a free press were quelled in Chicago when a reporter sought to cover Obama's Chicago activities via Annenberg and Ayers and "education reform."

Notice today his army of czars, all radical leftists, many race baiters, many anti-American globalists, all distinctly and angrily opposed to most traditional American values.

And now we have his media czar, Anita Dunn, singing the praises of Chairman Mao and bragging the Obama campaign controlled the media. All this coming at a time she calls Fox nothing more than a Republican mouthpiece. (Never mind that half of Fox's viewers are Democrats and Independents, according to a recent survey by the Global Marketing Research Center, a Dick Morris operation.)

If Dunn is correct, Fox is better off being a Republican mouthpiece compared to the entire Obama administration being a self-proclaimed mouthpiece for Chairman Mao.

Thanks to the Internet (which Obama seeks to control as well), those who are wise consumers of media and news have been paying attention. They know full well this president and his operatives are capable of most anything. The lies and misrepresentations increase almost daily.

Journalists with an ounce of integrity, among them Helen Thomas, see through the octopus ink being spewed in the water, for this is what the war on Fox is all about: clouding the issues, providing cover, defense, and retreat. How odd to see a radical leftist president in Nixonian garb. (Note that Helen Thomas is no longer on the scene.)

Fox has been the only news TV organization willing to challenge this president on both foreign and domestic policy. Fox is the only TV outfit with guts enough to run stories about ACORN corruption. Fox is the only television organization covering what at least half the people think about healthcare reform and cap and trade, doing so with real coverage of town hall meetings and Tea Parties. Fox is the leading news group asking the tough questions about Afghanistan along with talk radio, *The Weekly Standard*, *National Review*, *Heritage*, *IBD*, *Newsmax*, *Drudge*, *Breitbart*, and *Human Events*.

The rest of the major media are either silent, complicit, or cheerleaders for this government, a government populated in the main by radical leftists devoted to the destruction of our republic, traitors by any definition.

In case you have not noticed, the Constitution is taking a back seat to the EU and the UN, and economic freedom is being absorbed into the Socialist Kool-Aid served daily throughout DC, the media, and the public schools. Just watch what happens with the Copenhagen Treaty on global warming in December. Obama is expected to sign this monstrosity, ceding our sovereignty to an unelected foreign dictatorial body, which will direct our affairs to our own detriment. Even if the Senate refuses to ratify the Copenhagen Treaty, Obama will no doubt push its provisions as domestic policy, passing legislation to achieve the same ends: high taxation, submission to UN authority, and economic deprivation, all in the name of worshipping at the altar of radical environmentalism fueled by junk science and propaganda to install global socialist governance.

It is not about saving the planet. It is very much about controlling the planet.

Fox has challenged all this, and so Fox must pay. Fox must pay, as Limbaugh did last week, by being tied to the scourging post and beat with lies, slander, and condemnation, excoriated in public by the most vicious and cruel campaign ever witnessed, unless you consider how Obama operatives treated Sarah Palin and her family.

The beatings will continue.

The battle lines are clearly drawn.

The president has made a clear declaration of war on at least half of his own people. Obama and company have made it clear: if you disagree with this president, you will be hounded, threatened, condemned, and destroyed.

How Stalinist. How Maoist. (Dunn was not kidding.) Imagine the reaction had Bush attacked MSNBC. The shrieks from the rafters would have condemned him a Nazi. The silence of

Obama-controlled reporters, producers, and editors condemns them. And, indeed, Obama's war against Fox amounts to a war against freedom of speech and freedom of the press.

This is the change you voted for, and this is the hope you expected?

This is the dawning of a new American age of unity, purpose, and prosperity Obama promised?

The only remaining questions are: how long will the people put up with Al Capone in the White House, how far will Al Capone push things, what will be the end game (2010 or 2012?), and how many bodies will he leave in his wake, both at home and abroad?

THE BLESSINGS OF LIBERTY OR THE CURSE OF THE COLLECTIVE?

October 25, 2009

> The spirit of resistance to government is so valuable on certain occasions, that I wish it to be always kept alive. It will often be exercised when wrong, but better so than not to be exercised at all. I like a little rebellion now and then. It is like a storm in the atmosphere.
>
> Thomas Jefferson,
letter to Abigail Adams, February 22, 1787

Will this American republic survive the onslaught, or will we descend into violence? Will we remain a free and independent people or submit to dependency, domination, and despondency?

It is paralyzing when leadership stands opposed to the majority of the people. It is downright dangerous when leadership actually turns on the majority of people, provoking them, fomenting violence. We pray it does not come to that.

This president is hell bent on causing major upheaval. He is pushing people to the limit and beyond. This president governs through fear, invoking crisis at every opportunity, using intimidation and legislative blitzkriegs to exact his agenda. Look at the record.

The people oppose gay marriage. They support traditional marriage. This president is trying to repeal the Defense of Marriage Act. He will move to federalize the issue, denying individual conscience and states' rights. He wants more power concentrated in Washington.

The people oppose public money being spent on abortion, providing substantial profits to Planned Parenthood and others. This president's first act in office was to approve tax-funded abortion overseas. He is working to pass FOCA, an evil series of laws, codifying abortion on demand funded by your tax dollars. His healthcare plans include abortion as a "service" financed by taxpayers. He wants to federalize the issue. He wants to increase the power of the central government.

Most people abhor the idea of almost-born, late-term abortion (partial-birth murder). The president endorses it.

Most people are horrified by the idea full-term aborted babies have been thrown in the trash to die, cold and alone in the dark. This president voted several times to allow the practice.

Most people don't want the government telling their doctor what he/she can or cannot do on their behalf. This president insists it is the role of government.

Most people support the idea of doing all that is possible to sustain and extend life. Not this president.

Most people oppose bailouts and stimulus spending, viewing both as pork-laden wastes, having everything to do with federal control and acquisition of power, and little to do with economic recovery. He railroaded those measures anyway, providing the federal government more power to invade the private sector.

The majority opposes federal takeovers of private industry, rightly smelling a Marxist impulse in the mix. Obama proceeds anyway.

Forced acceptance of cap-and-trade legislation to address the unproven science of man-made global warming amounts to a federal tax on every citizen (without adequate representation) and a massive federal takeover of industry, especially the energy industry, all with the stroke of a pen, again contrary to the will of the majority.

The people want a sane energy policy that includes development of domestic petroleum and nuclear generation. Not this president.

The people want a strong defense. The president cuts defense.

The people do not want terrorists released from Gitmo. Obama releases terrorists from Gitmo.

The people do not want the president playing politics with the CIA. The president plays politics with the CIA.

The people want bipartisanship. The president delivers hyper-partisanship.

The people want a leader to unite them. Obama causes division.

The people do not want us to show weakness in the face of our enemies. The president routinely demonstrates weakness in the face of our enemies.

The people do not want the president apologizing for America as he visits foreign countries, and he does so over and over.

The people do not want education federalized even further. Obama promotes the contrary view.

The people do not believe a college education is a constitutional right, but the president does.

The people do not support wild federal spending, national debt, deficits, and the destruction of our currency, and this president and this Congress wallow in all of it.

The people want blind, impartial justice. Obama gives us preferential justice, situational ethics, discriminatory enforcement.

The people want adherence to tested and true principals, knowing traditional values and private virtue translate into public virtue and ethical government, or at least the approach thereof. Obama is a moral relativist.

The people do not want gun control. This president seeks gun control.

The people do not want federalized and duplicative hate crimes legislation, seeing it for what it is, a forced march to engineer society and bind and gag people of faith. Obama forces the agenda anyway.

The people do not want the government regulating speech or controlling journalism by means of a "fairness" doctrine, but Obama pushes it anyway.

The people want secure borders and a solution to illegal immigration. This president puts a halt to many efforts to secure borders and essentially talks about blanket amnesty for law breakers, no solution to the illegal immigration problem at all, and, in fact, he encourages more illegal migration by proposing national healthcare coverage extend to illegal residents.

We see ourselves as predominately a Christian people, but the president declares we are not a Christian nation, saying, rather, we have become one of the emerging Muslim nations.

The pattern is obvious: Obama consistently moves to acquire more federal power, which always means liberty lost. He squanders our resources when we call for thrift. And he contradicts majority sentiment at every turn. (Notice his move to repeal the Twenty-Second Amendment to pave the way for a third term.)

He is rather free with our money, don't you think? He spends massive amounts of our money in ways that contradict the public will. He is bankrupting the country, and if we object, his allies call us un-American, racist, saboteurs of democracy, fear mongers, evil, even Nazis.

Some will argue, "He won the election. He earned political capital. He is spending it. What is your beef? Is this a Republic or not?"

Granted. Assuming he was elected fairly and legally, he is the president, and, yes, he is doing what he said he would do. And, yes, this is not a Democracy; it is a Republic, and therefore we operate by the combined influences of majority will, elected representatives, and the rule of law.

What happens then when an elected representative appears to violate the rule of law in direct contradiction of the public will?

Strict constructionists will say it is unconstitutional for the government to be in the healthcare business, as it is unconstitutional to federalize private industry, bailout private industry, fund abortion, federalize issues surrounding marriage and reproduction, or otherwise run roughshod over individual and state's rights or violate conscience, as in the case of forcing doctors to perform abortions even if they raise a moral objection.

Furthermore, those of us who have always opposed Obama and his agenda remain opposed, and unless we missed another move to restrict freedom by this administration, we still have the right to dissent and voice opposition and debate the merits.

In all these discussions and developments, ongoing for decades but focused with the rise of Obama, the topic of the two Americas has been visited and revisited.

One America is rooted in the founders' vision: small, central government; states' rights; individual liberty and responsibility, strong national defense; limited foreign involvement beyond charitable contributions; low taxes; low national debt; economic freedom.

The founders' vision has been wildly successful, essentially dependent upon the success of the republican form of government and the good and proper exercise of economic freedom, free markets, capitalism, rightly regulated for the protection of all, all supported by the notion of virtue, person to person.

The other America is driven by what Hon. Janice Rogers Brown calls the "collectivist impulse" driven by a secularist religion, demanding diversity training (contradicting traditional morality), multiculturalism (diluting cherished sovereignty), centralized government power, government control cradle to grave, destruction of private property, redistribution of property, egalitarianism, utopian dreams, green czars, and globalism.

One America loves the founders' vision, desires preservation of tradition, expressing a willingness to work for a "more perfect union."

The other America wants a totally different America. This vision in truth works to disband the union, not perfect it.

And this president and his friends are working feverishly toward that end, whether you like it or not, and that is the definition of tyranny leading to the establishment of oligarchy, the very power structures the founders' fought and defeated in order to hand us the blessings of liberty.

The critical question facing Americans today: will we allow such a blessing to be destroyed?

Afterthought: this administration would have you believe Tea Party protesters and town hall activists are puppets of Republicans and lobbyists and insurance companies and so on. In truth, what the country is witnessing is a genuine, spontaneous citizen uprising, and the more the powerful look down their noses, leveling false and insulting accusations, the longer those noses grow.

Addendum: John Adams and Thomas Jefferson were frequently at odds, but on this much they agreed, agreeing with all the founding fathers: Americans must remain ever vigilant in opposition to the concentration of power in the federal government because that concentration presents the greatest threat to liberty imaginable. And so here we are.

Even though this is a long list of quotes from Jefferson and Adams, they are included here in hopes the reader will rediscover and embrace our first principles, and share them with others, all for the common good.

> Government is instituted for the common good; for the protection, safety, prosperity, and happiness of the people; and not for profit, honor, or private interest of any one man, family, or class of men; therefore, the people alone have an incontestable, unalienable, and indefeasible right to institute government; and to reform, alter, or totally change the same, when their protection, safety, prosperity, and happiness require it... Fear is the foundation of most governments; but it is so sordid and brutal a passion,

and renders men in whose breasts it predominates so stupid and miserable, that Americans will not be likely to approve of any political institution which is founded on it.

John Adams,
"Thoughts on Government," 1776

Public virtue cannot exist in a nation without private, and public virtue is the only foundation of republics. There must be a positive passion for the public good, the public interest, honour, power and glory, established in the minds of the people, or there can be no republican government, nor any real liberty: and this public passion must be superior to all private passions.

John Adams,
letter to Mercy Warren, April 16, 1776

Remember democracy never lasts long. It soon wastes, exhausts, and murders itself. There never was a democracy yet that did not commit suicide.

John Adams,
letter to John Taylor, April 15, 1814

That, as a republic is the best of governments, so that particular arrangements of the powers of society, or, in other words, that form of government which is best contrived to secure an impartial and exact execution of the laws, is the best of republics.

John Adams,
"Thoughts on Government," 1776

All, too, will bear in mind this sacred principle, that though the will of the majority is in all cases to prevail, that will to be rightful must be reasonable; that the minority possess their equal rights, which equal law must protect, and to violate would be oppression.

Thomas Jefferson,
first Inaugural Address, March 4, 1801

Cherish, therefore, the spirit of our people, and keep alive their attention. Do not be too severe upon their errors, but reclaim them by enlightening them. If once they become inattentive to the public affairs, you and I, and Congress, and Assemblies, Judges, and Governors, shall all become wolves.

Thomas Jefferson,
letter to Edward Carrington, January 16, 1787

Dependence begets subservience and venality, suffocates the germ of virtue, and prepares fit tools for the designs of ambition. Thomas Jefferson, *Notes on the State of Virginia*, Query 19, 1787
Every government degenerates when trusted to the rulers of the people alone. The people themselves, therefore, are its only safe depositories.

Thomas Jefferson,
Notes on the State of Virginia, Query 14, 1781

I consider the foundation of the Constitution as laid on this ground that 'all powers not delegated to the United States, by the Constitution, nor prohibited by it to the states, are reserved to the states or to the people.' To take a single step beyond the boundaries thus specially drawn around the powers of Congress, is to take possession of a boundless field of power, not longer susceptible of any definition.

Thomas Jefferson, "Opinion on the Constitutionality of a
National Bank," February 15, 1791

I think we have more machinery of government than is necessary, too many parasites living on the labor of the industrious.

Thomas Jefferson, letter to William Ludlow, September 6, 1824

In questions of power, then, let no more be heard of confidence in man, but bind him down from mischief by the chains of the Constitution.

Thomas Jefferson, fair copy of the drafts of the Kentucky Resolutions of 1798

On every unauthoritative exercise of power by the legislature must the people rise in rebellion or their silence be construed into a surrender of that power to them? If so, how many rebellions should we have had already?

Thomas Jefferson, *Notes on the State of Virginia,* Query 12, 1782

The natural progress of things is for liberty to yield and government to gain ground.

Thomas Jefferson, letter to Edward Carrington, May 27, 1788

The principle of spending money to be paid by posterity, under the name of funding, is but swindling futurity on a large scale.

Thomas Jefferson, letter to John Taylor, May 28, 1816

The republican is the only form of government which is not eternally at open or secret war with the rights of mankind.

Thomas Jefferson, letter to William Hunter, March 11, 1790

THOUGHT IS NOW A CRIME

October 28, 2009

It took twenty-five years, but 1984 has finally arrived, and with it, the fulfillment of Orwell's prophecy.

"The more the Party is powerful, the less it will be tolerant: the weaker the opposition, the tighter the despotism. There will be no loyalty, except loyalty towards the Party. There will be no love, except the love of Big Brother" (1984 by George Orwell).

Today, the president signed Hate Crimes legislation into law. Of course, these new laws are installed for the general welfare, the betterment of society, says the president. Never mind they are entirely duplicative, serving no purpose when it comes to improving law enforcement.

It is already against the law to hurt someone, kill someone or slander someone, regardless of race, sexual orientation or disability. Now however, if you say for example, that you think homosexuality is a sin, you can be brought up on charges. Your thought, your expressed opinion, has hurt someone's feelings you see, and this makes you a criminal. In fact, as of today, even writing this way subjects this author to special scrutiny, and the possibility of prosecution.

Hold the phone, insists our dear leader! We only wish to squash hate not prosecute thought or destroy freedom of speech!

Despite assurances, hate crimes law means, if you are shown to possess discriminatory thought toward certain people, during the commission of a crime, or otherwise, you will be prosecuted under a new set of rules carrying more stringent penalties.

Does anyone really believe this new set of laws will either act as a deterrent or change opinions when it comes to issues of conscience such as the controversy surrounding gay marriage?

From Orwell's 1984: "There is a word in Newspeak" said Syme, "I don't know whether you know it: duckspeak, to quack like a duck. It is one of those interesting words that have two contradictory meanings. Applied to an opponent, it is abuse; applied to someone you agree with, it is praise."...

Your comments will be reported to the moderator.

Big Brother is watching.

LETHAL NAÏVETÉ OR WILLFUL STUPIDITY: FORT HOOD SHOOTER

November 9, 2009

One commentator concluded the shootings were the act of a lone wolf, a crazy man, an aberration, no linkage to Islamic terrorism.

A US Army general says he is most concerned about dissention in the ranks thanks to this atrocity. Really? Not concerned about another Muslim deciding to randomly shoot people screaming "Allahu Akbar!"?

Leftists' throats are bellowing about Muslim victimhood, harassment, and the need to "understand" when people lash out as members of an oppressed people group.

Item: *Homeland chief warns against anti-Muslim backlash* (AP)

ABU DHABI, United Arab Emirates—The U.S. Homeland Security secretary says she is working to prevent a possible wave of anti-Muslim sentiment after the shootings at Fort Hood in Texas. Napolitano was in the United Arab Emirates on Sunday for talks with security officials and a meeting with women university students in Abu Dhabi.

Memo to Janet Napolitano:

You are a highly-placed official in the US government, and while visiting an Islamic country, your public reaction to the Fort Hood massacre is to warn of Americans attacking Muslims?

No offense intended, madam secretary, but are you the secretary of homeland stupidity? We suffer a murderous attack at our largest military post, and your main concern is a backlash against Muslims?

One would think your main concern would be securing our country against further attacks. Isn't that responsibility number one on your job description?

Your concern about a backlash against Muslims in America takes political correctness to new levels of insanity: you turn a blind eye to the origins of real terrorism and denigrate your fellow Americans as potential perpetrators.

Is it a practice of security experts to ignore actual threats and focus on potential threats from people who've never demonstrated aggression?

Rather than mourn the loss of American life, you placate our enemies with this?

We make the victims suspects and classify suspects as innocents persecuted?

It might interest you to know that in the wake of 9/11, after 2,996 of our citizens were murdered, only one revenge killing was documented.

It might interest the world to know our military goes out of its way to protect civilians overseas, self-restraining with rules of engagement so tight soldiers and marines make themselves sitting ducks most of the time.

Thousands of our boys have died protecting Muslim civilians, madam secretary.

Yet you are most concerned about Americans having negative sentiments toward Muslims or threatening Muslims in some way?

What planet are you from?

Obviously, Americans are tolerant, patient, fair-minded, and not overwhelmed by revenge, even after eight years of terrorist escalations worldwide.

Studies indicate through fourteen thousand attacks, about sixty-seven thousand people (67,000) have been murdered by Islamo-fascists since 9/11 in various countries. History, tradition, culture, and religious instruction repeated daily in mosques worldwide demonstrate a clear and present danger to anyone considered infidel, especially Danes, Americans, and Israelis.

Clearly Americans pose no comparable threat: Americans are the merciful, on balance.

Let us recall one of your first acts as secretary, shall we, Ms. Napolitano?

Remember the release of the DHS report earlier this year? You asserted a danger is presented by our own people, including returning vets. Your report claimed—without any supporting evidence—that single-issue activists concerned about abortion, illegal immigration, gun control, concentration of power in Washington, all "rightwing extremists," might very well recruit returning American soldiers, and these domestic terrorists might be planning acts of violence, strongly implying conservatives opposed to this administration should be held suspect.

President Obama recently repeated the "extremist" slander referencing conservative activists in our country.

So while you appear to virtually ignore our real enemies, you make enemies of fellow citizens, people you perceive are political opponents, and insult our military personnel in the process.

Incompetence and insanity revealed.

Secretary Napolitano: didn't you recently suggest we enlist the Boy Scouts to help with homeland security? No offense intended the Boy Scouts, but do you think they match up against a military officer armed with two 9mm pistols loaded with twenty-round clips, carrying armor-piercing rounds?

Furthermore, your department, the Department of Justice, and the entire Obama administration are trying to destroy Sheriff Arpaio of Maricopa County, Arizona. His crime? Enforcing the law and arresting illegal aliens, something the federal government trained him to do by the way.

By the way: breaking news—American intelligence knew the Fort Hood shooter had tried to contact al-Qaeda; there are direct ties between the shooter and the imam who "ministered" to at least two of the 9/11 hijackers; the shooter had declared he was Muslim first, American second; and America's war on terror he considered a war on his religion. He tried to convert injured soldiers to Islam. There are reports his mosque has direct ties to terrorists. He was reported enamored by a radical imam* who now exalts him a hero for killing Americans.

Still, Obama and Napolitano insist we not to jump to any conclusions since, presumably, the religion of political correctness must be preserved at all costs even if it means more Americans are murdered.

Considering all this, one final question remains: what on earth is wrong with you, madam secretary?

PS: Mr. President, please appoint a security expert to head up DHS, not another politician.

* Imam Anwar al Awlaki praises alleged Fort Hood shooter, according to this AP report, Nov. 9, 2009:

> *Washington* (AP) - A radical American imam on Yemen's most wanted militant list who had contact with two 9/11 hijackers praised alleged Fort Hood shooter Maj. Nidal Malik Hasan as a hero on his personal Web site Monday. The posting on the Web site for Anwar al Awlaki, who was a spiritual leader at two mosques where three 9/11 hijackers worshipped, said American Muslims who condemned the attacks on the Texas military base last week are hypocrites who have committed treason against their religion.

Lone wolf, isolated incident? Not according to this lieutenant colonel. Search "Allen West, The tragedy at Ft. Hood, Human Events, Nov. 9, 2009"

Other resources:

http://www.jihadwatch.org
http://www.thereligionofpeace.com
http://www.faithfreedom.org/
Must see scholarly documentary: *ISLAM-What the West Needs to Know*

TEA PARTY PEOPLE AND PARANOID POLITICIANS

November 11, 2009

It doesn't take a genius to figure out that 'progressives' are paranoid about Tea Party people and town-hall conservatives. Paranoids cannot stop talking about the object of their paranoia.

One case in point: Rachel Maddow of MSNBC. Rachel, who believes all evil can be traced to Christians and Republicans, cannot stomach mainstream Americans exercising their constitutional rights. She ruminates about 'insane' tea party folks quite often. The ever-snide and hysterical Rachel will have you know the Tea Party movement is obviously Astroturf because, well, that's the way she wants it to be, so, poof! It simply is as she says. Like her steamed colleague Keith 'the Visigoth' Olbermann, she wastes little time gathering facts or subjecting them to thoughtful analysis.

"Never fear!" she assures her miniscule audience: Tea Baggers are fake, fizzled, and frazzled. There is nothing grassroots about them! The regime is safe!

Curious how Keith and Rachel always spin the conspiracy there are big bad corporate meanies behind every movement opposed to their political orientation, while the big bad corporate meanies they agree with (Soros, NBC, et. al), well, you know, they're cool.

Recently their hero, Mr. Obama, sneered at 'tea bag people,' calling them 'extremists,' and 'anti-government people.' This was just before he was found making jokes, immediately prior to issuing a statement about the Fort Hood shootings, just before he failed to go directly to comfort the families, something Mr. Bush accomplished without fanfare. (In this regard, a Nov. 22, 2010 posting by Hillbuzz. org is worth the read: 'Thank you former President George W. Bush and former First Lady Laura Bush.')

Soon after Mr. Obama's denigration of Tea Party and town hall folks, Mr. Bill the Clinton (Oh no!) picked up the refrain: "The reason the tea-baggers are so inflamed is because we are winning." (It depends on what the definition of "winning" is. . . .)

Mr. Clinton issued these words of wisdom yesterday at an event designed to puff up Democrats who are feeling as low as Obama's approval rating. Recent Dem gubernatorial defeats in Virginia and New Jersey apparently did not come to Mr. Clinton's mind, occupied as it was with visions of tea bagging dancing in his head.

And we all recall the characterizations of Tea Party people and town hall conservatives made by folks like Nancy 'The Knife' Pelosi, Harry 'The Slender' Reid, and DNC officials: hate mongers, anti-American, right-wing extremist Republican nut jobs, a fringe birther mob, ugly, uncivilized. Only the paranoid would invoke such vitriol.

Can anybody remember this crowd objecting to anti-war/anti-G8 demonstrators defecating and urinating in the streets, blocking traffic, setting fires, destroying property, and causing injury? Not a peep. But let Grandma speak up at a town hall meeting, or let Grandpa carry a protest sign at a Tea Party, and, well, western civilization as we know it is done, finished, kaput.

The truth is paranoid politicians and putrid pundits saw huge turnouts nationally at several Tea Party events starting in April and running through September. They saw at least one million protestors in DC on September 12. They saw twenty thousand in the streets again recently protesting Obamacare. They saw packed rooms and vocal opponents at hundreds of town hall meetings throughout the summer. And just last week they saw the tangible results at the polls, proof an enormous backlash has crystallized in opposition to this president and this Congress.

The 2010 elections will likely be a Democratic massacre, and they sense it, so to divert attention or propagandize reality away or engage a little self-medication, they roll out Clinton and feed the egos at MSNBC or have Obama verbally jab, all in an attempt to put a smiley face on the miserable clown no one sees when no one's around.

Arthur C. Brooks of the American Enterprise Institute, writing last spring in the WSJ, agrees the Tea Party movement is a real grassroots ground swell of citizen activism representing the majority view:

> Voices in the media, academia, and the government will dismiss this ethical populism as a fringe movement—maybe even dangerous extremism. In truth, free markets, limited government, and entrepreneurship are still a majoritarian taste. In March 2009, the Pew Research Center asked people if we are better off in a free market economy even though there may be severe ups and downs from time to time. Fully 70% agreed, versus 20% who disagreed.

So, Mr. Obama, Mr. Clinton, the folks who object to an all-powerful federal government, reckless spending, creeping socialism, deficits, and trampling citizen rights may not be PhDs, but they are the backbone of this country, the majority, the ones who do most of the work, and the ones whose sons and daughters proudly wear the uniform.

What you don't realize is we now have a continuous Tea Party working twenty-four-seven to right the ship of state before you run it into an iceberg.

THE LEADERSHIP VACUUM: ADAPT, MIGRATE, OR BECOME EXTINCT

November 13, 2009
Good leadership is the talent to inspire people to cooperate for the greater good.
The ability to adapt is the mark of intelligence.
Intelligent leadership combines these elements.
For all the hoopla these past three years, characterizing Mr. Obama as the most brilliant political leader yet seen, little in the way of intelligent leadership has been demonstrated since January.
During the campaign he presented himself the slightly center-left patriot, capable of hobnobbing with radicals without contracting the disease. Yet the moment he swore the oath, he started breaking it along with his promise to govern from the center.
Now, only ten months into his term, his approval rating has fallen through the floor, his disapproval rating soars, more than half the country stands opposed, while 38 percent, according to Rasmussen, strongly disapprove; translation: mad as hell. Thirty-eight percent of 108 million voters equals 41 million. Add another twenty million who are seriously alienated, and the future for Democrats looks mighty dim.

Almost every Democratic policy initiative meets with strong opposition and controversy. Even with a big 'mandate' a year ago, and a huge majority in the House, Pelosicare only passed by two votes. Weak.

Obama appears incapable of strong leadership in foreign affairs or as commander in chief. Wild spending and crushing debt infuriate most voters. Healthcare reform has become a lightning rod to spark conservative resurgence. Cap and trade lunacy looms, another lightning rod.

And today the move to bring 9/11 'suspects' from Gitmo to New York for trial in civilian court fully televised, providing our enemies a global electronic platform to spew hatred, and whip up extremism, all this puts us at risk, evidence of Obama's DOJ on PC steroids.

Incredible that Holder and Obama would announce this ill-advised movement of 9/11 terrorists for trial only days after the Fort Hood massacre. The insensitivity displayed by this president right after that atrocity was bad enough. He compounds it today, bringing news he continues making excuses for killers.

But never mind. We wouldn't want to jump to conclusions about radical Islam, terrorists seething with murderous hatred in our midst, or rogue nations with nukes. Instead listen to the intelligent leader who would have us turn our ire on Israel and Tea Party people.

At some point one keeps expecting Mr. Obama to demonstrate some of this celebrated intelligence and adapt. At some point one hopes to see a change wherein he inspires a majority to cooperate.

Knowing full well the vast majority of people oppose closing Gitmo and oppose bringing terrorists from there to here, he goes ahead anyway. Few would condemn him (other than the hyenas on the left) if he stopped and said, 'Hey, after deep deliberation we've determined closing Gitmo is a bad idea because there aren't really any good alternatives, and we've decided, based on sound advice from both sides of aisle, it is better leaving justice in the hands of military tribunals, in part because that squares with the terrorists' insistence they are enemy combatants.'

If he did something like that and said something like that, his polling data would start to change overnight.

Further, adaptation on healthcare and cap and trade would be in order, given our financial situation.

Intelligent leadership, perceiving a narrowing dark hallway ahead economically, would make moves to broaden the road and open the options for more sunlight to pour in. In view of the worsening economy made worse by federal spending and plans to tax the marrow out of the very people who make the country work, the president has a ripe opportunity to make real changes that would give people real hope.

Adaptive wisdom would lead Mr. Obama to announce a return to proven policies: lower taxes, enhanced economic freedom through reduced regulation, encouragement of open markets and economic freedom, strengthened lines of credit for small business, and a focus on rebuilding our manufacturing base, all moves sure to create jobs and get the country moving again. You know, real stimulus.

Intelligent leadership would manifest in decisiveness with regard to Afghanistan and Iraq and Iran and North Korea and Russia, demonstrating to the world we stand by goodness and security and Israel no matter what.

And intelligent leadership would refuse to pander to hyper-partisans and foreign powers solely for the sake of holding fast the reins of power.

So far the leadership we have seen insists on riding a predetermined track no matter where it leads, no matter the serial failures, accelerating down the line without any ability to adapt, persuading people of one thing: this is no longer a government of, by, and for the people. The majority of people now realize they've been snookered. Few remain inspired, fewer still willing to cooperate.

By insisting on his way or no way, Mr. Obama has provoked a huge and growing backlash. By his refusal to listen to the people, he has created a leadership vacuum, a vacuum conservatives are working feverishly to fill in 2010, and 2012, praying Mr. Obama will continue on his track, doing most of the heavy lifting for them.

Mr. Obama is already a lame duck without even knowing it. Time to adapt, migrate, or become extinct politically.

Communism is like prohibition, it's a good idea but it won't work.

Will Rogers, 1927

US TAXPAYERS FUNDING TERRORISM: THE TIES THAT BLIND

November 16, 2009
What would you think if it was proven beyond doubt your tax money is getting into the hands of terrorists not altogether accidentally?

How would you feel if you discovered that the dollar you paid in income tax had been channeled by the federal government through a bank bailout law to Citigroup, which then 'invested' in an Islamic or Sharia-compliant organization that transformed that dollar invested into a payout which was used to support international terrorism?

Would you feel an outrage beyond furious?

The story has been out there for many months. Most Americans remain unaware, another indictment of the mean-streak media in this country.

First, one must understand a little about Sharia-compliant financing (SCF) and the linkage to Citigroup. (Note as well: what is happening in England is happening here.) Frank Gaffney of the Center for Security Policy explains in this excerpt from his Townhall column published March 9, 2009, titled "Farewell to Britain":

> The U.S. taxpayer now owns most of AIG and Citigroup, two companies massively engaged in Shariah-compliant transactions (SCF), at odds with our constitutional separation of church and

state,' wrote Frank Gaffney last March, Deputy Assistant Secretary of Defense during the Reagan administration, and founder of the Center for Security Policy. 'Promoters of this (SCF) industry, like 'Shariah advisor' and al-Jazeera host Sheikh Yusuf al-Qaradawi, have described SCF as 'financial jihad' and al Qaeda has publicly embraced its practice... (and British Prime Minister) Brown has declared he wants Britain to be the world capital of Shariah finance. The British government has refused to take punitive action against British-based Islamic 'charities' that provide money to terrorist organizations. The latest is Interpal, a Palestinian organization that even the BBC was able to figure out provides support to Hamas.

Investigative reporter Daniel Greenfield, noting the Obama-ACORN-Citi connections, explains further in this March 9, 2009 column published online in the Canada Free Press:

> Islamic Banking uses a Sharia board to vet permissible investments. That Sharia board is much the same for Citigroup and AIG. It consists of Saudi or Saudi affiliated "religious scholars" who have to give their okay on financial products that can be sold by a bank. This has obvious political implications. The terrorist connections aren't hard to find either. Citi Islamic Investment Bank is overseen by 'eminent' Sharia scholars. For example Nazih Hammad, President of Citi Islamic Investment Bank's Sharia board. Nazih Hammad is a board member of the North American Fiqh Council. The North American Fiqh Council is another one of the Saudi front groups operating in America, one of whose trustees was Alamoudi, an Al Qaeda fundraiser. The North American Fiqh Council's former President, Taha Jaber Al-Alawani, was an unindicted co-conspirator in the case of Islamic Jihad leader, Sami Al Arian. And there was board member Sheikh Muhammad al-Hanooti, who had extensive Hamas ties.

Thanks to the work of people like Frank Gaffney, Jack Cashill, Kevin J. Murray, Daniel Greenfield, and Melanie Phillips we know the truth.

More background and connections from the research by Cashill, Greenfield and Gaffney:

- Al-Waleed bin Talal, net worth 16.3 billion dollars, the man who helped Barack Obama get into Harvard Law School, is the second largest shareholder in Citigroup right behind the US government.
- Cashill reports: "As far back as 1988, however, Obama had serious pull. He would need it. As previously reported, Khalid al-Mansour, principle adviser to Saudi Prince Al-Waleed bin Talal lobbied friends like Manhattan Borough President Percy Sutton to intervene at Harvard on Obama's behalf. An orthodox Muslim, al-Mansour has not met the crackpot anti-Semitic theory he could not embrace. As for bin Talal, in October 2001, New York Mayor Rudy Giuliani sent his $10 million relief check back un-cashed after the Saudi billionaire blamed 9/11 on America."

Jack Cashill writes extensively on these matters in an article titled "Why Obama is Mum about Harvard, published online at WorldNetDaily, September 11, 2008. Here are some highlights:

- Citigroup pioneered the big bank embrace of Sharia finance back in the 1990s.
- Citigroup's Islamic banking operation represents the world's leading of Islamic loans and Sukuk bonds.
- Currently American taxpayers are in hock for forty-five billion dollars to bailout Citigroup, while the treasury, the FDIC, and the Federal Reserve cover 90 percent of Citi's three hundred thirty-five billion dollar losses.
- The American taxpayer is maintaining the number one Shariah finance bank in the world and that means the US government now officially owns a third of the largest Sharia finance

arranger in the world together with the Saudi royal family: Wahhabism's quest for global Islamic domination and the US government come together.

- AIG is also big into Shariah finance, even fielding Shariah finance offerings domestically.

- Another Obama connection: Citigroup provided half a million dollars to ACORN, essentially money directed for the Obama campaign's "Get Out the Vote" fraud program. Citigroup partnered with ACORN Housing Works to provide a specialized mortgage program for ACORN, the exact sort of program that caused the economic disaster in the first place.

There can be no doubt the US government is squandering taxpayer money, not only wasting it but using it in support of activities actually threatening to the future of the country.

Jack Cashill,
"Why Obama is Mum about Harvard,"
WND, Sept. 11, 2008

"The US government hasn't just bailed out Wall Street fat cats, but the centers of Islamic finance, rescuing the sizable investments of Saudi Arabia and the Abu Dhabi Investment Authority," reports Greenfield. "And American taxpayers are now in the position of funding the world's largest Sharia arranger, as well as the importation of Sharia finance to the United States through AIG. Lenin used to talk about the capitalists selling him the rope with which he would hang them. He had no clue that we would actually be buying the noose of Sharia Finance with which we're being hung, and paying through the nose for the privilege."

One US Marine, Kevin J. Murray, has decided to take direct action, filing a lawsuit directed at AIG's Sharia-compliant activities, calling the secretary of the treasury and the Federal Reserve to account.

As a Christian, a federal taxpayer, and a former U.S. Marine veteran of the war against Islamic terrorism, Plaintiff objects to and is harmed by the appropriation and disbursement of public funds to AIG and being forced as a taxpayer to contribute to the propagation of Islamic beliefs and practices predicated upon Shariah law, which is hostile to his religious beliefs and practices and which forms the basis for the global jihadist war against the West and the United States in particular.

Some have said all this criticism and concern is nonsense: Muslims simply tithe for charity, giving 10 percent to the less fortunate (*zakat*), something President Obama has praised.
Columnist Melanie Phillips clarifies:

> Sharia requires Muslims to tithe a percentage of their money to charity, called "zakat." But charity in Islam is more like solidarity. So some of this money donated to Islamic charities may well find its way to organisations promoting jihad and supporting suicide bombing including Hamas, Hezbollah, the families of Palestinian suicide bombers and Islamist madrassas in places like Pakistan.
>
> Source: Daily Mail, UK,
> "Britain's a world-leader in sharia banking,"
> Feb. 10, 2009

Other sources, search online:

Obama offers prime posts to campaign contributors, one from Citibank, Bloomberg
Obama and al-Waleed bin Talal connection, DarkSkiesBlog, Sept. 4, 2008
Forbes profile of al-Waleed bin Talal, Oct. 7, 2007

FORT HOOD KILLER: FACTS AND FANTASY

November 17, 2009

"O ye who believe! Fight those of the disbelievers who are near to you, and let them find harshness in you, and know that Allah is with those who keep their duty [unto him]" (Koran 9:123).

'Surely, the worst of all living, in the sight of Allah, are those who reject Faith, so they do not believe' (the message of Islam). So if you find them in war, make them an example (deterrent) for those behind them, so that they take a lesson.' (Koran 8:55–57).

"Remember thy LORD *inspired the angels (with the message): 'I am with you: give firmness to the Believers: I will instill terror into the hearts of the Unbelievers: smite ye above their necks and smite all their fingertips off them.'* " (Koran 8:12).

American television talking heads and reporters speculate Maj. Nidal Malik Hasan was motivated to kill fourteen (one in the womb) and wound thirty-one soldiers at Fort Hood because:

- he snapped psychologically,

- he was harassed by fellow soldiers for being Palestinian,

- he was suffering from pre-traumatic stress (related to anticipated trauma), an unknown malady,

- he was lonely without a wife and felt alienated in the army.

These experts assure us his murderous rampage had nothing to do with his Islamic beliefs, because, as everyone knows, Islam is a religion of peace.

No doubt Hasan's attorney will plead insanity, holding the Army and American society responsible. Perhaps Mr. Obama will insist on a trial in civilian court, arguing Hasan cannot possibly get a fair trial before a military tribunal.

Certain facts tell a plausible story gleaned from various news accounts:

- Nidal Malik Hasan, US born, is described by family and friends as a lifelong, devout Muslim.
- As he calmly and methodically fired about one hundred rounds (special 9mm armor piercing loads), he screamed *"Allahu Akbar."* He used two privately owned handguns, each with twenty-round clips, so he was prepared, and had to reload three times. There is no doubt this was a premeditated act.
- He had substantial contact with Anwar al-Awlaki, an Islamic cleric supportive of al-Qaeda, one endorsing violence and terrorism. The US-born cleric praised Hasan after the massacre as "a hero." This is the same al-Awlaki who "ministered" to at least two of the 9/11 hijackers.
- On his business card, Hasan identified himself as a "soldier of Allah."
- Classmates at military college reported Hasan held anti-American views, stated Islam was superior to the US Constitution, and supported suicide bombings.
- Not long ago he gave a medical lecture to Army colleagues, but instead of a medical lecture, he delivered a dawah, telling

his audience they would burn in hell unless they converted to Islam.

- His job in the army was to provide therapy for traumatized soldiers returning from battle. On many occasions, Hasan reportedly tried to convert the soldiers to Islam and threatened to charge others with war crimes, actually leveling charges in some cases.

- He sent money to terrorists in Pakistan.

- He told students, "I'm a Muslim first and an American second," according to Dr. Val Finnell, a lieutenant colonel. "I really questioned his loyalty," Finnell said.

- He told colleagues the US war against terror was a war against Islam.

- In various communications he celebrated Islamic martyrdom, a central tenet of Osama bin Laden's theology.

- The morning before the shootings, he was videotaped in a convenience store, wearing full Muslim attire described as Pakistani funeral garb worn by Muslim men either for attending a funeral or for a suicide mission.

Did he purposefully choose a Thursday to attack?

"For his journeys, the Holy Prophet liked a Thursday whether it was for Jihad of or some other purpose." (Maariful Qur'an, volume iv, p.489).

Moral: If it walks like a jihadist, talks like a jihadist, looks like a jihadist, says it is a jihadist, behaves like a jihadist, and jihadists recognize it as their hero, well, one supposes *it is a jihadist.*

It is unfathomable how people deny glaring factual evidence.

Terrible outstanding questions remain: why did the army ignore numerous warning signs for so long, why did the army promote Hasan, why did the FBI determine there was no basis for further investigation, and why did so many remain silent for so long?

Apparently the lessons of 9/11 and fourteen thousand Islamic terror attacks worldwide since have taught us little.

Can it possibly be the tyranny of multiculturalism strikes again? All hail diversity even if it means suicide?

PS: Remember this report last February?

The Muslim founder of BridgesTV*, an American cable network whose slogan is 'Connecting people through understanding' trying to 'improve the image of Muslims in the United States,' was arrested on Thursday for allegedly killing his estranged wife in a manner normally associated with Islamist terrorists: chopping off her head.

Remember the outcry then as well: the beheading had nothing to do with the teachings of authoritative Islam.

When was the last time you heard about a Lutheran decapitating his wife?

And Rifqa Bary has nothing to worry about?
http://rifqabary.com/
*Update on BridgesTV
http://www.danielpipes.org/blog/2009/02bridges-tv-a-wifes-beheading-and-honor-murder

KHALID SHEIKH MOHAMMAD PLAYS OBAMA

November 17, 2009

Pat Buchanan knows a lot. He has been around for a long time. He has seen a lot of people screw up in Washington. Pat says the Obama administration is a developing train wreck, and the latest car to buckle might very well jump the track.

Writing this week, Buchanan asks the central question: are we at war or not? If yes, then terrorists are enemy combatants, people who do not have US constitutional rights, people who should be treated the way we have always treated enemy soldiers who commit war crimes: capture, try, convict, punish or release, all within the military structure for handing justice in a time of war.

However, the president is making it clear he does not think we are at war. Apparently he thinks handicapping the American military further is in order, and apparently he does not trust the military to administer justice in the case of the 9/11 conspirators, contrary to what he said in 2006 as a senator.*

Attorney General Eric 'Nation of Cowards' Holder announced last week he and the president have decided to bring Khalid Sheikh Mohammad to NYC in about three weeks to stand trial in civilian court for plotting the 9/11 attacks. Standing in the dock with KSM will be four accused co-conspirators. Al-Qaeda perpetrators killed 2,976 Americans that day and injured more than six thousand. Khalid Sheikh Mohammad and his pals will be treated as if they are US citizens. They will be provided defense counsel and the ability to examine witnesses and introduce evidence and the whole bit.

Nothing like a full-color, televised reconstruction of 9/11 to add a little holiday cheer.

Holder practically guaranteed a conviction, saying he is asking for the death penalty. Presumed omniscience aside, Mr. Holder, there are no guarantees in court unless, of course, justice has been prearranged. In that case, why even talk about a fair trial, American justice, the rule of law?

"What do we do if the case against KSM is thrown out because the government refuses to reveal sources or methods, or if he gets a hung jury, or is acquitted, or has his conviction overturned?" writes Buchanan, November 16. "In America, trials often become games, where the prosecution, though it has truth on its side, loses because it inadvertently breaks one of the rules. The Obamaites had best pray that does not happen, for they may be betting his presidency on the outcome of the game about to begin."

If treated as a civilian, and if acquitted, would KSM be able to sue the United States for false imprisonment?

Game indeed. It is more difficult to get a conviction in a US civilian court compared to a military tribunal. Khalid Sheikh Mohammad and company were already in the process before a military commission at Guantanamo. Last December KSM and company pled guilty and asked for the death penalty. Under military law, and standing military commissions involved, this could still happen. Consequently, why the show trial?

Some at the *New York Times* speculated the Obama administration decided to bring KSM to New York as part of the process of closing Guantanamo, a move many see as politically motivated given Obama's campaign promises.

Andy McCarthy, former federal prosecutor experienced in bringing charges against terrorists and writer for *National Review*, sees the move as a Holder/Obama payoff to Bush-hating leftists central to Democratic political fortunes. He joins former New York mayor Giuliani and others, pointing out the security risks involved:

> Nothing results in more disclosures of government intelligence than civilian trials. They are a banquet of information, not just at the discovery stage but in the trial process itself, where witnesses' 'intelligence sources' must expose themselves and their secrets.

Khalid Sheikh Mohammad was water boarded. Evidence collected thereby may not be admissible. Many see this move by Obama as a way to put the Bush administration on trial, another political payoff.

Many people, including the governor of New York, fear for the safety of citizens during a lengthy trial. Average citizens can hardly believe the government would extend citizenship rights to Islamic terrorists with American blood on their hands.

And then there are the concerns about complications: who will sit on the jury, what will be allowed in the way of testimony and evidence, will the defense demand a change of venue, and what can the defense do when the defendant has no defense since he has already confessed? The only option then, as many have pointed out, is for the defense to put America on trial, providing an enormous propaganda platform for the terrorists worldwide.

Never mind the cost to the tax payers for the trial itself and the costs to the city of New York for added security, incarceration expense, and so on. The cost to Americans at home and abroad will certainly be enormous in blood and treasure and humiliation at the hand of our enemies, using our resources, in our courts, only blocks away from where the twin towers once stood.

One can only imagine what New Yorkers are thinking these days, especially those who lost loved ones on 9/11, but you can bet most are not rushing out to send the president a Christmas card or an ornament for the "Holiday tree."

*Speaking of Obama, did you know as a senator he called for KSM to be brought to justice before a military commission, citing our obligations under the Geneva Conventions? Now he is on the other side of the moon.

What changed?

Perhaps the best points are made by Bobbi Bennett, commenting on David Horowitz's column on this topic, FrontPageMag.com, Nov. 13, 2009, 'The Worst Decision by a U.S. President in History':

> There is no doubt that in specifically and purposefully targeting civilians and other non-combatants, terrorists committed war crimes. They should be tried for these by military tribunals according to the laws of warfare. No one seems to be considering the precedents that would be set by trying war-time enemy combatants in US civilian courts. In order to prosecute these acts of war as if they were civilian crimes certain rights citizens of the US are guaranteed would need to be denied, such as Miranda warnings and rules of evidence. Once the precedent is set of denying rights to one defendant in one case, we can't un-ring the bell.
>
> Obama, and others, at one point suggested we set up a two-tiered system of justice to handle "terrorists." There is grave danger in this for citizens since once a second tier is set up, what's to stop the federal government from determining that certain crimes committed by certain citizens deserve referral to the second tier?
>
> In addition, as I understand it, only some terrorists will be tried in civilian courts - those that the government feels it can prosecute successfully. Others will be tried by military tribunal. Not only does this fly in the face of all notions of equal treatment under the law, it sets the precedent that the government can capriciously choose the court that suits the strength of their case in order to achieve a pre-ordained result.
>
> I smell tyranny in the air.

The Post columnist Michael Gerson sums it up well:

> Holder's choices do not reflect the normal policy shifts between administrations. It is not typical that seven former directors of the CIA have publicly denounced Holder's assault on the institution they served. It is not typical that Holder's immediate predecessor, Michael Mukasey, has called the plan for trials in Manhattan a risky 'social experiment' that will raise the risk of attack 'very high.' Something unique and frightening is taking place: The ACLU is effectively being put in charge of the war on terror.

REAL GREATNESS: A VISIT TO THE REAGAN RANCH

November 30, 2009
This is a personal story. I will try to tell it objectively although that will be difficult because this story involves two of the men I love and admire most: my dad and Ronald Reagan.

Dad and Mr. Reagan have a lot in common: both hail from Illinois, both came from difficult circumstances growing up, both lacked a father figure, both were/are self-made men who love America with passion, both promoted traditional American values all their lives, living out their later years in or near the Santa Ynez Valley, and both loved ranching and horses.

Back in the 1960s a group of businessmen gathered small contributions to help Mr. Reagan explore the potential for running for governor of California. My Dad was one of those businessmen. When approached about running, in typical humble fashion, Mr. Reagan said he didn't think that was necessarily a good role for him to play, referencing his former Hollywood acting career. The small businessmen prevailed upon him, Mr. Reagan ran for office, and the rest is history. (He served as governor from 1967 to 1975.)

Recently, on a trip home to visit the folks for Thanksgiving, we planned a visit to Reagan's Rancho del Cielo. It is not open to the general public. The Young America's Foundation preserves the ranch as a tribute to Mr. Reagan's values and service to the nation, allowing only special visits to avoid overuse and related noise. Consequently, only registered YAF students, interns, contributors, and seminar hosts are granted access.

It was a perfectly beautiful day, November 24, just north of Santa Barbara' clear blue skies, temperature in the mid seventies, no wind, the sun glistening off the deep blue Pacific, the glorious Channel Islands in the distance.

The drive to Rancho del Cielo from the highway is only seven miles, but it takes twenty-five minutes. The road is narrow, steep, and riddled with ruts and switchbacks. The climb is breathtaking. At times it seems you are traveling straight up from sea level to about twenty-six hundred feet elevation.

Our host, ranch development director Rick Keith, one of the most gracious and friendly fellows you'll meet, explained during his presidency Mr. Reagan usually traveled to the ranch by helicopter. Upon landing in Marine One, the president would routinely walk north to the S.Y. Valley overlook and quote Psalm 121: 'I will lift up mine eyes unto the hills, from whence cometh my help. My help cometh from the LORD, which made heaven and earth.'

Listening to Rick tell the story that day, I think I will remember on my way out of this world. What an awesome experience to imagine Reagan, standing there, speaking those words, believing them in his soul, and relying upon the promise of help, the mark of true humility and greatness.

Ronald and Nancy Reagan bought the ranch in 1974, and all through his presidency (1981 89) they spent every Thanksgiving there. So it was especially meaningful for us to visit during Thanksgiving week and remember how much we have to be thankful for in this wonderful country, a country revitalized by Reagan's courage, vision, energy, optimism, and leadership.

As we arrived, a small herd of glossy, well-fed deer raced through the oak grove in front of our vehicle, bounding from the shadows, then racing off to the meadow to graze. They lingered the entire time we were there. As the ranch house came into view, we parked and walked out to the grounds, reverently reluctant to step on the meticulously manicured driveway and lawns, the surrounding silence broken only by the hoof falls and snorts of horses nearby and the giggles from our toddler daughter as she rolled in the grass.

At the entrance to the house was a bell Mrs. Reagan would ring to summon the president for meals. On the door, a plaque revealing the man's sense of humor read, "On this site in 1897, nothing happened."

It was obvious Mom and Dad were deeply touched, as we all were. Equally obvious, this beautiful and peaceful place was the ideal setting for the president to recharge and regroup during the eight years of toil on behalf of our country, and, indeed, the world. This is the place Mr. Reagan signed the biggest tax cut in American history, ushering in the prosperity of the late 1980s and the 1990s. This is the place he received news of the downing of Korean Airlines flight 007, shot down by the Soviets. And this is where he called all the families of the 221 Marines and others killed in Beirut by terrorists in 1983.

This was the cherished retreat for a straightforward man from Illinois who helped engineer the fall of the Soviet empire without firing a shot.

It was fascinating to learn Mr. Reagan built the fencing himself, extended the original adobe to create a very modest home, placed the flagstone for the front porch himself, and, with others, worked to clear twelve miles of riding trails. Reagan dug the lake himself and built by hand the small dock. He loved clearing brush to prevent fire, cutting firewood (the house had no central heat or AC), and doing most all the work by hand, even to the point of digging post holes manually, a tough job (I speak from experience) for anyone in ninety-five-degree weather during summer, let alone a man in his seventies.

One funny story related to the lake: Mr. Reagan stocked it with fish, but a bothersome heron would visit regularly to feed. Not wanting to kill the bird, one morning Reagan decided to scare it away by discharging his pistol a few rounds. You can imagine what that did to the Secret Service security staff!

We learned from Rick that Reagan first fell in love with riding horses after joining a riding club in his early years, followed by experience in the Army Reserve as a cavalryman, and movie roles requiring horsemanship followed by personal ranching prior to his political career. His lifelong love of the outdoors, of nature, and of riding carried through until that tragic day when his friend and fellow horseman, Secret Service agent John Barletta, had to tell him his riding days were done because of the affliction of Alzheimer's.

Rick showed us the location by the fireplace where John tearfully informed the president it just wasn't safe to ride anymore, Nancy seated nearby. Characteristic of Reagan's greatness and sympathy for others, he stood, walked over to where John was seated, placed his hands on John's shoulders to comfort him, and said, 'That's okay, John. It's all right. I know. I know.'

(Be sure to get and read John Barletta's book: *Riding With Reagan: From the White House to the Ranch*. Simply an excellent read.)

You see, Mr. Reagan's mother and brother had suffered Alzheimer's, and he knew full well what he was in for, saying later he only wished his could spare Nancy and his family the ordeal, an ordeal that would last for ten years from 1994 upon diagnosis through his parting in 2004.

It was amazing to see the interior of the house. It is very small, only about fifteen hundred square feet. The master bedroom is painted yellow to celebrate sunshine, akin to Reagan's sunny personality and endless optimism. Twin beds placed together with a stool at the foot of his side to accommodate his feet, for, you see, he was too tall for the bed itself. The tiny closet still containing his riding boots and attire and a bathroom so small only one person at a time could enter, the shower head a replica of the Liberty Bell. Modest furnishings throughout, all celebrating the West, Native Americans, nature, America, and our heritage. Over there, the chair by the fire where the president read every night, his favorite book besides the Bible, *Witness* by Whittaker Chambers. Over here, a small black-and-white television he watched rarely, preferring only *Jeopardy* and *Murder She Wrote*, one to match wits with contestants, the other to enjoy the moral of every story.

The tool barn where his vehicles and chain saws are stored was ordered just as he would see it every morning. The tack room was filled with saddles and bridles and all the materials and tools required. On the wall, a spoof movie poster from the Eastern Block, depicting the relationship between Reagan and Margaret Thatcher as if they were starring in *Gone With the Wind*, aggravating nuclear tensions, a mushroom cloud in the background.

Hating war and always seeking peace, Reagan shared a favorite story in a speech given only eighteen months into his term:

> Our Ambassador to Luxembourg wrote me a letter, and he said that he had been up on the East German border, visiting the Second Armored Cavalry Regiment. And he told me how great they looked. And then he said that one of these fellows, a 19-year old trooper, followed him over to his helicopter and asked him if he could get a message to me. And being an Ambassador, he allowed as how he could. And the kid said, "Well, will you tell the President that we're proud to be here, and we ain't scared o' nothin.'" I just thought you'd like to know about the attitude of those who are guarding our shores, because they are the real freedom fighters. It is by doing their job and doing it right that they can be a deterrent to war. And our goal is peace. And you've never gone into a war because you were too strong; you go into them when the other fellow thinks you aren't strong.

Growing up in the S.Y. Valley, Dad taught me to love my country, follow after God, do my best, and appreciate people like Mr. Reagan, people willing to sacrifice for our country, men and women who had the courage to hold to good principles, and the staying power to see them work miracles.

On the way home, we stopped at a guest ranch, the Circle Bar B, so the kids could take in a trail ride. Having worked as a wrangler, I hit it off immediately with the boys working the trail, all of them the real deal, as evidenced by their rough cut, good nature, and bowed legs. They soon learned about our visit to Reagan's place, each one sparking up saying, 'There was greatness. They don't make 'em like that no more…'

I'll take a wrangler's opinion over that of an ivy leaguer any day…

It is fitting to end with the rest of Psalm 121, words Mr. Reagan no doubt mediated on many times during his days at Rancho del Cielo:

> He will not suffer thy foot to be moved: he that keepeth thee will not slumber. Behold, he that keepeth Israel shall neither slumber nor sleep. The LORD is thy keeper: the LORD is thy shade upon thy right hand. The sun shall not smite thee by day, nor the moon by night. The LORD shall preserve thee from all evil: he shall preserve thy soul. The LORD shall preserve thy going out and thy coming in from this time forth, and even for evermore.

Note: Be sure to listen to the speech that launched Mr. Reagan's political career. Google the speech entitled 'A Time for Choosing,' given to support Goldwater's presidential ambitions in 1964.

DESTROYER OF WORLDS: GLOBAL WARMING TYRANTS RUN AMOK

December 7, 2009

> They call themselves Green because they are too Yellow to admit they're Red.
>
> Lord Monckton

One of the most critical issues facing Americans at this moment is the end of freedom, the end of America as we know it, thanks to what President Obama prefers to do soon in Copenhagen.

LORD Christopher Monckton, British journalist, business consultant and politician, who once served as science advisor to the Prime Minister, toured western countries recently sounding the alarm. He says man-made global warming is junk science, a hoax, a sham and a deliberate deception used to attack American sovereignty and accomplish global redistribution of wealth. His lecture is quite informative. Access it on YouTube easily by searching: "LORD Christopher Monckton Speaking in St. Paul."

Another credible source of information along this line can be found in the writing and lectures offered by *Dr. Richard Lindzen,

Alfred P. Sloan Professor of Meteorology, Department of Earth, Atmospheric and Planetary Sciences.

And then are the six hundred fifty scientists who met in Poland one year ago, all saying anthropogenic global warming in ridiculous.

Plus: Last March in New York, seventy scientists met to present similar findings.

And now we have ClimateGate, ignored by the mainstream media, ignored by the elitists in Washington, and condemned by the thoroughly mind-controlled green left, all leading one to believe a lot of Americans in name only truly want the UN to take over the world by bringing the United States to its knees.

They will try to destroy America by insisting bad science is truth, horrendous tax policy is benevolence, sinister environmental policy is responsible, and green economics profitable. Best newsspeak ever!

We believe the lies and thus commit suicide, or we embrace the truth and live free.

Do you require more proof? Read these articles:

Climategate: the final nail in the coffin of anthropogenic global warming by J. Delingpole, The Telegraph, November 20th, 2009

Morning Bell, Heritage Foundation: "The Copenhagen climate comedy," December 7, 2009, online.

*The aforementioned Dr. Lindzen says:

> Future generations will wonder in bemused amazement that the early 21st century's developed world went into hysterical panic over a globally averaged temperature increase of a few tenths of a degree, and, on the basis of gross exaggerations of highly uncertain computer projections combined into implausible chains of inference, proceeded to contemplate a roll-back of the industrial age.
>
> Massachusetts Institution of Technology Professor Richard Lindzen, PhD, Atmospheric Science

Consider the implications given this surgical remark:

> On such (climate) models we are supposed to wager trillions of dollars—and substantially diminished freedom.
> George F. Will, syndicated columnist, *Washington Post*

Update December 25, 2010: EPA Moving Unilaterally to Limit Greenhouse Gases

Washington (AP)—Stymied in Congress, the Obama administration is moving unilaterally to clamp down on greenhouse emissions, announcing plans for new power plants and oil refinery emission standards over the next year.

Who needs Congress when we have a messiah in the White House?

THE TRUTH ABOUT HOMOSEXUALITY AND CHRISTIANITY

December 8, 2009

Despite what media talking heads and others claim, the vast majority of Christians do not hate anybody, including homosexuals. Ours is the God of love who teaches us to love. However, this God does not promote a touchy-feely, lowercase love. He promotes divine love, sacrificial love, a love always seeking the highest good of the object of his affection.

That kind of love is the most intense form of love, and that kind of love is often tough.

It will not countenance sin because, quite frankly, sin is a disease brought by the evil one, a fatal disease spread about to destroy love. It would seem easier to accommodate sin and avoid conflict, but we are called to this divine, tough love, and this is why it is called the rugged road of the cross. When you take a stand for this kind of love, the fury of hell is unleashed against you.

Love is best described in 1 Corinthians chapter 13. As Christians we would be well-advised to consider this passage often before speaking out on this, or any topic. However, what is sometimes heard by the secular ear as harsh, is, in reality, a tough word spoken in love. Jesus often spoke tough words that sounded harsh, calling his own disciples evil at one point, but he was always speaking truth in love. John the Baptist spoke tough words to Herod. They were tough words spoken in love. Let us not confuse straight talk applied medicinally with condemnation leading only to strife and division.

As believers we are commanded to obey the law of love, which requires we speak the truth in love.

The Scripture clearly teaches that homosexuality is sin, and, as sin, it is a killer. Science confirms this claim. Physical and psychological maladies occur at much higher rates in the homosexual community. If you conduct a Google search with key words 'incidence of illness homosexuals' at the top you will get a listing titled 'Scholarly articles for incidence of illness homosexuals," with 23,000 items, many peer reviewed. One especially useful entry: "The Health Risks of Gay Sex," by John R. Diggs, Jr., M.D.

If we say we love the homosexual but ignore that which is killing him or her, we cannot say in good conscience we love that person. Watching someone kill themselves or be devoured by sin without saying a word is not seeking the highest good of the object of our affection. It is not an act of love to stand silent. Rather, it is an act of cowardice.

(And, let's be very clear, the Scripture also teaches that all have sinned and fallen short of the glory of God, which means no one has any right to claim superiority. We are all miserable sinners this side of God's redeeming grace.)

As a matter of faith, science, conscience, morality and social stability Christians cannot endorse homosexual practice, or the demand the lifestyle be normalized.

Christians and others in the faith community cannot go along with the idea of same-sex marriage because it violates everything we understand to be true about the law of love, the nature of marriage, the essential building blocks of family and society, and the tenets of morality taught by the God we serve.

Asking us to endorse same-sex marriage is asking us to repudiate our LORD, and insisting we do so is forcing us to commit heresy. We simply cannot go there. For us, it is as much an act of love to obey the LORD as it is for us to speak truth into the debate concerning homosexuality and same-sex marriage.

Casting Christians as hate-filled homophobes is a lie from the pit of hell, but an effective lie used to denigrate our faith. The lie forwards a grim political agenda, for if the homosexual lobby is successful instituting same-sex marriage, it means Christians will be forced to choose.

We will be forced to choose to serve man or God. Serving God has usually meant persecution and suffering, long the history of the world when darkness and light collide. Believe it or not, Christians are the most persecuted group in history, see 'Theophobia and Persecution' in this book.

Finally, look around the world. Where are homosexuals enjoying the most freedom, prosperity, acceptance, and safe passage? Why are they enjoying these benefits? What religious tradition or philosophical orientation provides the culture or environment giving rise to this kind of tolerance and diversity?

An honest appraisal will conclude Western Civilization founded in the Judeo-Christian tradition is the place where, on balance, love and acceptance and diversity and tolerance are practiced, indeed, where these notions originated. And there is a reason for this: it is because we chose to follow and obey the LORD of love and reject the selfish impulse of the flesh and the lies of the evil one.

God wants the highest good for the greatest number of people. He is the ultimate good Father. If we would only follow his lead, we would all be so much better off. God wants what is best for everyone, including homosexuals, and, as his people, Christians seek the highest good for the greatest number as well, including homosexuals.

Resource:

"The Slippery Slope of Same Sex Marriage," FRC.org

ONWARD CHRISTIAN SOLDIERS: THE MANHATTAN DECLARATION

December 10, 2009

The Manhattan Declaration is a Christian call to activism in the name of righteousness. Many people have signed in support of the declaration, yet respected Christian leaders have also declined to support the initiative, namely Alistair Begg and R.C. Sproul. Here is a summary:

The Manhattan Declaration: A Call of Christian Conscience

Christians, when they have lived up to the highest ideals of their faith, have defended the weak and vulnerable and worked tirelessly to protect and strengthen vital institutions of civil society, beginning with the family.

We are Orthodox, Catholic, and evangelical Christians who have united at this hour to reaffirm fundamental truths about justice and the common good, and to call upon our fellow citizens, believers and non-believers alike, to join us in defending them. These truths are:

- the sanctity of human life
- the dignity of marriage as the conjugal union of husband and wife
- the rights of conscience and religious liberty.

Inasmuch as these truths are foundational to human dignity and the well-being of society, they are inviolable and non-negotiable. Because they are increasingly under assault from powerful forces in our culture, we are compelled today to speak out forcefully in their defense, and to commit ourselves to honoring them fully no matter what pressures are brought upon us and our institutions to abandon or compromise them. We make this commitment not as partisans of any political group but as followers of Jesus Christ, the crucified and risen Lord, who is the Way, the Truth, and the Life.

MEETING SAUL ALINSKY ON THE BACKSIDE OF HISTORY

December 12, 2009

> A Marxist begins with his prime truth that all evils are caused by the exploitation of the proletariat by the capitalists. From this he logically proceeds to the revolution to end capitalism, then into the third stage of reorganization into a new social order of the dictatorship of the proletariat, and finally the last stage—the political paradise of communism.
>
> Saul Alinksy

Alinsky operated according to the law of the jungle: dominate or be dominated, the overarching rule is there are no rules.

Saul Alinsky was the genius sociopath godfather of the contemporary radicalized American left, i.e., the modern-day Democratic Party. Saul Alinksy is the patron saint of the Obama machine. Think of it: the most influential men in Obama's life are Saul Alinsky, Jeremiah Wright, Bill Ayers, and Franklin Davis Marshall, all perverts, all America haters, all communists.

To this day, most Americans do not fully understand what they are up against, and it may be too late for them to open their eyes to see their executioner clearly.

One can get a good sense of the heart of Alinksy's philosophy and methodology from the following quotes from his writings:

> ...the primary assault would be on Biblical absolutes and Christian values.
> Yesterday's immoral terrorist is today's moral and dignified statesman.
> Ridicule is man's most potent weapon. It is almost impossible to counteract ridicule. Also it infuriates the opposition, which then reacts to your advantage.
> One acts decisively only in the conviction that all the angels are on one side and all the devils on the other.
> In a fight almost anything goes. It almost reaches the point where you stop to apologize if a chance blow lands above the belt.

Read all of Alinsky's poison in his 1971 book, *Rules for Radicals,* which he dedicated to Lucifer. (Not kidding.)

He was a prophet of revolution, preaching any means are justified in the war against capitalism: the only moral value is victory.

He encouraged his followers to pose as middle-class traditionalists, urging them to infiltrate, grab power, and attack. For Alinsky, those standing in his way were the enemy, and they had to be destroyed.

So now you understand what has been happening since January 20, 2009.

Alinsky nurtured a special hatred for Christians.

Among Alinsky's devoted disciples are Barack and Michelle Obama, Bill and Hillary Clinton, Nancy Pelosi, Bill Ayers, Jeremiah Wright, and most of the people drawing salaries in the executive branch, including Rahm Emanuel and David Axelrod.

I met Saul Alinsky once. He came to our college campus to speak. At the time I was part of the student group sponsoring his appearance. Although I did not spend a lot of time with him, perhaps two hours, it was enough to see he was an angry man, seething, agitated, vindictive, arrogant, tough, mean, vengeful. Chain smoker. Dark circles under his eyes. He spoke about the evils of capitalism with passion and hate. He said revolutionary change was the only option at any cost, using any means, because that was the only way the powerless could overcome the powerful.

When he was done, he grabbed his check and left without so much as a thank you.

Saul Alinsky was the kind of man who would use his own activists to shoot and kill his own comrades if he thought he could blame it on his enemies. The means justify the ends. You know, like what the Sandinistas did to skewer the Contras: line up your own people dressed like the enemy, shoot them, then blame the opposition.

Dr. Martin Luther King Jr. was a Christian activist motivated by love, using the tactic of non-violence to achieve social justice.

Saul Alinksy was altogether otherwise, an atheist thug, motivated by hate, using violence to achieve only strife and division, packaged as the march to social justice, change, hope. Sound familiar?

Which man does Barack Obama most closely resemble?

Is it any wonder then we have SEIU union thugs attacking a man opposed to Obamacare outside a town hall meeting recently? What is especially grievous is the union thug is black, and the conservative activist protesting Obamacare is black. Please remember, Obama exalts the SEIU, has worked on their behalf, and loves Alinsky's *Rules for Radicals*, which sanctions violence and thuggery like this. So much for the post-racial unifier. Obama is nothing more that a tool of radicals, a willing participant in promoting anarchy.

This is not about unifying the country. It is about dividing us and conquering.

Leftists, like Alinsky, are constantly angry, resentful, and seething with envy. They can never gain political ground showing their true face, so they recruit golden boys like Obama to be their front men. As a group they refuse to take personal responsibility, always blaming someone else and demanding the rich pay their bills. Since the rich are in the minority, the rich are an easy target because they cannot adequately defend themselves.

But that is only part of the story.

The left hates the middle class—the hated bourgeoisie—always has, always will. The ultimate coup is demonizing the rich then lulling the middle class, pretending to be allies then plundering the middle class via government grants to fund stuff like ACORN, the Apollo Alliance, MoveOn.org, Code Pink, Public Allies, AmeriCorp, The Annenberg Challenge, the Woods Fund, Media Matters, Soros, SDS, NARAL, and the DNC, a virtual army of Alinsky assassins, Obama allies.

And if you are poor, do you think these people really care about you?

Ask the poor in Russia or North Korea or Cuba or Venezuela about their lot. Any improvements in the last eighty years, anywhere? How about all those poor folk Obama organized in Chicago. Do you think they are better off today than they were twenty years ago? What tangible difference for the good has Obama or Alinsky or Soros or Ayers ever contributed?

Zero, zip, nada.

You see, the truth is the rules for radicals only apply for the purposes of creating exclusive access for elitists like Obama, Hillary, Ayers, Axelrod, Emanuel, and Pelosi. Once they are in power, everybody else can go to hell. Still, they have to put up a good show. And that is what healthcare "reform" is all about. It is also about gaining more iron-fisted control, for the left is all about control, total control.

Funny how the cherished proletariat always get stuck under Alinsky's dictatorship. The "paradise of communism" never ever shows up.

Bottom line: man without God is a beast. Beasts like Alinsky and Obama now roam the country, occupying the halls of power, invading every aspect of life, dictating to us what we will and will not do. The beasts are thoroughly self-serving.

Increasingly, people see them for what they really are, and it is quite possible their end is near.

The American republic, populated by citizens endowed by their Creator with certain unalienable rights, still offers the greatest good for the greatest number of people.

Are we going to let Alinsky's flying monkeys destroy it? Alinksy's son believes the flying monkeys are succeeding:

> "Obama learned his lesson well. I am proud to see that my father's model for organizing is being applied successfully beyond local community organizing to affect the Democratic campaign in 2008. It is a fine tribute to Saul Alinsky as we approach his 100th birthday."
>
> Letter from L. David Alinsky, son of Saul Alinsky, printed in the Boston Globe, letters to the editor, 8.31.08, headlined: "Son sees father's handiwork in convention."

In the following excerpt the connections are made as strongly, from an article by Richard Lawrence Poe, November 26, 2007, contributing editor to NewsMax, titled "Hillary, Obama and the cult of Alinsky:

> True revolutionaries do not flaunt their radicalism, Alinsky taught. They cut their hair, put on suits and infiltrate the system from within. Alinsky viewed revolution as a slow, patient process. The trick was to penetrate existing institutions such as churches, unions and political parties.... Many leftists view Hillary as a sell-out because she claims to hold moderate views on some issues. However, Hillary is simply following Alinsky's counsel to do and say whatever it takes to gain power.
>
> Barack Obama is also an Alinskyite.... Obama spent years teaching workshops on the Alinsky method. In 1985 he began a four-year stint as a community organizer in Chicago, working for an Alinskyite group called the Developing Communities Project.... Camouflage is key to Alinsky-style organizing. While trying to build coalitions of black churches in Chicago, Obama caught flak for not attending church himself. He became an instant churchgoer.

More resources, search:

BHO and the Strategy of Manufactured Crisis, by Jim Simpson (American Thinker)

Former KGB agent, the process of demoralization, Yuri Bezmenov (You Tube)

Overview of America, John McManus, March 12, 2009 (You Tube)

KHALID SHEIKH MOHAMMED PUTS AMERICA AND ISRAEL ON TRIAL

December 22, 2009
This individual should have faced a firing squad months ago. Instead, thanks to our president, he will enjoy global celebrity status.

Khalid Sheikh Mohammed, 9/11 mastermind, confessed to murdering three thousand Americans.

Reversing himself from when he as a US senator, Barack Obama last month declared through his attorney general that KSM will not be brought to justice before a military tribunal. Instead he will be brought to New York to stand trial in a civilian court as if he were an American citizen with full constitutional rights.

Anybody see a problem with this?

For one, KSM is not an American citizen. So from now on, will every terrorist enemy combatant have the right to a fair trial in our courts at our expense?

Is it fair to the people of New York to bring this terrorist and his four co-conspirators to NYC to put them on trial just blocks away from ground zero?

What is the purpose for creating this expensive show trial when it would be perfectly legal to have KSM stand trial in military court in

Cuba or elsewhere? Is it important for people to know KSM confessed last year during preliminary proceedings in Cuba? Will those confessions be thrown out because of enhanced interrogation techniques used on KSM?

Why spend enormous sums of taxpayer money to hold court in NYC?

Will this trial attract fanatics, terrorists, and other nut jobs, encouraging them to perpetrate acts of violence in NYC?

The president and others on the hard left insist holding this trial in NY will demonstrate to the world our system of justice is fair. However, AG Eric Holder has guaranteed a conviction. How is it fair to guarantee a conviction before the trial starts?

Many security experts have said a public trial like this will compromise American security because the accused will be able to use the trial for propaganda purposes, and intelligence and military personnel will be called to testify, putting classified material at risk. All that, they say, puts American soldiers at risk.

What chance is there for acquittal? Since KSM was water boarded, some say chances are good he will walk if tried in a civilian court.

Many other observers say the president's motivation is purely political, that in the face of horrendous poll numbers, he is trying to bolster his base and denigrate the former administration by holding this show trial, by extension, a trial of the Bush administration as well.

CBS reported last month 54 percent of Americans are opposed to bringing KSM and his killers to the Big Apple. CNN reported last month 64 percent believe KSM and company should be tried in military court, with 34 percent agreeing with Obama.

Jay Sekulow of the ACLJ and Sen. Lindsey Graham (Republican, South Carolina) are pushing legislation that would prohibit terrorists from being tried in civilian courts.

Khalid Sheikh Mohammad and his friends will not stand trial in NY. America will stand trial.

How is that fulfilling your oath, Mr. President?

THOMAS JEFFERSON LOVED CHRIST

December 22, 2009
Few would call Jefferson a traditional Christian, but it is likewise inaccurate to portray him a deist or a humanist, in view of these quotes from *The Jefferson Bible,* "Introduction," by Henry Wilder Foote.

Originally, part of [Jefferson's] purpose was to compile a simple account of Jesus, giving his ethical teaching in his own words, in a form suited to the comprehension of the American Indians... (Foote)

> The practice of morality being necessary for the well-being of society, He (God) has taken care to impress its precepts so indelibly on our hearts that they shall not be effaced by the subtleties of our brain. We all agree in the obligation of the moral precepts of Jesus, and nowhere will they be found delivered in greater purity than in his discourses.
>
> Thomas Jefferson
> letter to James Fishback, Sept 27, 1809, Bergh 12:315. (1809)

Jefferson wrote in 1819, "I never go to bed without an hour or half an hour's reading of something moral, whereon to ruminate in the intervals of sleep"—to which Randall adds, "The book oftenest chosen... was a collection of extracts from the Bible."

He was passionately devoted to the gospel of Jesus, which stirred him to the depths of his being and was the most powerful motive force in his life.

> Donald S. Harrington, "Foreword," *The Jefferson Bible,* p. 11

Speaking of "the widespread denunciation of him by his political opponents as an anti-Christian infidel or atheist," Foote observes, "[I]t is one of the minor ironies of history that such slanders should have been so generally and so long believed about the man whose knowledge of and admiration for the teachings of Jesus have never been equaled by any other president." (p. 18)

Jefferson attended church regularly all his life. Throughout his two terms as president, he regularly attended worship services in the US Capitol building, at the time the largest church in the Capitol.

BEN FRANKLIN IS PRAYING FOR US

December 22, 2009

> A good conscience is a continual Christmas.
>
> Benjamin Franklin

Everyone who has looked into the matter realizes most of the Founding Fathers were devout Christians, men who prayed daily. Benjamin Franklin may not have been a dyed-in-the-wool churchman, but he was not simply a deist either. A deist believes God set the world in motion, and assumed a distant, hands-off posture.

What may surprise many is Ben Franklin appealed often to the God of the Jews and the Christians, perceiving him highly involved in human affairs, the source of wisdom and morality.

Reading *The Autobiography of Benjamin Franklin,* Barnes & Noble Books, 1994, page 101, we find he describes his early Presbyterian education and his objections to certain dogma, declaring:

> I was never without some religious principles. I never doubted, for instance, the existence of a Deity—that he made the world and governed it by his providence—that the most acceptable service to God was doing good to man—that our souls are immor-

tal—and that all crimes will be punished and virtue rewarded, either here or hereafter.

During the Constitution Convention of 1787, when the delegates were deadlocked, Franklin urged prayer, invoking the words of Christ and making references to the Old Testament. A treatment of the circumstances at the Convention, and the official recording of Franklin's statement (below) can be readily accessed at Wallbuilders.com, searching on the site for 'Franklin's Appeal for Prayer at the Constitutional Convention':

> In this situation of this Assembly, groping as it were in the dark to find political truth, and scarce able to distinguish it when presented to us, how has it happened, Sir, that we have not hitherto once thought of humbly applying to the Father of lights to illuminate our understandings? In the beginning of the Contest with G. Britain, when we were sensible of danger we had daily prayer in this room for the divine protection. "Our prayers, Sir, were heard, and they were graciously answered. All of us who were engaged in the struggle must have observed frequent instances of a Superintending providence in our favor. To that kind providence we owe this happy opportunity of consulting in peace on the means of establishing our future national felicity. And have we now forgotten that powerful friend? I have lived, Sir, a long time, and the longer I live, the more convincing proofs I see of this truth- that God governs in the affairs of men. And if a sparrow cannot fall to the ground without his notice, is it probable that an empire can rise without his aid? We have been assured, Sir, in the sacred writings, that "except the LORD build the House they labour in vain that build it." I firmly believe this; and I also believe that without his concurring aid we shall succeed in this political building no better than the Builders of Babel: We shall be divided by our little partial local interests; our projects will be confounded, and we ourselves shall become a reproach and bye word down to future ages. And what is worse, mankind may

hereafter from this unfortunate instance, despair of establishing Governments be Human Wisdom and leave it to chance, war and conquest.

I therefore beg leave to move, that henceforth prayers imploring the assistance of Heaven, and its blessings on our deliberations, be held in this Assembly every morning before we proceed to business, and that one or more of the Clergy of the City be requested to officiate in that service.

The deadlock was broke. A nation was born.

At the close of the Constitutional Convention of 1787, a woman approached Franklin as he left Independence Hall. The lady asked him, "What have you given us, Dr. Franklin, a republic, or a monarchy?"

He replied, "A republic, Madam, if you can keep it."

Source: "The American form of government," Wimp.com/thegovernment/, transcript here, "Overview of America," by John McManus, 2007, www.justpullit.com, pdf.

THE AGE OF INCOHERENCE

December 29, 2009
Saying good-bye to the first decade in this brave new century, one is reminded of New Year's Eve 1999. Champagne in hand, we toasted the twenty-first century and gladly said so long to the twentieth. Oh, to be primarily concerned about Y2K again. For all the euphoria of the 90s surrounding the technology explosion, economic expansion, and the sense of liberation from the Cold War, this first ten years in the new millennium has delivered something quite surprising on the heels of the knowledge age and the information age.

Fleetwood Mac and the Clintons urged us to keep thinkin' about tomorrow, but in typical boomer fashion, we neglected the business of today, rejecting so much of value from yesterday in the process.

One would think advances in science and computing would enlighten us. Logically you would assume enormous improvements in communications and knowledge base might contribute to greater understanding, tolerance, unity, and international cooperation. We've never before penetrated such depths of the subatomic universe. Our ability to see far beyond our own galaxy is fantastic: science fiction becoming reality. We move mountains, feed nations, run faster, and cram more activity into smaller spaces than ever before in all of human history. More Americans have attended college and graduate school in the last twenty years than in all our previous history.

Yet in truth, as Will Durant pointed out: 'Our knowledge is a receding mirage in an expanding desert of ignorance.'

For all our technology and learning, are we more intelligent, wiser?

Is virtue at an all-time high?

Have we appropriated greater measures of happiness and peace?

Has our approach to problem-solving improved?

Have we become a kinder, gentler nation?

Is government more efficient, effective?

Is the war on poverty over?

Have we conquered racism?

After pouring trillions of dollars into social programs, do we have a healthy society?

How tragic to think we've actually lost ground in these areas despite vast increases in knowledge and capability. We can build a city in a few months, but can we build a friendship with a neighbor? We seem to keep trying to conjure up goodness from within, not realizing that is something gifted from beyond. Always reaching for the brass ring, we keep falling off the carousel only to remount and grasp for the unreachable, again, in vain. Why do we keep on believing all will be well by the sheer force of will and work? Why do we settle for false hope?

With a few taps on a keyboard, the universe opens up, yet have we gained deeper understanding embracing this avalanche of data?

No. We've not grown wiser. We've not become friendlier. We aren't happier. We do not enjoy peace. In fact, a sober assessment of our situation leads to the conclusion we have regressed. We enjoy watching people bloody one another on computerized videos streamed globally in a heartbeat. The most bizarre violence and sexual behaviors are freely available to anyone with access to a computer. Things our grandparents would never even imagine are today common fare, even on television, promoted to children. We pollute our minds and our souls and call it freedom of expression.

Incoherence.

Unborn children are officially deemed non-human and viewed inconvenient, valued only for their stem cells. A few days ago the court of appeals in Oregon ruled unborn children are non-human. The court says they are non-persons.

A pregnant woman was accused of recklessly endangering her unborn child by using drugs. The court found that "an expectant mother's use of methamphetamine while pregnant does not meet the standard for the crime of recklessly endangering another person." Why? The court says the fetus is not a person, so how could the mother possibly endanger it?

Incoherence.

An enormous UN convention in Denmark during the course of ten days intended to take drastic action to solve a problem yet to be defined involving the transfer of trillions of dollars from wealth-producing countries to the third world, all designed to save the planet, achieve "justice," and end poverty wound up producing only chaos, violence and vitriol.

Incoherence.

For at least fifty years, the world has witnessed an escalation of violence and mass murder perpetrated routinely by Muslim males between the ages of eighteen and forty-five. When an atrocity occurs at Fort Hood involving an assailant who, once again, fits the profile, the president tells us not to jump to conclusions: Islam is a religion of peace. His secretary of security says the real security concern is the fear of potential revenge against Muslims, a fear never realized.

Incoherence.

Every place it has been tried, socialism has failed, miserably. Spreading the wealth always destroys prosperity, preventing the poor from improving their lot. In the end the only thing spread is misery; the only booming industry prisons. Socialist economies are regularly imposed by communist regimes, always leading to tyranny and depravation. Even so, we allow our leaders to push the agenda down the same, dark, dead end.

Incoherence.

We stand mute as a safe schools czar is appointed to teach students about non-existent safe sex, the glories of man-boy "love," and the crime of intolerance toward pornography on campus. School boards ignore the concerns of parents, students run amok, and teachers call it education.

And we ban DDT for no good reason, thereby allowing resurgent mosquito populations to carry malaria and kill millions more people annually, a man-made epidemic, especially in Africa, and we call ourselves wise stewards, benevolent and caring.

A Hollywood starlet who committed adultery to establish her out-of-wedlock relationship allows for infidelity in that relationship but insists if she does get married, she could never forgive infidelity, all this while she and her 'insignificant other' adopt children and lend advice on parenting, citizenship, and responsible living.

The attorney general guarantees a conviction even before the trial starts, telling us he is the champion of due process. In that light humorist Dave Barry writes in his 2009 year in review column:

"Attorney General Eric Holder announces that, to maintain the principle of due legal process, alleged Sept. 11 mastermind Khalid Sheikh Mohammed will be tried in federal court in New York City, but as a precaution, 'he will be executed first.' "

The president says one thing and does another multiple times and he is hailed the man of integrity. He fans the flames of war and gets the Peace Prize.

We tell people to buy things they cannot afford then act surprised the country is smothered in debt. The government uses tax money to subsidize home buying on behalf of people who can't otherwise qualify, and when the housing market crashes, well, it's Bush's fault.

Too many men are largely absent from their duties as fathers and husbands and we scratch our heads and ask why society is falling apart.

We elect corrupt people who fund corruption and they mount false fights against corruption, wasting our money on a charade, and then we wonder why we are corrupt, and broke.

The volunteer soldier defending Americans in some god-forsaken hellhole is falsely accused by a terrorist enemy, then prosecuted for war crimes by his own people. We slay our protectors and protect our executioners and can't understand why peace escapes us.

On practically every front we reject success and embrace failure, then blame someone else for our sorry state. We say virtue is irrelevant then demand it of one another.

And the Creator who endows human rights, the eternal Giver and Lover of our souls, is either ignored or slandered, more chapters writ in the endless, tragic story of a loving God rejected by sinful man.

We hear tell about the Iron Age, the Ice Age, the Bronze Age, the Enlightenment, the Industrial Revolution, and the Information Age, but from sifting through the available evidence, it appears we have entered the Age of Incoherence.

Truly, Will Durant was entirely correct stating: "The greatest question of our time is not communism versus individualism; not Europe versus America; not even the East versus West. It is whether men can live without God."

PREZ SAYS MOTOR CITY UNBOMBER "ISOLATED EXTREMIST"

December 29, 2009

"This incident, like several that have preceded it, demonstrates that an alert and courageous citizenry are far more resilient than an isolated extremist," President Obama said (CNSNews.com).

To be fair, perhaps he meant the terrorist who tried to blow up Flight 253 over Detroit Christmas day was alone, isolated in the sense of acting alone at that particular time and place. However, that goes without saying, so why say it?

Furthermore, a number of observers reported their impression was the president was portraying the perpetrator as being a lone wolf, someone without ties to an established organization, without a stated affection for a worldview motivating terrorist activity.

If this is accurate, it presents another troubling series of incidents, showing the president making judgments about circumstances before an investigation is complete prior to a more complete picture taking form, as if he hopes to direct public opinion along a pre-determined line of reasoning.

The suspect, Umar Farouk Abdulmutallab, has reportedly stated he is a jihadist with ties to al-Qaeda in Yemen. Yemeni authorities have established UFA had spent considerable time in Yemen. UFA's father tried to warn United States officials his son was running with the wrong crowd. There are now established links between UFA and Anwar al-Awlaki, the American-born Muslim cleric who encouraged the Fort Hood shooter, a cleric known to be associated with al-Qaeda in Yemen.

And for UFA to even get close to destroying an American commercial aircraft, he had to have had extensive support, training, and financing. And now we learn it is likely some of that support came from former Gitmo detainees.

ABC News reports that "two of the four leaders allegedly behind the al-Qaida plot to blow up a Northwest Airlines passenger jet over Detroit were released by the U.S. from the Guantanamo prison in November, 2007, according to American officials and Department of Defense documents" (Center for Security Policy).

Then, there is this report out of the UK:

> Hundreds of al-Qaeda militants are planning terror attacks from Yemen, the country's Foreign Minister said today. His (report) came after an al-Qaeda group based in Yemen claimed responsibility for the failed Christmas Day airliner bomb plot. Umar Farouk Abdulmutallab...was in the country only days before the failed attack.

So it is clear UFA was no isolated extremist. Can anyone seriously doubt the president was not in possession of all this information yesterday, and even if he was not, shouldn't he have refrained from jumping to conclusions?

At times this president seems to weigh in too late to no effect.

At other times, he issues preconceived conclusions while the jury is still out. Examples are "police acted stupidly" in Cambridge involving Professor Gates and jumping to conclusions about the Fort Hood shooter, at the same time telling us not to do so.

While it is true courageous Americans are more resilient than any 'isolated extremist,' the real question is: is this administration more resilient than untold thousands of terrorists working together to cripple America?

Given the administration's performance so far, confidence is not rising, especially in view of an AG who has worked to free terrorists and a secretary of homeland security that thinks American conservatives are a greater threat than jihadists.

An even more troubling question: can we rely on Mr. Obama's judgment to make reliable decisions in our defense should the country be threatened by a nuclear or other WMD attack.

Will he pull the trigger too soon or too late or not at all?

LIMBAUGH: TEDDY BEAR GLADIATOR

January 5, 2010

At his press conference, Rush Limbaugh seemed a changed man. The severe chest pains that had driven him to call for help remain a mystery. Doctors have given him clearance to return to work. Talking about the experience, he referenced mortality and urged anyone with unique and intense chest pain to seek attention immediately.

"Don't try to tough it out. It's not worth the risk," he said. He appeared relieved, grateful, and philosophical, noting the experience was a blessing in disguise, reminding him he is not bulletproof.

Rush is one of the most misunderstood people in America, which is ironic since he has expressed himself clearly for many hours daily on radio during the course of twenty-six years. He is one of the most influential people in the world. For many, however, he is a fiend, a hard-hearted blowhard, a carnival barker. Others love him zealously. There is little in between with Rush. Perhaps eight people in the country react lukewarm. He is provocative and bombastic by design.

One truth about the man: few match his passion. If one takes the time to listen, really listen, not satisfied to settle for sound bites served up by those always prowling and snarling, you discover somebody who cares deeply about the country and about people. This is another enormous irony: the man many vilify as an uncaring loudmouth is, in reality, one who passionately cares about America and about people.

He believes people, and the country, are best served by the preservation of liberty and that liberty is best sustained and expanded by the straightforward conservative ideas embraced by the founders: small government, low taxation, strong defense, virtue, the individual, economic freedom and the power of free people to creatively pursue their dreams. It is not a touchy feely love of country and people. It is rather a principle-driven love because he has seen the results in history and in his own life.

He is a straight shooter in an increasingly crooked world, a plain-spoken man in a world yearning for soothing reassurances, a broadcast combat soldier engaging the culture war long before most people knew it had been declared.

Another irony about Rush: while his critics call him a caveman, he is, in fact, an original, a pioneer, one acting far ahead of the curve, an innovator, an adventurer. It is commonplace today, this thing so reviled by so many called talk radio, but in 1984, when Rush started, it was rare and provincial. When he took his show national in 1988, few thought he'd succeed. Possessing a confidence that spans the country, he made it work, and EIB and *The Rush Limbaugh Program* became wildly successful, paving the way for hundreds of others, including liberals. He remains the number-one rated talk host in the country, enjoying an audience of twenty million.

Another irony comes to mind. The man so many misunderstand, calling him aloof, prideful, harsh, judgmental, and severe, is, in reality, according to those who know him best, the opposite: humble, gentle, engaging, attentive, even soft-hearted, and full of humor. He is an enigma, a combination of Ronald Reagan and Don Rickles: the ultimate individual in a time when collectivists reign.

The truth is he aggressively takes on ideas he believes dangerous to the general welfare, and he does so with incomparable effectiveness. Understandably, his adversaries hate him for it, which is perhaps the highest compliment.

This medical incident may have changed him in some ways, given him a renewed appreciation for life and how short it really is, but his critics won't change, and neither will his attitude toward his calling.

He is in it for the duration, and many of us are very glad about that. After all, there are millions more to inspire, Rush!

THE LAST BEST HOPE OF MAN ON EARTH

January 13, 2010

> We have plenty of Confidence in this country, but we are a little short of good men to place our confidence in.
>
> Will Rogers

> Your Description of the Distresses of the worthy Inhabitants of Boston, and the other Sea Port Towns, is enough to melt an Heart of Stone. Our Consolation must be this, my dear, that Cities may be rebuilt, and a People reduced to Poverty may acquire fresh Property: But a Constitution of Government once changed from Freedom, can never be restored. Liberty once lost is lost forever. When the People once surrender their share in the Legislature, and their Right of defending the Limitations upon the Government, and of resisting every Encroachment upon them, they can never regain it...
>
> John Adams to Abigail Adams–July 7, 1775

> What is conservatism? Is it not the adherence to the old and tried against the new and untried?
>
> Abraham Lincoln

It appears clearer day by day the voters misplaced their confidence by electing this new regime, realizing the "new," now tried, is turning disastrous.

No matter how you slice it, Obama and company are perceived as weak and ineffective. Across the board, this administration's policies fail. People of good will hoped for a better outcome. Many believed Obama when he implied he would govern from the center, even though he promised on many occasions to steer the country left.

Essentially, the people were sold a bill of goods, and now that the bill is past due there's no good to be found.

The number one issue is the economy. Massive, debt-ridden, pork-filled stimulus is impotent. Instead of job creation, government spending promises massive tax increases, measures that kill economic recovery. No rational person can look out at the current landscape and see anything but a worsening situation. The people are not fools. They know the responsibility lies squarely on the shoulders of the president and Congress, a Congress that has been dominated by leftists for almost four years, leftists who were largely responsible for the meltdown to begin with, as we all know, thanks to federal encouragement of risky home loans that Wall Street bundled and sold under false pretenses.

On the economy, government is the problem, the cause, and the agent of continuing decline. The people agree: according to Gallup, 56 percent disapprove of the way the president is handling the economy (58 percent disapprove of his handling of healthcare reform.).

Yet what does the president call for? More government interference, more government control, more government management by bureaucratic decree, all of it contrary to American traditions of free enterprise and constitutional republic.

The truth is we are in serious economic crisis. Unless we redirect this Titanic immediately by cutting government spending radically and freeing up the creative, free market energies of the people, we face ruin. That is not hyperbole; it is fact. And without economic recovery, we continue the downward slide in terms of national security. What enemy needs an army when they can bring us to our knees by default and bankruptcy?

In reality, the "new" promised by Mr. Obama was repackaged "old," discredited, far left policies from the past. Reaching back to FDR and appealing to LBJ with a modernized Carter spin on things, Obama sold us a lie boxed up as something new, wrapped in shiny new paper, containing nothing more than a globalist/collectivist agenda, driven by socialist utopian fantasies. The results speak for themselves: bankruptcy, demoralization, loss of standing internationally, emboldened enemies from every angle, and the very real threat of American demise.

Sensing the crisis, the people are rising up to reclaim their God-given right to take back control from professional politicians, radicals, and bureaucrats who have obviously lost touch with what it means to be an American. The only good news is the crisis has reawakened the people to realize the "old and tried" is our only salvation, a salvation originally delivered by the founders who brought forward a viable new experiment in self-governance by the only genuine revolution in history, one that really brought forward something entirely new and workable. It may be considered today "old and tried," but the truth is for more than two hundred years, this new experiment in freedom has survived continuous assaults from tyrants because the people have always stepped forward to defend and protect the shining city.

And so it is today: the people see clearly those who threaten liberty itself.

Consequently, Democratic congressmen and senators are on the bubble.

Miraculously, a conservative Republican has a shot at being elected to the Senate from the state of Massachusetts. If that is not a bellwether, then there is no such thing this election season.

The people obviously thirst for genuine, common sense citizen politicians who will bring fiscal sanity and strong national defense back to the center of governance. They yearn for good men and women they can trust, and, step-by-step, good men and women are coming forward to heed the call.

We are witnessing again the miracle of self-governance the founders gifted to us. Our gift to them, and to ourselves, will be the preservation of Republic and a rebirth of freedom behind a repudiation of statists, big government, central control, and limousine liberals.

It is one of those exhilarating times in human history. Everything is on the line. Will we step up and turn the tide or sentence our children to doom?

> You and I have a rendezvous with destiny. We will preserve for our children this, the last best hope of man on earth, or we will sentence them to take the first step into a thousand years of darkness. If we fail, at least let our children and our children's children say of us we justified our brief moment here. We did all that could be done.
>
> Ronald Reagan 1964

THE ELECTION OF SCOTT BROWN: "THESE HAVE NO EARS"

January 20, 2010

> Barack Obama has finally achieved transparency. On Tuesday, the voters of Massachusetts proved that they could see right through him.
>
> Sally Vaci

Last night, Mr. Obama congratulated Scott Brown on his victory in the Massachusetts special Senate election then immediately ordered passage of healthcare reform with all speed, followed quickly by a statement urging the Congress not to "jam" a bill through, followed by multiple statements from WH operatives blaming Bush for the anger in the Bay State. Sounds like hysteria has hit the WH.

Apparently some people are slow learners.

The election in Massachusetts last night was a stern warning from across the nation: stop healthcare legislation, stop the insane spending, fix the economy, secure the country, or else.

Still, the emperors have no ears. But they have plenty of mouth!

There is no telling how many people outside Massachusetts shouldered the wheel to help Scott Brown. Small donations in the millions poured in from out of state. Many thousands of calls were placed, encouraging a vote for Brown. Massachusetts became the voice for the majority, a majority energized and focused on removing elitists, statists, and tyrants from the halls of power.

Nine months ago Americans started demonstrating against the tax and spend policies of this administration, angrily condemning fiscal irresponsibility, massive debt, and looming tax increases. For the first time in their lives, average Americans, most of them middle-aged and elderly, took to the streets to express their outrage.

Several Tea Party events meshed with numerous town hall protests against healthcare "reform," culminating in a massive demonstration in DC in September, a huge gathering the president pretended not to notice. The media in the main either ignored the protests or mocked the people involved.

Mr. Obama and his colleagues in the Congress, including Pelosi and Reid, all turned a deaf ear. They refused to hear the people. They actually had the audacity to denigrate the people, calling them un-American and evil-mongers, ridiculing them, calling them stupid and uninformed, characterizing the movement Astroturf funded by Republicans or other unnamed sinister forces.

Joining Obama and company, most of the mean-stream media, the talking heads ridiculing the people, calling them tea baggers, an insult meaningful only to the depraved.

The arrogance of these elitists was exceeded only by their contempt for the common man and woman.

And with every lie and insult, the movement grew.

Then came more outrage. More spending, more proposed spending, more debt coupled with fools errands in the war on terror prosecuting the intelligence community, closing Gitmo, granting terrorists access to civilian courts, indecisive and incoherent Afghan policy, the general call to retreat.

Throughout the summer and fall it seemed the president was going out of his way, daily, to insult and provoke the very people he was elected to serve.

Then came the elections in November with Republican governors winning in Virginia and New Jersey.

Still the elitists refused to listen, refused to acknowledge the ground swell, insisting all was well, despite poll after poll confirming the grassroots opposition was growing in numbers and intensity.

Then came Fort Hood, the act of terrorism in Detroit on Christmas Day, the murder of CIA agents in Afghanistan.

And then last night and Scott Brown's resounding victory.

Olbermann mumbled about tea baggers and condemned Brown with the same tired insults, insulting the majority of Americans. Maddow frantically sifted sand for an explanation, desperately avoiding the glaringly obvious. At least Chris Matthews was marginally honest. He acknowledged the opposition had an argument and had prevailed, his leg tingle giving way to a spine chill.

Today we have the president and Pelosi and Reid and others blowing the bugle and ordering the charge: same policies, same direction, same arrogance, same dismissive attitude: "Let them eat cake."

Others scurry about, trying to find ways to prevent Scott Brown from voting on healthcare, a crass attempt, once again, to derail the will of the people, a move that will only inflame and energize the opposition further.

All of this brings to mind a history lesson from 1876.

Prior to the battle of Greasy Grass Creek, Sitting Bull performed a sun dance, cutting himself bloody until he had a vision of cavalry falling down, as a voice said, 'I give you these because they have no ears.'

Later, General George A. Custer insisted on riding down the valley into the Little Big Horn, ignoring warnings there were four thousand furious, well-armed Sioux and Cheyenne warriors ready to welcome him. He led his 263 men to their deaths.

After the battle, a Cheyenne woman hammered an awl deep into each of Custer's ears so he would be able to listen in the afterlife. Another report: Custer's ears were cut off as a penalty for refusing to listen in this life.

General Custer thought a great victory at the Little Big Horn would pave the way for him to assume the White House, but he had no ears.

Mr. Obama's political Little Big Horn comes in stages: first, last night; next in November; then in 2012 (because he has no ears.).

As the Japanese learned in WWII, it is a grave error to awaken the sleeping giant: worse to underestimate him once awakened.

WAR FOR OIL AND THE US MARINE CORPS

January 26, 2010

Headline out of Iraq yesterday: *Marines hand over command to Iraqis in Anbar.*

A few years ago my oldest, Ian, at seventeen came to me, saying because of 9/11 and the war on terror he wanted to sign up to be a Marine. He had spent time with a dear family friend, Walter Jamieson, a WWII Marine who'd been wounded in the South Pacific, a Marine who told him the unvarnished truth about Marine Corps training and war. (For more about Walter Jamieson, get the book "'Once a Marine Always a Marine," by Jay A. Jamieson, MD, Dog Ear Publishing, 2008.)

Ian had been through Devil Pups. He knew what he was getting into.

Filled with patriotism and a desire to serve, he got on the bus, rode south all night, and started recruit training in San Diego. First step: feet on the paint. Recruit training is some of the toughest in the world, producing warriors feared everywhere.

After basic on their way west by ship for their first tour in Iraq, Ian's regiment was diverted Christmas Day 2004 to provide tsunami relief in Indonesia, that government requiring the Marines bring supplies unarmed.

The Marines I've met never want to talk about combat; they aren't looking for a pat on the back, and they don't serve to get rich or famous. They join for various reasons, but in the end, they fight like hell for one another and love of country.

Like so many others in many branches of service, Ian served two tours in Iraq. Miraculously he survived four roadside bomb attacks and various close calls from snipers, mortar fire, RPG, and small arms. Several of his buddies were not so fortunate. Many died. Many more were severely wounded.

Thanks to my son's courage and service, I became a member of an exclusive group, Marine dads. One friend lost his son Marcus in April 2006. Another friend lost his son Derek in October 2006. We met Debbie later when Ian came home. Her son James didn't make it. James was killed by a sniper in al Anbar in July 2006. Debbie is raising money for a memorial for Americans lost since Vietnam, The National Fallen Heroes memorial.

Marcus Glimpse, Derek Jones, and James Higgins all lost their lives in Anbar.

Another friend's son Garrett lost his leg in Iraq. Another friend's son Joe was disfigured. All of them emotionally scarred for life, part of the high price all combat veterans pay.

Thousands of young men and women across this country volunteered to fight for us these last few years, and yesterday the news was mission accomplished: freedom for the people of Iraq purchased by the blood of young Americans.

They served and continue to serve despite all the political games played and all the false accusations leveled.

They serve and suffer and die in freedom's cause, killed and wounded for folks back home, for each other, and for strangers, all for the love of an idea, the simple idea that all men and women yearn for freedom and have a right to pursue it. On the occasion of the news out of Iraq yesterday, it would have been nice to see our political leaders stop and acknowledge the sacrifice and success of our young men and women in uniform.

It is bizarre how some people take so much for granted and express so little appreciation.

Semper Fi anyway, and God bless the USA and all those who wear the uniform.

> Some people spend an entire lifetime wondering if they made a difference in the world. Marines don't have that problem.
>
> Ronald Reagan, President of the United States, 1985

POTUS ATTACKS SCOTUS, HARMS REST OF US

January 28, 2010

Obama has a special talent for stirring up division. In his State of the Union speech last night, he managed to disregard the Massachusetts mandate, attack Republicans, threaten conservative Democrats, attack the former administration, demagogue some in the financial community, and humiliate the justices of the Supreme Court.

The attack on the justices was especially noteworthy. Here is what the President said to them as they sat directly in front of him:

> With all due deference to separation of powers, last week, the Supreme Court reversed a century of law that I believe will open the floodgates for special interests, including foreign corporations, to spend without limit in our elections. I don't think American elections should be bankrolled by America's most powerful interests or, worse, by foreign entities. They should be decided by the American people. And I urge Democrats and Republicans to pass a bill that helps correct some of these problems.

Polls show the American people are split over the court's decision, an opportunity the President exploits.

Justice Kennedy, writing for the majority, stated in the decision:

When government seeks to use its full power, including the criminal law, to command where a person may get his or her information or what distrusted source he or she may not hear, it uses censorship to control thought. This is unlawful. The First Amendment confirms the freedom to think for ourselves.

As many will recall, the McCain-Feingold campaign finance reform act was controversial. Critics said it infringed upon freedom of speech by limiting contributions and allowing government to regulate elections communication by organizations, including corporations and labor unions. The recent Supreme Court decision on a five-to-four vote overruled many of the provisions of McCain-Feingold, calling them unconstitutional infringements on free speech.

The president insisted the court's ruling will allow foreign money to pour into the system. This is simply not true. The court let stand provisions in McCain-Feingold that prevent foreign contributions, contributions from overseas that Mr. Obama enjoyed via the Internet when he was running for the White House, contributions impossible to trace.

The most disturbing aspect of the president's criticism of the court last night is this: while he wants us to believe he respects the separation of powers, his attack on the justices demonstrates his lack of respect for that central constitutional structure of government. He would manipulate the legislative to control the judicial, giving the executive more power, the act of a king.

THE WAR ON CHRISTIANITY I

January 31, 2010

From the moment Jesus proclaimed himself divine, preaching in the synagogue in Nazareth, people tried to kill him and the message. Read all about it in Luke 4:14-30.

All the people in the synagogue were furious when they heard Jesus say he was God. They got up, drove him out of the town, and took him to the brow of the hill on which the town was built in order to throw him down the cliff (Luke 4:28–29).

For three years thereafter he was frequently confronted by angry mobs looking to stone him. Eventually, they found accomplices in the Romans and had him crucified.

The Romans were especially accomplished killing Christians. Nero had them impaled then set ablaze to serve as lanterns for his outdoor orgies. Christians were drawn and quartered, employing the power of four horses driven in separate directions, tearing people apart. Believers where sawn in half lengthwise. They were fed to lions or butchered by gladiators in the arena.

For all the savagery directed at Christians down through the ages, we know from authoritative studies approximately seventy million have been martyred since Christ was crucified, most of them, forty-five million, killed in the twentieth century alone.

Christians learn to expect trouble. Jesus, noting the world hated him, told his followers it would hate them as well (John 15:18). He added, in John 16:

> I have told you these things, so that in me you may have peace. In this world you will have trouble. But take heart! I have overcome the world... in fact, a time is coming when anyone who kills you will think he is offering a service to God. *They will do such things because they have not known the Father or me.*

And so it continues to this day. Christians are killed around the world at a rate of about eighteen per hour, 432 per day, one hundred fifty-seven thousand per year. Their crime? Testifying about the LORD of love. (Online source, continuously updated, "Center for the Study of Global Christianity, |FCO|EmphasisWorld Christian Trends: The demographics of Christian martyrdom, AD 33- AD 2001," |FCC|by Dr. David B. Barrett and Dr. Todd M. Johnson, *Gordon-Conwell Theological Seminary.*)

Right here in America, the persecution has not so far burned intensely enough to take the form of outright killing. Here in America the war on Christianity takes other forms: a disturbing pattern of persecution escalating in recent years.

Here is a sampling of the attacks happening daily throughout the country, this first example reported by United Press International online.

> *Item:* 'Judge goes to court over Ten Commandments' Jan. 29, 2010
> *Columbus,* Ohio (UPI) An Ohio judge is back in court for the second time defending a courtroom poster featuring the Ten Commandments. The poster bears the title 'Philosophies of Law in Conflict' and contrasts the 'moral absolutes' of the Ten Commandments with the 'moral relatives' of 'humanist principles.'

Item: World War I memorial in the Mojave Desert, a cross, located in a remote location, must be removed, says the ACLU. The fight has gone on for ten years.

Item: San Diego war memorial to honor veterans, the Mount Soledad Cross, again, the ACLU insists it must be removed, citing separation of church and state. The twenty-one-year court battle continues.

Item: Atheists' 'hate' sign blasted in lawsuit. A political candidate in this week's primary election for the office of comptroller in Illinois has filed a lawsuit against the state charging it officially expressed 'hate' and 'hostility' toward Christianity and other religions that include a belief in God by allowing atheists to post a sign in a state building at Christmas.

Item: 'Professor calls student a 'fascist bastard' for speaking out against gay marriage. Attorneys with the Alliance Defense Fund Center for Academic Freedom filed a lawsuit against officials of the Los Angeles Community College District Wednesday. The lawsuit comes after a professor censored and threatened to expel a student following a speech about his Christian faith, including passing reference to the topic of marriage, during an open-ended assignment in a public speaking class.

Item: "Christian Photographer Accused of 'Discriminating' Against Lesbian Couple." The Human Rights Commission of New Mexico ruled on Wednesday that an evangelical Christian photographer discriminated against a lesbian couple because he refused a job to photograph the couple's same-sex commitment ceremony. The commission ordered Elaine and Jon Huenins, owners of Elane Photography in Albuquerque, N.M., to pay the lesbian couple $6,600 in attorney fees.

Item: "Youth pastor arrested for talking to people at a mall"

Jan. 2010: Arguments have moved to the appellate court level in a California case in which a man talking to two willing strangers in a shopping mall was arrested because the subject of the conversation was God.

Item: "Husband and wife arrested for preaching to get brand new trial" August 2008. "It's hard to believe that we've come to a point in our country where Christians are arrested for sharing the Gospel on a public street corner," said ADF Litigation Counsel David LaPlante. Alliance Defense Fund attorneys filed suit against the City of Elmira, N.Y., after police threatened to arrest three Christians if they did not remove a shirt and stop sharing biblical messages during a "gay" pride event at a public park.

Item: "Christians arrested at homosexual event" *Demonstrators spend 21 hours in jail, charged with felonies* Eleven Christians who were demonstrating at a public homosexual-rights event in Philadelphia have been arrested and charged they say unjustly.

Item: Pastor Jailed for Pro-Life Witness Writes Letter from Prison to "Men of the Cloth" OAKLAND, California, April 3, 2009 (LifeSiteNews.com)

"It is Thursday, March 26th, 2009 and I am sitting on the top of the second of fifteen bunks in housing unit thirty-four east of the Santa Rita jail in Dublin, California," begins a recent letter from Oakland pastor Walter Hoye, who was sent to jail on March 23 for peacefully counseling and picketing at a local abortion facility.

Rev. Hoye is an African-American pastor who says he feels a special calling to work for the end of what he calls the genocide by abortion taking place in the African-American community. As part of his efforts, he stands in front of an abortion facility in Oakland with leaflets offering abortion alternatives and a sign reading, "Jesus loves you and your baby. Let us help."

Today many atheists and others continue the drumbeat, persecuting homeschoolers, redefining the doctrine of church/state separation to fashion it a weapon, suing school districts for so-called violations, and petitioning to expunge every vestige of Judeo-Christian tradition from every aspect of public life, going so far as to suggest CBS anathema for airing a pro-family, pro-life message during the upcoming Super Bowl or restricting the free speech rights of Christians via legislation based on the myth of hate crimes and muzzling military chaplains who wish to pray in Jesus' name.

The war on Christianity rages.

In America the lions have been replaced by courts and legislatures and human rights commissions, and the Romans and Nero have been replaced by atheists, humanists, secularists, 'progressives,' and other assorted tyrants.

It will get worse. Much worse.

THE WAR ON CHRISTIANITY II

February 1, 2010

'God damn America. That's in the Bible for killing innocent people.' So says the president's pastor for twenty years, Jeremiah Wright. When a so-called Christian minister sounds exactly like Osama bin Laden, one has to wonder what is happening in America and why.

People like Jeremiah Wright used to be the exception. Today, extreme leftists and liberation theologians occupy pulpits across the land. Moderate and conservative pastors appear less and less willing to confront heresy or address the great moral issues of the day: abortion, infanticide, gay marriage, embryonic stem cell research, assisted suicide, euthanasia.

The war on Christianity is being waged from outside and from inside the church. Why is the God of love under such assault? What is the objection from secularists to a tradition that teaches we are all better off when we love one another as Christ loved us? Why is there so much hatred expressed toward Christianity, a system of belief resulting in far more blessing than any other, especially in America during the course of three centuries?

Part of the explanation lies in a traditional understanding of western art and scholarship, what has been called "The Great Conversation." Classical education has always fed the idea that learning is best engaged by a free and open inquiry into all aspects of life in order to discuss, examine, and debate the great questions: what is life about, why are we here, what is our purpose, what is morality, how best do we proceed, what is goodness, what is truth?

The rules of logic, grammar, and rhetoric traditionally guided those inquiries, giving practitioners masterful tools to achieve critical thinking. And those tools, first provided by the ancients, were refined and perfected in Christian universities throughout Europe and the Americas.

Today, however, the Great Conversation, classical education, and critical thinking have given way to prejudicial thinking. In other words we don't go about looking for truth and arriving there after careful examination of the evidence according to the scientific method. Instead we define truth ahead of time and go about looking for 'evidence' to support the presuppositions. We prefabricate 'truth' and then self-justify or rationalize.

For example we say ahead of time a presupposition is women are enslaved by their biology, and, therefore, they can only be liberated if granted exclusive rights to reproductive outcomes. Hence abortion becomes a high moral calling, and men are irrelevant. What was once considered murder is made mandatory at the altar of liberation theology, and the relationships between men and women, once ideally based on mutual trust and respect, are now politicized, casting men to the margins as agents of oppression. A kind of secularist religion installed by judicial fiat dictates the sentiment of the minority to the exclusion of the majority, despotism light by any definition.

This one example—and there are many more, of course—illustrates the great divide in the Great Conversation. On the one hand, there are the traditionalists who embrace the idea of moral absolutes, transcendent moral authority, acknowledging the limitations of human intellect. On the other hand, there are those who embrace the idea that man can perfect man, that human reason and capability are sufficient for the just ordering of society apart from transcendent authority and that moral relativism is the true path to tolerance and diversity.

The trouble is the former has borne good fruit while the later has routinely failed throughout history.

Traditionalists, operating from the Christian notion of the fall of man, accept the idea that people are largely selfish and prone to sin and that any ordering of society must take that central truth into consideration. The founders did so, and thus you have the idea of covenant between God and man, and between men, referenced throughout our founding principles, yielding a structure of checks and balances so as to thwart the corrosive power of power itself vested exclusively in the hands of fallen man.

Interestingly, those who would refashion the American republic— the system of representative government, separation of powers, and checks and balances— acknowledge their only means of doing so requires destroying the Constitution. Short of destroying it outright, they suggest the Constitution is a 'living' document, subject to radical change in the face of change. This is simply another way to destroy the Constitution while appearing supportive of it. They make no secret of their desire to replace a republican form of government with a statist structure. All one need do to verify this is read Saul Alinksy (Obama's mentor), members of the Frankfurt School, Marx, Lenin, Mao, and professors Cloward and Piven, a story originally broken by Jim Simpson, American Thinker.

And globalist—most everyone employed by the White House— argue rightly that world governance requires the removal or restructuring of America, making it subservient to the UN or other international governing body.

Thus the glue of western civilization—do unto others as you would have them do unto you—is under assault. The motto the secular world prefers is we will all do right unto one another when the right government is in place run by the right people who work to make sure everyone is provided for equally.

The separation point between the two mottos distills down to opposing views of human nature: is man perfectible in his own strength, or is man inherently flawed, civilized only via cooperation with transcendent moral authority?

For traditionalists it also boils down to the struggle between good and evil, for their analysis of history demonstrates that man left to his own devices exclusive of divine influence will always trend despotic, even murderous.

In America the essential link between God-given rights and freedom as articulated in the Declaration protects citizens from the excess of government and thwarts the ambitions of secularists eager to turn the Constitution on its head so that statists can take over and engineer equal outcomes.

Hence the war on Christianity.

Christianity focuses on the individual, not the collective, just as our Declaration and our Constitution focus on the individual. The emphasis is on individual rights, individual freedom, individual responsibilities, and individual virtue, honor, and duty.

The antithesis—the collectivist worldview—demands the individual submit to the interests of the collective as defined by some powerful individual or group. Thus the rights of the individual are washed away by the priority emphasis on the compelling interest of the group, as defined by central authority.

One model says fallen people can become virtuous, thanks to divine intervention, and such virtue is required for a constitutional republic to exist, the only foundation for freedom and prosperity, the only proven way people are encouraged to hold one another in mutual respect.

The other model says people are essentially good and can be perfected without any regard for transcendent moral authority, that people as part of a larger society are perfectible by society governed by a self-generated morality, a consensus morality, a morality that changes with changing times and preferences.

These two worldviews cannot coexist. They emerge from entirely different sets of assumptions and suggest vastly different methods for the ordering of society. They are antagonistic toward one another and always have been.

For now, in America, the battle rages as never before. Mr. Obama and his allies see an America transformed by the secularist, collectivist impulse, codified in an all powerful central government that presumes to know better than the individual what is best for the individual and for society.

And the only barrier to their ambitions is a populace that continues to uphold the ideas of traditional morality, the individual and constitutional republic.

This, then, explains the essential reason for the war on Christianity: it stands in the way of secular ambitions to establish manmade socialist utopia on earth.

For if you cannot prevail in The Great Conversation by debating the merits, then your only option is to destroy the opposition, making it a one-sided conversation, something atheists, humanists, and 'progressives' fight for daily throughout the western world, finding themselves bedfellows with the likes of Mao and bin Laden and Jeremiah Wright.

THE WAR ON CHRISTIANITY III

February 2, 2010
Thomas More Law Center sues Obama administration on behalf of pastors claiming hate crimes laws are unconstitutional.

Spiritual warfare is difficult to discuss with people who have no regard for spiritual matters, a situation Christ confronted almost daily during his ministry. The book of John is especially revealing. Christ was constantly confronted by those who sought an argument or his death. Given the following exchange, it's no wonder.

Speaking to the religious leaders of the day, Jesus, as usual, focused on their essential problem, a problem shared by many people today:

> If God were your Father, you would love me, because I have come to you from God. I am not here on my own, but he sent me. Why can't you understand what I am saying? It's because you can't even hear me! For you are the children of your father the devil, and you love to do the evil things he does. He was a murderer from the beginning. He has always hated the truth, because there is no truth in him. When he lies, it is consistent with his character; for he is a liar and the father of lies. So when I tell the truth, you just naturally don't believe me! Which of you can truthfully accuse me of sin? And since I am telling you the truth, why don't you believe me? Anyone who belongs to God listens gladly to the words of God. But you don't listen because you don't belong to God.
>
> John 8:42–47

It is truly amazing to hear people say they love or respect Jesus Christ when they completely ignore him or contradict him. Careful reading reveals his life on earth was a full-time engagement in spiritual warfare: confronting the evil one, seeking to save that which was lost in the garden.

More than anyone in the Scriptures, Christ talked about Satan, the spiritual realm, the constant warfare with the forces of evil, and the coming kingdom that will settle the matter once and for all. Spirit-filled Christians therefore realize that people who come against Christ are goaded by the spiritual forces of darkness, that though they be unawares, they are nonetheless being used as pawns in Satan's game.

Here is an example of what happens when spiritual warfare is manifest in the physical world.

In November of 2008 there was a demonstration in Palm Springs concerning Proposition 8, the measure that eventually passed in California prohibiting gay marriage.

Present that evening was a sixty-nine-year-old grandmother, a Christian, who was peacefully making her opinion known, supporting the measure. She was attacked by gay activists, pushed, hit, and spat upon (sound familiar?), and then the cross she was carrying was ripped from her hands, thrown to the ground, and trampled. The story received national television coverage and the video can easily be located on YouTube.

Notice at the end of the local coverage the male anchor claims there was a lot of "hate being expressed on both sides," a total lie.

A grandmother prayerfully exercising her constitutional right to free speech, freedom of assembly, and the right of conscience assaulted no one either verbally or physically, but she, rather, was assaulted, then made the perpetrator by her assailants.

When people give themselves permission to behave in this fashion at the same time casting their opponents as hate-filled bigots, when in truth the hate and bigotry resides with them, one witnesses the strategy and tactics of the evil one working through human beings.

Of course, those with no spiritual sensitivity or understanding will scoff, but they do so to their own injury, for Satan would prefer people deny his existence. Such denials make his work most easy: the hell harvest.

Observe the president as he joins the forces of darkness to force a gay agenda on the military whose leaders have long opposed the agenda. Even Bill Clinton saw the wisdom of backing off.

The issue is sustaining the most effective military articulation possible, but it will be recast, redefined, and restated as a human rights issue, an equal rights issue, and all those opposed will be condemned and ridiculed, as always, characterized as hate-filled bigots and homophobes, another manifestation of the spiritual battle constantly raging in the unseen.

And through the ages, Christ wages war on our behalf, reminding us:

> The thief comes only to steal and kill and destroy; I have come that they may have life, and have it to the full.
>
> John 10:10

> The darkness is getting darker but it has not and never will overcome the Light.
>
> John 1:5

*Related:

Three pastors sue Obama administration, challenging constitutionality of federal hate crimes legislation recently enacted, more on the story here: "Holder sued over 'Hate Crimes Act' by Thomas More Law Center (TMLC) on behalf of three Michigan pastors and the president of the American Family Association of Michigan," by Bill Bumpas, OneNewsNow, February 9, 2010.

DO YOU WONDER WHAT IS HAPPENING IN AMERICA TODAY?

February 12, 2010

> Liberty is not built on the doctrine that a few nobles have a right to inherit the earth. No! No! It stands on this principle: that the meanest and lowest of the people are, by the unalterable, indefeasible laws of God and Nature, as well entitled the benefit of the air to breathe, light to see, food to eat, and clothes to wear, as the nobles or the king. That is Liberty! And Liberty will reign in America!
>
> John Adams

From our earliest days, the founders, even before declaring independence, asserted that human rights flow from the Creator. This single principle, more than any other, promoted the idea of democratic republic while simultaneously repudiating the idea a king or mere human institution was, or ever could be, the purveyor of rights.

Now a few 'nobles' believe they have a right to inherit the earth, and these 'nobles' are the monarchs apparent, those presuming assumption to the throne, extremists led by Obama, those gathered to destroy the spirit of independence, individualism, and liberty itself. They deny our Judeo-Christian heritage, which gave birth to freedom, and they work feverishly to remove the Creator from all considerations of public policy. Thus they set themselves against the very spirit of Americanism and face a growing and aggressive opposition from people who refuse to be dominated.

One does not need to be a Christian or a person of faith to understand the essential protection to liberty provided by the Creator, that one's individual rights are unalienable thanks to that protection, that liberty is thereby preserved, and government can never convince the people to forfeit, for as the Creator reigns, so reigns liberty.

This was the idea all the founders gathered around, agreed to, promoted, and sustained all through the rumblings of discontent in the colonies, right through the Declaration, the darkest days of the revolution, and afterward when the fledging republic struggled to find its legs.

What is happening today is a repeat of history, a repeat of inspired dissent, a rebirth of inspiration in American hearts in love with liberty, realizing again the debt we owe so many who bought this precious freedom with their own blood.

While the nobles sneer, the meanest and lowest take to the streets to protest government usurpations.

While the nobles dine and congratulate one another, lusting to inherit the earth, the meanest and lowest organize and communicate and fashion weapons of resistance, given full expression at the ballot box, and thank God for that box, for without it real bullets would fly.

While the king and his nobles scheme to dominate and manipulate the people by taxation, executive orders, administrative rules, legislative trickery, judicial activism, bureaucratic despotism, and the ceding of sovereignty to foreign powers, the meanest and the lowest rediscover the strength that flows from the Creator's endowments, fueling a new revolution, which will again throw off the cruel chains of slavery.

And while the nobles and their king squander the hard-won fruit of the people's labor, gorging themselves at the people's table, the meanest and the lowest redouble their efforts, recruiting an army of rebels devoted each day to the utter defeat of those who would lead us into years of darkness.

On this, Abraham Lincoln's birthday, we would be wise to heed his words:

> Our reliance is in the love of liberty which God has planted in our bosoms. Our defense is in the preservation of the spirit which prizes liberty as the heritage of all men, in all lands, everywhere. Destroy this spirit, and you have planted the seeds of despotism around your own doors.
>
> September 11, 1858, Speech at Edwardsville

We planted those seeds in November 2008. We are reaping the harvest. Now it is time to clear the land, cultivate, and replant in hopes of harvesting a new crop of liberty and prosperity for our children and our children's children. *

CHENEY VERSUS OBAMA-BIDEN — WAR OR CONTINGENCY?

February 14, 2010

This week VP Joe Biden declared Iraq is one of the greatest successes of the Obama administration.

Today, asked about Biden's remark, former VP Dick Cheney chuckled then said, "I'm glad he now believes Iraq is a success."

Anyone who has been paying attention these last few years knows very well that Mr. Biden and Mr. Obama were constant critics of Bush/Cheney both in terms of the war in Iraq and the war on terrorism.

Obama opposed the surge, which led to success in Iraq, and now he claims credit for things he had no hand in.

Obama opposed the Iraq invasion despite the vote in Congress in October 2002, authorizing the use of force. (The full text of that authorization is included below. It is very interesting to read all the whereas clauses and compare them to the anti-war rhetoric we've heard during the last seven years. Keep in mind Congress passed this measure, paving the way for invasion in 2003.)

It is also interesting to note that Biden voted yes to authorize the use of force but today says the invasion of Iraq was not worth the price, at the same time insisting Iraq is a crowning achievement of the Obama administration.

Perhaps the rules of logic are different in Delaware?

In April 2008, restating his opposition to the surge in Iraq, saying the surge was a failure and Iraq was becoming a complete disaster, Joe Biden said this: "I believe the president (Bush) has no strategy for success in Iraq. His plan is to muddle through, and hand the problem off to his successor."

Today, can we rightly ask who is muddling?

Obviously, when it comes to Iraq, Obama deserves no credit whatsoever.

And as to national security...

What we do know can be derived from the track record. Comparing the two administrations with regard to the war on terror and securing the homeland, we find no attacks on the homeland in seven years under Bush, but under Obama we've seen three attacks in one year.

One year ago Cheney warned of coming attacks:

"When we get people who are more concerned about reading the rights to an Al Qaeda terrorist than they are with protecting the United States against people who are absolutely committed to do anything they can to kill Americans, then I worry."

American forces, demoralized under Obama, continue to do their duty under adverse conditions created by Obama's policies, most notably:

- reverting to a pre-9/11 posture, making terrorism a criminal matter rather than addressing terrorism as an act of war;
- assuming a defensive rather than an offensive posture;
- hamstringing and demoralizing intelligence agencies by removing the very successful tool of enhanced interrogation, and announcing the threat of prosecution;

- releasing top-secret CIA memos against the best advice in the intelligence community;
- projecting weakness by retreating from military commissions, Gitmo, and aggressive intelligence gathering.

Mr. Bush and Mr. Cheney inherited an escalating terrorist threat, thanks to the soft policies of Mr. Clinton. Unlike Mr. Obama, they did not whine or complain about the circumstances handed to them. Rather, they acted, achieving tremendous results despite mistakes regarding the prosecution of the Iraq war in some respects. Bush was a liberator and a freedom fighter: he prevented further attacks on American soil, liberated fifty million people in Iraq and Afghanistan, put the fear into terrorists and their sponsors worldwide, and decimated al-Qaeda.

In one year, Mr. Obama has turned much of that good work on its head.

Results speak louder than pontification, Mr. Biden.

Authorization To Use Force In Iraq

Oct 18, 2002—Enrolled Bill. This is the final text of the bill or resolution as approved by both the Senate and House. This is the latest version of the bill currently available on GovTrack.

H.J.Res.114
One Hundred Seventh Congress of the
United States of America

At The Second Session

Begun and held at the City of Washington on Wednesday, the twenty-third day of January, two thousand and two Joint Resolution To authorize the use of United States Armed Forces against Iraq.

Whereas in 1990 in response to Iraq's war of aggression against and illegal occupation of Kuwait, the United States forged a coalition of nations to liberate Kuwait and its people in order to defend the national security of the United States and enforce United Nations Security Council resolutions relating to Iraq;

Whereas after the liberation of Kuwait in 1991, Iraq entered into a United Nations sponsored cease-fire agreement pursuant to which Iraq unequivocally agreed, among other things, to eliminate its nuclear, biological, and chemical weapons programs and the means to deliver and develop them, and to end its support for international terrorism;

Whereas the efforts of international weapons inspectors, United States intelligence agencies, and Iraqi defectors led to the discovery that Iraq had large stockpiles of chemical weapons and a large scale biological weapons program, and that Iraq had an advanced nuclear weapons development program that was much closer to producing a nuclear weapon than intelligence reporting had previously indicated;

Whereas Iraq, in direct and flagrant violation of the cease-fire, attempted to thwart the efforts of weapons inspectors to identify and destroy Iraq's weapons of mass destruction stockpiles and development capabilities, which finally resulted in the withdrawal of inspectors from Iraq on October 31, 1998;

Whereas in Public Law 105–235 (August 14, 1998), Congress concluded that Iraq's continuing weapons of mass destruction programs threatened vital United States interests and international peace and security, declared Iraq to be in 'material and unacceptable breach of its international obligations' and urged the President 'to take appropriate action, in accordance with the Constitution and relevant laws of the United States, to bring Iraq into compliance with its international obligations';

Whereas Iraq both poses a continuing threat to the national security of the United States and international peace and security in the Persian Gulf region and remains in material and unacceptable breach of its international obligations by, among other things, continuing to possess and develop a significant chemical and biological weapons capability, actively seeking a nuclear weapons capability, and supporting and harboring terrorist organizations;

Whereas Iraq persists in violating resolution of the United Nations Security Council by continuing to engage in brutal repression of its civilian population thereby threatening international peace and security in the region, by refusing to release, repatriate, or account for non-Iraqi citizens wrongfully detained by Iraq, including an American serviceman, and by failing to return property wrongfully seized by Iraq from Kuwait;

Whereas the current Iraqi regime has demonstrated its capability and willingness to use weapons of mass destruction against other nations and its own people;

Whereas the current Iraqi regime has demonstrated its continuing hostility toward, and willingness to attack, the United States, including by attempting in 1993 to assassinate former President Bush and by firing on many thousands of occasions on United States and Coalition Armed Forces engaged in enforcing the resolutions of the United Nations Security Council;

Whereas members of al Qaida, an organization bearing responsibility for attacks on the United States, its citizens, and interests, including the attacks that occurred on September 11, 2001, are known to be in Iraq;

Whereas Iraq continues to aid and harbor other international terrorist organizations, including organizations that threaten the lives and safety of United States citizens;

Whereas the attacks on the United States of September 11, 2001, underscored the gravity of the threat posed by the acquisition of weapons of mass destruction by international terrorist organizations;

Whereas Iraq's demonstrated capability and willingness to use weapons of mass destruction, the risk that the current Iraqi regime will either employ those weapons to launch a surprise attack against the United States or its Armed Forces or provide them to international terrorists who would do so, and the extreme magnitude of harm that would result to the United States and its citizens from such an attack, combine to justify action by the United States to defend itself;

Whereas United Nations Security Council Resolution 678 (1990) authorizes the use of all necessary means to enforce United Nations Security Council Resolution 660 (1990) and subsequent relevant resolutions and to compel Iraq to cease certain activities that threaten international peace and security, including the development of weapons of mass destruction and refusal or obstruction of United Nations weapons inspections in violation of United Nations Security Council Resolution 687 (1991), repression of its civilian population in violation of United Nations Security Council Resolution 688 (1991), and threatening its neighbors or United Nations operations in Iraq in violation of United Nations Security Council Resolution 949 (1994);

Whereas in the Authorization for Use of Military Force Against Iraq Resolution (Public Law 102–1), Congress has authorized the President 'to use United States Armed Forces pursuant to United Nations Security Council Resolution 678 (1990) in order to achieve implementation of Security Council Resolution 660, 661, 662, 664, 665, 666, 667, 669, 670, 674, and 677';

Whereas in December 1991, Congress expressed its sense that it 'supports the use of all necessary means to achieve the goals of United Nations Security Council Resolution 687 as being consistent with the Authorization of Use of Military Force Against Iraq Resolution (Public Law 102–1),' that Iraq's repression of its civilian population violates United Nations Security Council Resolution 688 and 'constitutes a continuing threat to the peace, security, and stability of the Persian Gulf region,' and that Congress, 'supports the use of all necessary means to achieve the goals of United Nations Security Council Resolution 688';

Whereas the Iraq Liberation Act of 1998 (Public Law 105–338) expressed the sense of Congress that it should be the policy of the United States to support efforts to remove from power the current

Iraqi regime and promote the emergence of a democratic government to replace that regime;

Whereas on September 12, 2002, President Bush committed the United States to 'work with the United Nations Security Council to meet our common challenge' posed by Iraq and to 'work for the necessary resolutions,' while also making clear that 'the Security Council resolutions will be enforced, and the just demands of peace and security will be met, or action will be unavoidable';

Whereas the United States is determined to prosecute the war on terrorism and Iraq's ongoing support for international terrorist groups combined with its development of weapons of mass destruction in direct violation of its obligations under the 1991 cease-fire and other United Nations Security Council resolutions make clear that it is in the national security interests of the United States and in furtherance of the war on terrorism that all relevant United Nations Security Council resolutions be enforced, including through the use of force if necessary;

Whereas Congress has taken steps to pursue vigorously the war on terrorism through the provision of authorities and funding requested by the President to take the necessary actions against international terrorists and terrorist organizations, including those nations, organizations, or persons who planned, authorized, committed, or aided the terrorist attacks that occurred on September 11, 2001, or harbored such persons or organizations;

Whereas the President and Congress are determined to continue to take all appropriate actions against international terrorists and terrorist organizations, including those nations, organizations, or persons who planned, authorized, committed, or aided the terrorist attacks that occurred on September 11, 2001, or harbored such persons or organizations;

Whereas the President has authority under the Constitution to take action in order to deter and prevent acts of international terrorism against the United States, as Congress recognized in the joint resolution on Authorization for Use of Military Force (Public Law 107–40); and

Whereas it is in the national security interests of the United States to restore international peace and security to the Persian Gulf region: Now, therefore, be it

Resolved by the Senate and House of Representatives of the United States of America in Congress assembled,

Section 1. Short Title.

This joint resolution may be cited as the 'Authorization for Use of Military Force Against Iraq Resolution of 2002.'

Sec. 2. Support For United States Diplomatic Efforts.

The Congress of the United States supports the efforts by the President to—

1. strictly enforce through the United Nations Security Council all relevant Security Council resolutions regarding Iraq and encourages him in those efforts; and

2. obtain prompt and decisive action by the Security Council to ensure that Iraq abandons its strategy of delay, evasion and noncompliance and promptly and strictly complies with all relevant Security Council resolutions regarding Iraq.

Sec. 3. Authorization For Use Of United States Armed Forces.

A. *Authorization-* The President is authorized to use the Armed Forces of the United States as he determines to be necessary and appropriate in order to—

1. defend the national security of the United States against the continuing threat posed by Iraq; and
2. (enforce all relevant United Nations Security Council resolutions regarding Iraq.

C. *Presidential Determination-* In connection with the exercise of the authority granted in subsection (a) to use force the President shall, prior to such exercise or as soon thereafter as may be feasible, but no later than 48 hours after exercising such authority, make available to the Speaker of the House of Representatives and the President pro tempore of the Senate his determination that—

   1. reliance by the United States on further diplomatic or other peaceful means alone either (A) will not adequately protect the national security of the United States against the continuing threat posed by Iraq or (B) is not likely to lead to enforcement of all relevant United Nations Security Council resolutions regarding Iraq; and
   2. acting pursuant to this joint resolution is consistent with the United States and other countries continuing to take the necessary actions against international terrorist and terrorist organizations, including those nations, organizations, or persons who planned, authorized, committed or aided the terrorist attacks that occurred on September 11, 2001.

C. War Powers Resolution Requirements—

   1. *Specific Statutory Authorization*—Consistent with section 8(a)(1) of the War Powers Resolution, the Congress declares that this section is intended to constitute specific statutory authorization within the meaning of section 5(b) of the War Powers Resolution.

2. *Applicability Of Other Requirements-* Nothing in this joint resolution supersedes any requirement of the War Powers Resolution.

Sec. 4. Reports To Congress.

A. *Reports-* The President shall, at least once every 60 days, submit to the Congress a report on matters relevant to this joint resolution, including actions taken pursuant to the exercise of authority granted in section 3 and the status of planning for efforts that are expected to be required after such actions are completed, including those actions described in section 7 of the Iraq Liberation Act of 1998 (Public Law 105–338).

B. *Single Consolidated Report-* To the extent that the submission of any report described in subsection (a) coincides with the submission of any other report on matters relevant to this joint resolution otherwise required to be submitted to Congress pursuant to the reporting requirements of the War Powers Resolution (Public Law 93–148), all such reports may be submitted as a single consolidated report to the Congress.

C. *Rule Of Construction-* To the extent that the information required by section 3 of the Authorization for Use of Military Force Against Iraq Resolution (Public Law 102–1) is included in the report required by this section, such report shall be considered as meeting the requirements of section 3 of such resolution.

Speaker of the House of Representatives.
Vice President of the United States and
President of the Senate.

IRAQ, BUSH, "TORTURE," AND THE WAR ON TERRORISM

February 15, 2010

> And you will know the truth, and the truth will set you free.
>
> Jesus Christ

There are still those who believe the invasion of Iraq was illegal, a war for oil, a vast conspiracy of the Bush family in league with the Saudis playing a global chess game against the Russians and the Iranians.

Yet the more we know, the more we find the invasion was executed for precisely the reasons delineated in the Congressional Authorization to use force passed in October 2002.

Despite the full power of the mainstream media and Democrats and extremists declaring Bush a war criminal for years starting three months after the invasion, as the smoke and BS clear, thanks to real historians, we see an administration carefully addressing serial threats to American security, going out of its way to engage military and intelligence authorities, legal counsel, the UN, and allies around the world in the crafting of tactics and strategy.

Contrary to the hysterical hand wringing on the left over Gitmo (a model prison by any estimation), water boarding (used only on three high-value terrorists when nothing else would work, resulting in thousands of saved American lives), and other intelligence gathering techniques (never forget Obama voted in favor of FISA), we now learn we do indeed face ruthless enemy combatants who've declared unconditional war, and, therefore, we have one of two options: kill them or incarcerate them to stand trial in a military setting.

We can be thankful for truth tellers like Mike Hayden (former CIA director), Marc Thiessen (former Bush speech writer and author of *Courting Disaster*), and John Yoo (law professor, former DOJ official, author of numerous books, most recently *Crisis and Command: A History of Executive Power*).

Hayden has been forthright about what is required in this war on terrorism. His endorsement of Thiessen's work lends a great deal of credibility to the entire discussion about the success of enhanced interrogation and the terrible risks brought forward by Obama's policies and actions. (Search: "Thiessen's 'Courting Disaster' a must-read," Daily Caller, 2.15.10, and read all of Hayden's evaluation of Thiessen's work.)

Thiessen has been actively promoting his book, *Courting Disaster: How the CIA kept America safe, and how Barack Obama is inviting the next attack*. He has been hammered on CNN and MSNBC and elsewhere, but his argument prevails. Why? Because he has carefully documented what was done and why, and when someone tells the truth, it is virtually impossible to destroy him.

This morning on Laura Ingraham's radio program, Yoo articulated the essential truth about what DOJ attorneys advised when asked by Bush administration officials for advice concerning the rules governing interrogation. Yoo stated the CIA and the administration wanted to get the most information possible from enemy combatants but only within the rule of law, both in view of American law and international agreements. Yoo reports no pressure was brought by the administration to force a particular recommendation, that DOJ attorneys advised certain enhanced interrogation techniques, consistent with what US soldiers experience in training, would be acceptable. Further, enhanced techniques could include water boarding, not considered torture, if used only in very exclusive cases for compelling reasons having to do with severe threats to American lives and national security.

Thanks to John Yoo, who has been vilified by the left and the MSM, we know the truth about what was done and why. We also know that Obama administration threats to prosecute Yoo and his colleagues are groundless, that such threats amount to political grandstanding.

And thanks to Marc Thiessen, we know water boarding saved thousands of American and European lives, gave our military and intelligence heroes the tools they needed to prevail against a viciously enemy, turning the tide against al-Qaeda and related groups.

Thanks to Hayden, Thiessen, and Yoo, we also realize the grave danger we are now facing because of Obama's policies to appease, capitulate, retreat, and accommodate.

By releasing top-secret CIA documents last year, documents that detailed our tactics involving interrogation, Obama hurt our side and helped the terrorists. Why would a president do such a thing?

By insisting we close Gitmo, Obama helps them and hurts us. The same holds true for trying KSM and others in civilian court, threatening prosecution of CIA and DOJ officials doing their duty in the former administration, assuming a defensive rather than offensive posture, remaining impotent in the face of Iranian nuclear ambitions, Mirandizing terrorists, outlawing enhanced interrogation and failing to put in place a substitute program. All this encourages an enemy fanatically devoted on our destruction.

People are awakening to the truth and will vote accordingly in upcoming elections.

On a personal note: if the CIA or the military are forced to water board a known terrorist in order to save the life of my four-year-old daughter, I say have at it boys.

By the way, the argument Gitmo and water boarding are recruiting tools for Jihad, BS. Islamic fanatics don't need our help. The promise of glory and eternally submissive virgins to a huge population of sex-starved, unemployed, and hopeless men is sufficient to recruit all the suicide bombers needed. Besides, many of these young men are so indoctrinated from an early age—to hate us and love death—they willingly become terrorists.

Parting shots: read and consider these excerpts from the aforementioned books by Yoo and Thiessen. If nothing else, they provide a great deal of perspective and clarification:

> An American president faces war and finds himself hamstrung by a Congress that will not act. To protect national security, he invokes his powers as commander-in-chief and orders actions that seem to violate laws enacted by Congress. He is excoriated for usurping dictatorial powers, placing himself above the law, and threatening to "breakdown constitutional safeguards."
>
> One could be forgiven for thinking that the above describes former President George W. Bush. Yet these particular attacks on presidential power were leveled against Franklin D. Roosevelt. They could just as well describe similar attacks leveled against George Washington, Thomas Jefferson, Andrew Jackson, Abraham Lincoln and a number of other presidents challenged with leading the nation through times of national crisis.

"Crisis and Command: A History of Executive Power from George Washington to George W. Bush, "by John Yoo, front flap, 2009, Kaplan Publishing.

This extended excerpt from Thiessen's book reads like a novel, but it reports actual events:

Just before dawn on March 1, 2003, two dozen heavily armed Pakistani tactical assault forces move in and surround a safe house in Rawalpindi. A few hours earlier they had received a text message from an informant inside the house. It read: "I am with KSM."

Bursting in, they find the disheveled mastermind of the 9/11 attacks, Khalid Sheikh Mohammed, in his bedroom. KSM lunges for a rifle and shoots one of the Pakistani soldiers in the foot before being finally subdued. He is taken into custody along with another senior al Qaeda operative, Mustafa al-Hawsawi, the paymaster of the 9/11 plot. In the safe house, they find a treasure trove of computers, documents, cell phones, and other valuable "pocket litter."

Once in custody, KSM is defiant. He refuses to answer questions, informing his captors that he will tell them everything when he gets to America and sees his lawyer. But KSM is not taken to America to see a lawyer. Instead he is taken, via a third country, to a secret CIA "black site" in an undisclosed location.

Upon arrival, KSM finds himself in the complete control of Americans. His head and face are shaved. He is stripped naked, his physical condition is documented through photographs, and he undergoes a medical exam and psychological interview. He does not know where he is, how long he will be there, or what his fate will be.

Despite his circumstances, KSM still refuses to talk. He spews contempt at his interrogators, telling them that Americans are weak, lack resilience, and are unable to do what is necessary to prevent the terrorists from succeeding in their goals. He has trained to resist interrogation. When he is asked for information about future attacks, he tells his questioners scornfully:

"Soon, you will know."

It becomes clear he will not reveal the information using traditional interrogation techniques. So he undergoes a series of "enhanced interrogation techniques" approved for use only on the most high-value detainees. The techniques include water boarding.

His resistance is described by one senior American official as "superhuman." Eventually, however, the techniques work, and KSM becomes cooperative—for reasons that will be described later in this book.

He begins telling his CIA de-briefers about active al-Qaeda plots to launch attacks against the United States and other Western targets—information that leads to the arrest of operatives tasked to carry them out. He holds classes for CIA officials, using a chalkboard to draw a picture for the CIA of al-Qaeda's operating structure, financing, communications, and logistics. He identifies al-Qaeda travel routes and safe havens, and helps intelligence officers make sense of documents and computer records seized in terrorist raids. He identifies voices in intercepted telephone calls, and helps officials understand the meaning of coded terrorist communications. He provides information that helps our intelligence community capture other high-ranking terrorists, some of whom are also taken into CIA custody and questioned—resulting in still more intelligence on the enemy's plans for new attacks.

KSM's questioning, and that of other captured terrorists, produces more than six thousand intelligence reports, which are shared across the intelligence community, as well as with our allies across the world.

In one of these reports, KSM describes in detail the revisions he made to his failed 1994–1995 plan known as the "Bojinka plot"—formulated with his nephew Ramzi Yousef—to blow up a dozen airplanes carrying some 4,000 passengers over the Pacific Ocean.

Years later, an observant CIA officer notices that the activities of a cell being followed by British authorities appears to match KSM's description of his plans for a Bojinka-style attack. He shares this information with British authorities. At first they are skeptical, but soon they acknowledge that this is in fact what the cell is planning. Intelligence from terrorists at Guantanamo Bay provides further insight into the cell's plans for the use of liquid explosives.

In an operation that involves unprecedented intelligence cooperation between our countries, British officials proceed to unravel the plot. On the night of August 9, 2006—just over a month before the fifth anniversary of the 9/11 attacks—they launch a series of raids in a northeast London suburb that lead to the arrest of two dozen al Qaeda terrorist suspects. They find a USB thumb drive in the pocket of one of the men with security details for Heathrow airport, and information on seven trans-Atlantic flights that were scheduled to take off within hours of each other: United Airlines Flight 931 to San Francisco departing at 2:15 p.m.; Air Canada Flight 849 to Toronto departing at 3:00 p.m.; Air Canada Flight 865 to Montreal departing at 3:15 p.m.; United Airlines Flight 959 to Chicago departing at 3:40 p.m.; United Airlines Flight 925 to Washington departing at 4:20 p.m.; American Airlines Flight 131 to New York departing at 4:35 p.m; and American Airlines Flight 91 to Chicago departing at 4:50 p.m. They seize bomb-making equipment and hydrogen peroxide to make liquid explosives. And they find the chilling martyrdom videos the suicide bombers had prepared—including those quoted above scolding Americans that "Sheikh Osama warned you" and promising "you will never know peace."

While there is no way to know precisely what day they planned to launch the attack, American intelligence officials believe that the plot was just weeks away from execution.

This is only one of the many attacks stopped with the help of the CIA interrogation program established by the Bush Administration in the wake of the September 11, 2001, terrorist attacks.

Information from detainees in CIA custody led to the arrest of an al Qaeda terrorist named Jose Padilla, who was sent to America on a mission to blow up high-rise apartment buildings in the United States.

Information from detainees in CIA custody led to the capture of a cell of Southeast Asian terrorists which had been tasked by KSM to hijack a passenger jet and fly it into the Library Tower in Los Angeles.

Information from detainees in CIA custody led to the capture of Ramzi Bin al-Shibh, KSM's right-hand-man in the 9/11 attacks, just as he was finalizing plans for a plot to hijack airplanes in Europe and fly them into Heathrow airport and buildings in downtown London.

Information from detainees in CIA custody led to the capture of Ammar al-Baluchi and Walid bin Attash, just as they were completing plans to replicate the destruction of our embassies in East Africa by blowing up the U.S. consulate and Western residences in Karachi, Pakistan.

Information from detainees in CIA custody led to the disruption of an al Qaeda plot to blow up the U.S. Marine camp in Djibouti, in an attack that could have rivaled the 1983 bombing of the U.S. Marine Barracks in Beirut.

Information from detainees in CIA custody helped break up an al Qaeda cell that was developing anthrax for terrorist attacks inside the United States.

In addition to helping break up these specific terrorist cells and plots, CIA questioning provided our intelligence community with an unparalleled body of information about al Qaeda—giving U.S. officials a picture of the terrorist organization as seen from the inside, at a time when we knew almost nothing about the enemy who had attacked us on 9/11.

Until the program was temporarily suspended in 2006, intelligence officials say, well over half of the information our government had about al Qaeda—how it operates, how it moves money, how it communicates, how it recruits operatives, how it picks targets, how it plans and carries out attacks—came from the interrogation of terrorists in CIA custody.

Consider that for a moment: without this capability, more than half of what we knew about the enemy would have disappeared.

Former CIA Director George Tenet has declared: "I know that this program has saved lives. I know we've disrupted plots. I know this program alone is worth more than what the FBI, the Central Intelligence Agency, and the National Security Agency put together have been able to tell us."

Former CIA Director Mike Hayden has said: "The facts of the case are that the use of these techniques against these terrorists made us safer. It really did work."

Former Director of National Intelligence John Negroponte has said: "[T]his is a very, very important capability to have. This has been one of the most valuable, if not the most valuable … human intelligence program with respect to al Qaeda. It has given us invaluable information that has saved American lives. So it is very, very important that we have this kind of capability."

Former Director of National Intelligence Mike McConnell has said: "We have people walking around in this country that are alive today because this process happened."

Even Barack Obama's Director of National Intelligence, Dennis Blair, has acknowledged: "High value information came from interrogations in which those methods were used and provided a deeper understanding of the al Qaeda organization that was attacking this country."

Leon Panetta, Obama's CIA Director, has said: "Important information was gathered from these detainees. It provided information that was acted upon."

And John Brennan, Obama's Homeland Security Advisor, when asked in an interview if enhanced interrogation techniques were necessary to keep America safe, replied: "Would the U.S. be handicapped if the CIA was not, in fact, able to carry out these types of detention and debriefing activities? I would say yes."

Indeed, the official assessment of our intelligence community is that, were it not for the CIA interrogation program, "al Qaeda and its allies would have succeeded in launching another attack against the American homeland."

And in his first forty-eight hours in office, President Barack Obama shut the program down.

Update: May 3, 2011—And now we know that Osama bin Laden was located and executed thanks in large part to the enhanced interrogation techniques the CIA employed, grounds for CIA prosecution according to Obama and Holder.

Furthermore, I have it on excellent authority from a confidential source that the CIA and the DOD went forward with killing Osama bin Laden *without* first getting the green light from the POTUS. Imagine that. A president so disconnected and disrespected by the military he supposedly commands, he is left out of the loop, and then lies about it, attempting to take credit.

GIVE ME LIBERTY OR GIVE ME MY CHECK: THAT IS THE QUESTION

February 22, 2010

American politics has always been a full-contact sport. Thomas Jefferson hired an investigator to dig dirt on John Adams during the presidential campaign of 1800. In 1804 a longstanding war between Aaron Burr and Alexander Hamilton ended in a duel that also ended Hamilton's life. Jefferson Davis and Abraham Lincoln loved America and held vastly different views about her future, yet they shared a love of freedom. The Civil War was the ultimate contact sport.

In almost every administration from Washington forward, you can find pitched battles, fierce struggles, loud and exaggerated rhetoric, and power plays, all exercised to define Americanism, arguments usually centered on the proper role of government and how best to preserve freedom.

The difference today is the argument is no longer about refining Americanism to preserve freedom. It is no longer a debate about how best to work toward a more perfect union. No, the argument is about completely redefining and remaking America into something that would have horrified the founders.

Where Adams and Jefferson and Burr and Hamilton fought about how best to preserve freedom, as do many conservatives, today, half the country is fighting with the other half questioning if freedom is even worth the trouble.

As George Will rightly pointed out during his recent CPAC speech, the battle line drawn between liberals and conservatives separates competing visions of what liberty means.

"Conservatives stress freedom. They are therefore willing to accept greater disparities of social outcomes, and they are inclined to regard the multiplication of entitlements and the mentality it breeds as inimical to the attitudes and aptitudes essential for free citizens of a free society," stated Will. "Liberals today tend to stress equality. Not equality of opportunity but equality of outcome, and therefore they tend to regard the multiplication of entitlements and that entitlement mentality as enhancing the public good. Therefore they are for spreading dependency. Dependency on government is not an unfortunate corollary of what they are advocating; it is their agenda."

It is an agenda the founders would have rejected out of hand, knowing as they did that freedom declines the more government prevails and government prevails the more citizens are dependent, precisely the objective of the Obama administration, which is why you never hear the president invoke the founders in any relevant way.

> I think we have more machinery of government than is necessary, too many parasites living on the labor of the industrious.
>
> Thomas Jefferson,
> letter to William Ludlow, September 6, 1824

FROM THE ABUNDANCE OF THE HEART, THE MOUTH SPEAKS

February 26, 2010

What has the heart to do with politics, other than recent news involving Bill Clinton and Dick Cheney or references to bleeding-heart liberals and hard-hearted conservatives?

It is interesting to think about the heart, knowing also that according to the latest research, the heart also "thinks" about the brain. There is constant interaction between the two.

Philosophers and poets have long probed the mysteries of the heart, saying it is the seat of the soul, the fountainhead of love, the residence of spirit and character, personality and emotion.

Religion appeals to the heart. All religious traditions place special emphasis on the heart.

Christians assert salvation comes only when the intellectual confirmation of faith takes firm root in the heart: when the mortal heart blends with the immortal heart of Christ. In Buddhist tradition, peace comes from the balance between heart and mind through meditation upon oneness with everything. In Judaism the heart is the special place where human imagination and wisdom exist, a place where good and evil exist, leading the penitent to request God circumcise the heart to remove sin.

In the New Testament tradition, the Master speaks of removing our stony hearts and giving us a heart of flesh, imagery pointing to spiritual renewal, the purging of the sin nature, the advent of the spirit walk. That same tradition enlightens an understanding: whether of stone or flesh, what takes up the most heart space issues forth in our language.

Therefore, the condition of our hearts has everything to do with our politics because our politics are all about language. Language expresses orientation and philosophy, of course, but it reveals our heart motivation as well: does one seek office to serve others or self?

In considering someone for public service or considering a political philosophy to support, listening closely to the language is a strong guide to true heart motivation.

In reading Carl Sandburg's biography of Lincoln, we see a president whose heart was definitely in the right place, as evidenced by his consistently cordial, intelligent, and compassionate speech, even in the face of horrendous circumstances and the worst treatment imaginable.

We forget Lincoln was in office only for a few weeks when the Civil War broke out, that even before he was sworn in, there were very real attempts to assassinate him.

Everyone tends to think their present problems are paramount and incomparable, but with Lincoln, he was virtually alone, assailed on every side, handicapped by an emotionally and psychologically impaired wife, surrounded by political adversaries, critics in the press, and lethal enemies on every side. He was blamed for corruption and racketeering. The Union Army was frequently commanded by incompetents. Again, Lincoln was blamed. One man became the lightening rod for all the rage and hate and turmoil of the period.

The weight of the war was made all the heavier by the death of Lincoln's beloved little boy Willie.

And still the president spoke of healing the nation's wounds, preserving the Union, and promoting the right of all men to live free.

The very heart of Lincoln is displayed on the right hand wall of his memorial in Washington. The words of his second inaugural address (March 4, 1865) carved in stone there bring tears to those in touch with the tragedy of civil war, slavery, and racism:

> One eighth of the whole population were colored slaves, not distributed generally over the Union, but localized in the Southern part of it. These slaves constituted a peculiar and powerful interest. All knew that this interest was, somehow, the cause of the war. To strengthen, perpetuate, and extend this interest was the object for which the insurgents would rend the Union, even by war; while the government claimed no right to do more than to restrict the territorial enlargement of it. Neither party expected for the war, the magnitude, or the duration, which it has already attained. Neither anticipated that the cause of the conflict might cease with, or even before, the conflict itself should cease. Each looked for an easier triumph, and a result less fundamental and astounding. Both read the same Bible, and pray to the same God; and each invokes His aid against the other. It may seem strange that any men should dare to ask a just God's assistance in wringing their bread from the sweat of other men's faces; but let us judge not that we be not judged. The prayers of both could not be answered; that of neither has been answered fully. The Almighty has his own purposes. "Woe unto the world because of offences! for it must needs be that offences come; but woe to that man by whom the offence cometh!" If we shall suppose that American Slavery is one of those offences which, in the providence of God, must needs come, but which, having continued through His appointed time, He now wills to remove, and that He gives to both North and South, this terrible war, as the woe due to those by whom the offence came, shall we discern therein any departure from those divine attributes which the believers in a Living God always ascribe to Him? Fondly do we hope—fervently do we pray—that this mighty scourge of war may speedily pass away. Yet, if God wills that it continue, until all the wealth piled by

the bond-man's two hundred and fifty years of unrequited toil shall be sunk, and until every drop of blood drawn with the lash, shall be paid by another drawn with the sword, as was said three thousand years ago, so still it must be said "the judgments of the Lord, are true and righteous altogether."

With malice toward none; with charity for all; with firmness in the right, as God gives us to see the right, let us strive on to finish the work we are in; to bind up the nation's wounds; to care for him who shall have borne the battle, and for his widow, and his orphan—to do all which may achieve and cherish a just and lasting peace, among ourselves, and with all nations.

In only a few short weeks, this heart-of-gold president would be assassinated by a drunken actor with a heart of a different sort.

Someone once said, "Love is a decision not an emotion."

Lincoln consistently demonstrated his love for our country by making very difficult decisions based on principle, not emotion, even though emotions tore him apart.

For our politics to be useful, our hearts must be in the right place, not the place of emotion, but the place of rational love.

Sadly, our language too often reveals a heart far removed from that good and useful place.

GOOD-BYE AMERICA: LAND OF THE "ME," HOME OF THE KNAVE

March 1, 2010

Item: January 3, 2010* "...for the first time since the Great Depression, Americans took more aid from the government than they paid in taxes."

> There is a soft despotism driven by the collectivist impulse that drains the life out of a people "...and finally reduces each nation to being nothing more than a herd of timid and industrious animals of which government is the shepherd..."
>
> Alexis de Tocqueville

The sickening reality: America is being destroyed from within. Liberty, the lifeblood of Americanism, is chained to the floor, pistol-whipped by massive government and bureaucratic totalitarianism, all installed and promoted by a herd mentality focused on safety, an illusion of safety, and the false promise of state-guaranteed equality.

We used to be a can-do people. Increasingly, we are becoming a you-do-for-me group of toddlers dependent on government.

A once-great nation, inspired by individualism and adventure and the excitement of creative risk taking is bowing its head, submitting to the harness, the stallion now found gelded, half starved, dragging a plow through bleached and desiccated soil.

More than 10 percent of the people are on food stamps.

Every man, woman, and child is in debt about two hundred thousand dollars, thanks to the government's wasteful, binge spending. Every American family is in debt about 678 thousand dollars, thanks to government spending, waste, and mismanagement.

More than half the federal budget is consumed by entitlement spending. The government has promised to spend upwards of fifty trillion more in social spending during the next fifty years, money we do not have, money we will never have.

As it is, we are enslaved to the federal government, thanks to the debt load. That is the simple truth of the matter. That debt load is destroying prosperity. And what is the government's answer? More debt, more regulation, more engineering (AKA healthcare reform, cap and trade) to deepen citizen dependency on the federal government.

*The chilling reality is it may be too late. According to this Washington Times report, Americans rely on government like never before, story by Patrice Hill, March 1, 2010:

> Without record levels of welfare, unemployment and other government benefits as well as tax cuts last year, the income of U.S. households would have plunged by an astonishing $723 billion—more than four times the record $167 billion drop reported last month by the Commerce Department. Moreover, for the first time since the Great Depression, Americans took more aid from the government than they paid in taxes.

Welcome to the herd. There's your feedbag, and your stall.

We are living on thin air, funny money, and the illusion of recovery. We are, in reality, in denial. We are sleepwalkers.

The greatest engine for good government, providing the greatest good for the greatest number, is sputtering, faltering, and seizing up, thanks to tons of sugar (debt) poured into the fuel tank, the sugar of government promises: free lunch, free dinner, subsidized housing, healthcare, retirement, education, the works.

Communists, socialists, atheists, humanists, and anarchists have consistently chewed at the roots of the republic for decades, cutting off nourishment. The tree of liberty is dying. The republic established by the framers, the union saved by Lincoln, is being plowed under by Karl Marx while half the population stands by with hands out, begging for more.

Hope for change? Only if we take severe, immediate action and return to tried and true principles of limited government, virtue, and economic freedom.

Two recent declarations, if taken seriously and applied to our public policy, hold the promise for American renewal: The Mount Vernon Statement and the Manhattan Declaration, both found easily online. Well worth reading.

It is glaringly obvious: unless we pivot radically, we will soon become, and irrevocably remain, the land of the *me* and the home of the *knave*.

FULL STERN AHEAD: WORKERS UNITE (OR ELSE)

March 2, 2010
Andy Stern, very serious.

Many of us on the right have been trying to tell the people of America for a long time that the ultimate goal of the left is the dismantling of the US Constitution and the installation of global socialist government.

For years, seeking cover, the left has howled this assertion is ludicrous.

Notice how President Obama sneers and mocks those who level the accusation. He knows, as do his allies, their cover is blown, but they believe their time is now, that it is no longer necessary to pretend they are free market patriots, except in a pinch.

Obama and his friends believe the balance has shifted sufficiently. They believe they have enough support here in the US and around the world to flip the switch. But as they flip, they are meeting with massive resistance.

Let's just look at a couple of examples of statements now being made by Obama and his friends, keeping in mind the ultimate reason this administration is pushing healthcare reform is because the longer term goal is universal care, which, of course, means the government will have complete control over about one-sixth of the entire US economy. (Whenever you think of the words *liberal* or *leftist* or *Democratic*, please also think of *control*, for control is what they are all about.)

When they get control over who lives and who dies, who gets treatment and who does not, getting control of the rest is fairly easy: control of your money, your work, where you live, the kind of schools your kids attend, what your retirement looks like, where you can travel, what you can own.

Andy Stern states flat out the agenda is global socialism. Mr. Stern is the former president of the SEIU, an enormous labor union, where the workers of the world unite.

Stern is very close to the president. So close, in fact, Obama appointed Stern to the National Commission on Fiscal Responsibility and Reform (NCFRR). What is the NCFRR? Well, created by presidential decree, it is a commission of big wigs sitting around, talking about our bankrupt government with a bunch of other big wigs, all of them inevitably agreeing we must raise taxes. (As it turns out they eventually made several good recommendations for righting the financial Titanic we are on, but, the President completely ignored those recommendations.)

The politicians will never cut spending. The only way to salvage the sacred government then is to raise taxes.

Who will take the hit? The so-called rich. That actually means the middle class. The super rich know how to hide their money. The nominally rich are already taxed to the gum line. So the middle class gets the hit. But we'll call them rich so as to justify the envy, stir up hate and resentment, and rationalize government confiscation of private property. (Trouble is, once you kill the goose, where will you get golden eggs?)

According to the president and Stern and like-minded people, the "rich" don't deserve their wealth, and since the little guy has been crushed for centuries, justice demands that the rich pay the government to take care of the little guy, you know, to pay for Social Security, Medicare, prescription drugs, food stamps, subsidized slum housing, unemployment and government jobs, all unionized, of course.

(Oh, and just for giggles, remember we are now 118 *trillion* dollars in debt to SS, Medicare, and prescription drugs, looking out a few decades.)

Unionize the whole country or most of it? That's why we need card check folks. It's for your own good. This interim stage of development for people like Obama and Stern was aptly described by Saul Alinsky many years ago when he said once the socialists take over, there has to be a period of 'despotism of the proletariat.' This is necessary to stabilize things after the revolution, translation, solidify the power of the oligarchs. Afterwards, they will usher forward the 'paradise of communism,' insisted Mr. Alinsky.

Trouble is everybody always gets stuck in that "despotism of the proletariat" thing.

OBAMA STIMULUS: FRAUD, CORRUPTION, FAVORITISM, WASTE

March 4, 2010
No bid stimulus contracts?
For all the bright projections and promises of recovery, thanks to massive stimulus spending, the results continue to defy White House assurances.

And now comes a report government spending is subsidizing foreign companies, not creating green jobs at home as promised.

This Bureau of Labor statistics chart tells the story from an overview perspective, full analysis here, Heritage Foundation, *The Foundry*—"In Pictures: The Obama and Pelosi Job Gaps."

No matter how hard one tries, it is difficult if not impossible to find anyone with glowing reports about the efficacy of Obama's stimulus spending, especially when it comes to creating jobs.

Indeed, news agencies and analysts across the board report little if any positive impact on job creation. Most have concluded the so-called bump in GNP does not reveal real growth but is rather the result of government jobs increasing, pay increasing in government jobs, some inventory being moved at huge discounts, and some consumer spending attributed to government spending.

Many others including Greenspan see little reason to indicate a recovery, given the continuing declines in housing and automobile manufacturing. With credit card debt mushrooming, more bank failures, increasing national debt, and a predicted second round of foreclosure both in commercial and residential mortgage markets, the picture looks bleak.

Now comes a report that substantial portions of the stimulus money intended to create green jobs in the United States is actually being consumed by foreign interests.

A *US News & World Report* opinion piece today reports:

> ...allowing 80 percent of the money spent on wind turbines to go to foreign firms, as an American University study claims, is pure folly. The Obama administration and the industry dispute the study, but the figures provided to the Washington Post by the American Wind Energy Association aren't much better. According to the industry trade group, from 37 to 47 cents out of every dollar spent on the wind farm program has gone overseas.

Reportedly, several Democrat lawmakers are telling the president this is entirely unacceptable.

Here is the lead from the *Washington Post* coverage today:

> A group of Democratic senators called Wednesday for the government to halt a federal stimulus program aimed at building wind farms and other clean-energy projects, arguing that too much of the money spent so far has gone to create jobs overseas.

Critics of Obama's stimulus plans said a year ago there were two essential problems with the proposed 862 billion-dollar spending package: government spending to stimulate the demand side of the economy has never resulted in long term economic recovery; massive spending is unmanageable and subject to fraud and abuse.

In December the GAO reported large percentages of government contracts are being awarded without competitive bidding for allocations of stimulus funding.

No bid contracts are being let through various federal agencies including HUD, NASA, SBA, EPA, Commerce, Transportation, Homeland Security, and Agriculture. As of October 2009, no-bid federal stimulus spending had run about 7.8 billion dollars.

The *Sacramento Bee* reported last month fraud activity is high in California, and the FBI is warning that 7 to 10 percent of stimulus money could be wasted through fraudulent activity. At the higher end that could mean about 86 billion dollars in waste, enough to bailout California two and a half times, reference Sacramento Bee, Feb. 14, 2010, 'Stimulus Watchdog Warns about Fraud.'

The kicker: the 862 billion dollars of "stimulus" approved by Congress and the president last year—it's all borrowed money.

*Who gets stimulus money? Mostly Obama's friends, reference Michelle Malkin.com, "Stimulus High Marks."

ISLAMIZATION OF THE WEST: "ISRAEL IS FIGHTING FOR ALL OF US."

March 19, 2010

Robert Spencer, author and expert on Islam, said recently, "the Wilders trial ought to be an international media event; seldom has any court case anywhere had such enormous implications for the future of the free world."

Geert Wilders, Netherlands MP, warns of Islamization: "Europe is on the verge of collapsing." For stating truth, Wilders is put on trial for hate speech. Wilders says Europe is being destroyed from within, and America is next.

Producer of the banned film *Fitna* and outspoken critic of radical Islam, Geert Wilders, must have constant bodyguard and security protections due to serial death threats from Muslims.

Muslims publicly threaten Wilders with death in the UK. Those threatening to kill Wilders roam free.

Wilders was at one time denied a travel visa to visit Great Britain. Towns in Germany have shunned him.

When a Dutch citizen is prevented from free speech and prosecuted while those who openly advocate murder and overthrow of the government are ignored, something is severely out of balance.

If Wilders is only a harmless loon, as many in America and Europe claim, why do Muslims take him so seriously, and why are his civil rights being violated?

Wilders is increasingly influential because he is telling the truth about the dangers of political Islam and warning about the possible destruction of western civilization.

Note this excerpt from a speech he gave in New York in 2008, a speech titled 'America as the Last Man Standing':

> Let no one fool you about Islam being a religion. Sure, it has a god, and a here-after, and 72 virgins. But in its essence Islam is a political ideology. It is a system that lays down detailed rules for society and the life of every person. Islam wants to dictate every aspect of life. Islam means 'submission.' Islam is not compatible with freedom and democracy, because what it strives for is sharia. If you want to compare Islam to anything, compare it to communism or national-socialism, these are all totalitarian ideologies. Now you know why Winston Churchill called Islam 'the most retrograde force in the world,' and why he compared Mein Kampf to the Quran. The public has wholeheartedly accepted the Palestinian narrative, and sees Israel as the aggressor. I have lived in this country and visited it dozens of times. I support Israel. First, because it is the Jewish homeland after two thousand years of exile up to and including Auschwitz, second because it is a democracy, and third because Israel is our first line of defense. This tiny country is situated on the fault line of jihad, frustrating Islam's territorial advance. Israel is facing the front lines of jihad, like Kashmir, Kosovo, the Philippines, Southern Thailand, Darfur in Sudan, Lebanon, and Aceh in Indonesia. Israel is simply in the way. The same way West-Berlin was during the Cold War. The war against Israel is not a war against Israel. It is a war against the West. It is jihad. Israel is simply receiving the blows that are meant for all of us. If there would have been no Israel, Islamic imperialism would have found other venues to release its energy and its desire for conquest. Thanks to Israeli parents who

send their children to the army and lay awake at night, parents in Europe and America can sleep well and dream, unaware of the dangers looming.

> Text of full speech accessed here:
> JihadWatch.org, Sept. 2008,
> "America as the last man standing"

Personal note: in 1986 I was working at a Christian radio station in California. During that time part of my job was conducting live interviews. In that year I met Abraham Rababy from Beirut. Abraham speaks Arabic, knows Islamic culture inside and out, and is ordained in the Church of God. He has put his life on the line many times reaching out to Muslims. He told me two central truths twenty-four years ago, truths that have been confirmed many times since:

1. Islam requires all believers to obey the call to jihad
2. Jihad is coming to America

In the 1980s and 90s, Abraham tried to warn State Department officials about the coming jihad. They ignored him, until September 11, 2001.

In this Washington Times commentary, March 17, 2009, by Frank Gaffney, Founder of the Center for Security Policy, we see the same kind of resistance to the truth in the halls of power:

> President Obama on Friday (3.12.10) reiterated for the umpteenth time his determination to develop a 'new relationship' with the Muslim world. On this occasion, the audience were the leaders of Saudi Arabia, Indonesia, and the Philippines.
>
> Unfortunately, it increasingly appears that, in so doing, he will be embracing the agenda of the Muslim Brotherhood an organization dedicated to promoting the theo-political-legal program

authoritative Islam calls Shariah and that has the self-described mission of 'destroying Western civilization from within.'

Sixteen thousand, five hundred deadly attacks were perpetrated by Muslims worldwide since 9/11, and some people still advise we not jump to conclusions (www.thereligionofpeace.com).

OBAMA "CORRUPT," SAYS GINGRICH

March 22, 2010
Romney says Obama has violated his oath.
Conservatives believe the Obamacare vote in the House yesterday was actually a good thing. That vote focused two things for us: the legislative and executive branches are corrupt, and the battle lines are more clearly drawn than ever.

Significant efforts have already commenced to repeal Obamacare.

Like the usurpations of King George, the actions of the Obama cabal have sparked a spirit of resistance, which would amount to revolution were the usurpers lodged solely in the halls of power. Given that 42 percent of the population stands with the cabal opposed to traditional Americanism as defined by the founders, preferring the slavery of national socialism/fascism, we face civil war.

The worst aspect of the Obamacare vote in the House yesterday was seeing systemic corruption paraded about as some kind of victory. After a year of secret dealings, under-the-table payoffs, pandering to special interests, political corruption and outright disregard for public opinion, tattered and piecemeal legislation, opposed by a solid majority of Americans, was hailed a major breakthrough.

The president and Democratic leaders had for many months cut deals with the drug and insurance companies, with the hospital lobby, with labor unions, and with physician organizations; they had pressured legislators, threatened others, abused their authority, and railroaded a corrupt agenda only for the sake of concentrating more power in the central government.

And the mind-numbed dependency class, the willing sheep being led to slaughter, applauded their own execution.

'Sunday was a pressured, bought, intimidated vote worthy of Hugo Chavez but unworthy of the United States of America,' writes Newt Gingrich today in Human Events. Gingrich continues:

> The American people will not allow a corrupt machine to dictate their future. Together we will pledge to repeal this bill and start over. Together we will prove that this will not stand. 2010 and 2012 will be among the most important elections in American history. These elections will allow us to save America from a leftwing machine of unparalleled corruption, arrogance and cynicism.

Mitt Romney weighed in as well:

> America has just witnessed an unconscionable abuse of power. President Obama has betrayed his oath to the nation. His health-care bill is unhealthy for America. It raises taxes, slashes the more private side of Medicare, installs price controls, and puts a new federal bureaucracy in charge of health care. It will create a new entitlement even as the ones we already have are bankrupt. For these reasons and more, the act should be repealed. That campaign begins today.

The campaign Romney and Gingrich refer to, the new civil war, will be fought in the streets with demonstrations, in the courts, in the legislatures, and in elections. It will be expensive and time consuming, but those are the unavoidable results of an Obama approach to government: division, conflict, acrimony. There are few alternatives when a leader positions himself in opposition to the majority.

Afterthought: healthcare "reform" is not benevolence. It's not about helping those without coverage; it's about people in power helping themselves to more power by stealing from the people. Obama thinks you are tired of paying the price for liberty. He thinks it is time to merge the state with corporate power. Is he right?

AMERICA ON THE BRINK: LIBERTY OR DEATH

March 30, 2010

The vision of George Washington versus the vision of Karl Marx. Which vision will prevail?

Very soon the survival of American freedom will depend on young Americans.

Events are unfolding rapidly.

Battle lines are being clearly defined. Momentous history is in the making.

Older and middle-aged Americans form the ranks of resistance, presently joined by growing numbers of young people, but those of us getting on in years are fading, and unless the young step up to save her, America may be lost forever.

What we are witnessing in Washington by the hand of this president is an attempt to completely transform the country from government by the people to government by the powerful few.

Historically, that has always meant the end of freedom and the beginning of tyranny. When common people cannot voice their legitimate opinion without being viciously condemned by the powerful, something is broken in America. Obama's personally directed attacks against Sarah Palin during the campaign and his officially sanctioned attacks against the Tea Party are clear warning signs we have a tyrant in the White House.

When politicians who claim to be champions of the common people turn on them instead and denounce them as hate mongers and racists and gun-toting morons, something is broken in America.

When government enacts the largest entitlement program in history funded by the largest tax increases in history to steal from one citizen to give to another and all of it is done secretly in corrupt ways in clear contradiction to the will of the majority, we are approaching a real crisis.

The fabric of society is being ripped apart. Disorder looms.

In the process the free spirit of the plains buffalo and the eagle is being replaced by the domesticated, submissive, spiritless nature of the steer (read: *Animal Farm*).

Americans accusing Americans of terrorism as in the case of the DHS report by Napolitano, in order to gain political advantage, indicates our rhetoric is at such fever pitch, real, sustained violence is likely. Ironically, the ones voicing the loudest accusations and the fiercest criticisms are the very ones responsible for inflaming passions, those with their hands on the levers of power.

Consider the record. Embrace the truth. Study history. Ask the hard questions.

On the one hand, you have Frank Rich at the *New York Times* accusing Tea Party people—the common people—of horrendous things. He wrote recently that the common people protesting this government's power grabs and wasteful spending and excessive taxation, these common people, are ignorant racists.

Imagine: Americans resisting tyranny are somehow racists and fools, as if the founders should be cast likewise.

To justify his slander, Rich decries alleged incidents of violence supposedly perpetrated by Tea Party patriots despite the complete lack of evidence.

On the other hand, read Pat Buchanan's excellent column "The real anti-Americans." He makes the case for freedom, recounting the true history of leftist violence in this country, saying they engage the 'politics of desperation' while pointing out, "If the tea-party folks think it is leftist elites who detest and wish to be rid of the America they grew up in and love, they are right."

Buchanan names the hard left now in power the real anti-Americans, proving historically they are the perpetrators of violence and unrest even to this present day. They are anti-American because in being pro-big government, they are anti-freedom; by being pro-central control, they are anti-economic freedom; by being pro-communist, they are indeed anti-individual.

Imagine what we have come to: forced to face facts and proclaim the president and his Congress are anti-American.

As to present-day violence, while the left falsely accuses Tea Party people, the truth is the left is guilty, as documented by two glaring examples:

Republican leader Eric Cantor receives a death threat, and the perpetrator is arrested. Karl Rove is assaulted during a book-signing event. He rightly characterized the protestors as the anti-American totalitarian left.

People like Keith Olbermann are really no different than the Code Pink people you see on the Rove video. Their stock and trade is disruption and provocation to violence. They've no interest in rational discussion, discovering the truth, or examining real solutions to real problems.

And isn't it interesting to witness Obama's aggressive and dismissive attitude in the wake of the passage of Obamacare even as the flaws in the law are revealed almost daily sparking even more dissent and division?

It's as if the president is enjoying the escalating civil unrest, neglecting the real terrorist threat as he encourages Napolitano to use the FBI to hunt down a few clowns in Michigan, an obvious exercise in more political gamesmanship. Timing is everything, especially when you are playing lethal games.

But this is no game.

No American alive knows firsthand what it was like during the Civil War, but we understand from reading history that violence was widespread before and after that terrible conflict. We also know that in the middle of that war, twenty thousand men could fall in a single day, and, overall, six hundred thousand gave their lives.

Today, the internal conflict centering again on different visions of the future burns hotter every day, drawing us closer to serious unrest, even violence. The people who treat it like a game, leveling false accusations and intentionally stirring strife to take advantage of the situation for political gain, these are the people who will be held responsible regardless of the outcome.

But there is no doubt about this much: by the president's actions, he encourages more conflict, and if Americans remain devoted to freedom, Obama will be a one-term president.

THOU SHALT NOT SPEAK ILL

March 31, 2010

Few would disagree with the assertion our contemporary rhetoric has become ridiculous and extreme in many respects.

Many leftists insist conservatives are Nazis.

Many conservatives insist leftists are Nazis.

Good LORD, we can't all be Nazis.

Democrats say Republicans are evil.

Republicans say Democrats are evil.

Does that mean only Libertarians and Independents have halos?

There can be little argument that Obama Democrats and Reagan Republicans have enormous differences of opinion about the future of the country and about the definition of Americanism.

Obama Democrats favor increasing federal power, redistribution of wealth, government control of the economy, collective rights versus individual rights, and a more submissive foreign policy.

Reagan Republicans favor small, central government, private property rights, states' rights, economic freedom, individual rights, and a strong, assertive foreign policy.

These are competing visions of Americanism, as different as night and day. There is no question which one is most closely aligned with the founders' vision. Nor can there be much argument as to which vision has been proven most successful: collectivist regimes routinely fail economically as they ordinarily reduce individual liberties of necessity. After all, that is what control is all about.

Therefore, the conservative argument must always remind people of the virtues of individualism as articulated by the founders, appealing to our traditional love of freedom, and, we must always bring evidence to demonstrate our ideas have always proven worthy from known results in practical application.

Two of the most admirable thinkers in the contemporary conservative movement are Michael Medved and Marvin Olasky. Both men have traveled far. Both were once leftists—Olasky the more radical, given his communist/atheist sympathies years ago. Both men are thoughtful intellectuals regularly engaged in the culture war, both encouraging reason and sound debate. Today, each man posts a column, presenting an interesting convergence and divergence.

On the one hand, Medved confronts extremist rhetoric from the right that would whip partisan frenzy casting Obama the evil puppet master hell bent on creating despotic communism in the United States. He argues our political fortunes are damaged by such rhetoric, encouraging instead issue-oriented debate filled with fact-based, logical persuasion. In so arguing, Medved is critical of people like Glenn Beck without naming him directly. (Michael Medved, Townhall.com, 'Obama, Outright evil or simply wrong?' March 31, 2010)

On the other hand, Olasky writes about the tendency of the left to rig our discussions so as to forward just such a far-left agenda, noting the useful contributions of Glenn Beck in his recent debates with Jim Wallis. Olasky urges us, therefore, to be wise as serpents, gentle as doves. Thus, Olasky agrees and disagrees with Medved, acknowledging the value of Beck's more aggressive and colorful approach. (Marvin Olasky, Townhall.com, 'Beck vs. Wallis,' March 31, 2010)

Most notably, Medved and Olasky agree conservatives are better off articulating reasoned debate as the best means of confronting the hyperbole of the left.

All well and good. One might also argue there is room for passionate confrontation, for evil is evil wherever it is found, and good men and women dare not shrink for such confrontation although Medved's point is well taken. After all, if people are found running around, hysterically calling everything under the Democratic sun evil, credibility wanes.

On the other hand...

David Horowitz and Andrew Breitbart encourage us to embrace a more in-your-face approach to dealing with the communists within. Noteworthy too, both Horowitz and Breitbart were also radical leftists before seeing the light.

And let us also recall and consider that recently Howard Dean, Al Sharpton, and Jim Wallis have all agreed the Obama Democratic agenda is decidedly communistic, which is in and of itself decidedly anti-American, always a blueprint for economic failure, the platform for general assaults on liberty.

Overall, even if we back off from calling Obama evil, as Medved advises, and even if we heed Olasky and give Beck credit where due, we'd still be wise to consider the effectiveness of a Horowitz and a Breitbart, all the while remembering Reagan's eleventh commandment: Thou shalt not speak ill of any fellow Republican.

Perhaps we can be permitted to modify the commandment to read, "Thou shalt not speak ill of thy fellow conservative," for many a Republican left conservatism long ago.

There is enough ill-speaking from the left to go around, and there are compelling reasons to fight their fire with our own. The stakes are too high for us to keep quiet, or screech like our enemies. We must never retreat, never capitulate, never compromise and never miss an opportunity to win the debate on the merits. As Larry Elder says: "We've got a country to save!"

PS: Mr. Wallis, the gospel is not all about redistribution of wealth as you claim. It is about God himself paying the penalty for our sin so that we might be reconciled to him.

Bonus material: a thoughtful analysis of the central issue: "The politics of Debt," by Brit Hume, Breitbart TV.

DISINFORMATION AND NATIONAL DECLINE

April 5, 2010

Yelling fire in a crowded theater when there is no fire is a crime, especially if people get hurt. Yelling a false alarm like that is not protected speech. It is considered irresponsible, even criminal.

Recently, Sean Penn, the actor, informed us he believes anyone who calls Hugo Chavez a dictator should be jailed for telling lies.

Why is the first example criminal and not the second? Or perhaps you agree that both forms of speech are criminal. Maybe you believe neither represents criminal or irresponsible speech.

When someone yells fire, knowing there is no fire, causing panic, and putting people in harm's way, it's called reckless endangerment, a crime. Intentionally putting people in danger engaging this kind of speech is illegal throughout the United States.

In the state of Washington, it is considered reckless endangerment to deal illegal drugs. Such trafficking is seen as putting others at risk, increasing the likelihood of drive-by shootings. Perhaps pedaling the drug of disinformation is likewise reckless endangerment.

The reason Sean Penn is entirely incorrect to suggest jail time for anyone calling Chavez a dictator is fairly clear: Chavez is a public figure. The statement asserting he is a dictator can be substantially proven, and, in any case, it amounts to protected speech in America because it is opinion and does not amount to reckless endangerment. In fact, identifying and confronting dictators can help deliver people from the endangerment of tyranny and reckless people like Chavez. Penn is free to say he believes people should be jailed. Only the court of public opinion holds him accountable. Penn is therefore free to be wrong, free to be foolish. He is not free to endanger others.

But consider this: what should happen when an editorial writer or a reporter or a blogger or an actor publishes opinions that provoke people to violence? Is that protected speech, or it is reckless endangerment? Furthermore, what should happen when politicians are found practicing intentional disinformation, resulting in substantial harm to others? Is that at least a violation of their oath? Should they be prosecuted for reckless endangerment?

In America, the right to freedom of expression is so precious we have historically tolerated a lot of abuse and irresponsible behavior in the press and in public debate in order to make sure that our God-given right to free expression is not infringed. Indeed, the majority of people have tolerated various smaller groups who abused rights and privileges frequently; such toleration often seen as necessary in order to preserve the rights of everyone. For example, the KKK was tolerated so long as it did not violate the law, engage reckless endangerment, or perpetrate violence. Violent speech is even tolerated to a point. Such tolerance was extended to the Weather Underground, Students for a Democratic Society, and the Black Panthers. Today, we extend it even to the likes of Ed Schultz and Keith Olbermann.

We even tolerate Jeremiah Wright and Louis Farrakhan and their inflammatory speech against whites and Jews, allowing both men to continue encouraging blacks to be suspicious of whites, both men claiming whites in government unleashed the AIDS virus in order to kill blacks. Farrakhan actually accused Jews of using AIDS to kill blacks.

How many of you would tolerate a prominent white preacher insisting all blacks be held in contempt based solely on the remarks of Wright and Farrakhan? Why, then, do we put up with Wright and

Farrakhan? Why do we tolerate certain people who go head hunting for Christians and conservatives in the media every day?

Many say Wright and Farrakhan have crossed the line many times, but few object. Our silence is compliance.

Inciting blacks to hate whites and Jews is considered reckless endangerment by many people in this country but apparently not so in the US attorney's office. When Jesse Jackson said during the campaign he wanted to remove Mr. Obama's testicles with a knife, apparently the DOJ decided he was just having a Sean Penn moment.

On the other hand, recently a group of people in Michigan, obviously delusional, stated their intention to kill police and take over the government. Neither Christian nor militia but rather a small rag tag group of IQ challenged white people—they were set upon by the FBI in full combat gear using tanks and helicopters. For saying much the same uttered by Bill Ayers and associates with the Weather Underground in the 60s and 70s, the Hutaree faced the full force of federal law enforcement, were arrested, and now face charges. Bill Ayers roams free, freely expressing his hatred for most things American. The admitted bomb thrower responsible for police deaths whose wife celebrated Susan Atkins killing Sharon Tate and her unborn child with a dinner fork, these people are now college professors, Chicago celebrities, people central to the launching of the president's fortunes.

Obviously the speech of the Hutaree was deemed more than reckless endangerment but their treatment compared to the treatment of others serves to demonstrate how political correctness has infected our law enforcement and judicial deliberations. Anyone who thinks justice is blind at DHS or DOJ should take a second look.

Otherwise, consider these contrasts:

Item: Black Panthers, November 4, 2008 in Philadelphia, standing outside a polling place on election day, threatening voters, an incident caught on tape, a felony, was prosecuted and the suspects found guilty, but Obama's DOJ refused to follow through with the penalty phase.

Item: Tea Party people demonstrating peacefully in DC, recently, falsely accused of spitting on a black congressman and falsely accused of calling people 'nigger.' Politicians are seen actually attempting to provoke an incident, and afterward they are seen running to the media to 'report' their outrage. Nancy Pelosi, House Speaker, third in line to the presidency, parades through the crowd with a huge gavel, practically daring someone to cross the line, and when it doesn't happen, she floats falsehoods. Even Jesse Jackson got in the act, ridiculing demonstrators, inviting conflict.

Item: Andrew Breitbart, who covered the DC Tea Party, offered one hundred thousand dollars to anyone who could prove a Tea Party protestor called someone a nigger. No takers so far. Representative Cleaver, a black congressman, has withdrawn his claim someone spit on him.

Obviously the double standard is glaring, and the disinformation machine is in high gear, just as it was the moment after McCain announced Sarah Palin his running mate. Once again today, the Obama smear machine is revved up to destroy all opposition, by any means, including disinformation.

Where do we draw the line when it comes to public officials and even journalists or wanna-be journalists in the blogosphere?

Pelosi promised the most ethical Congress in history, and yet she is seen pulling every dirty trick imaginable to advance Obama's legislative agenda, with his encouragement, going so far as to incite racial tensions and provoke physical violence, confronting Tea Party demonstrators, essentially calling them racists. Harry Reid, and many others, are culpable.

Others yelling fire in a crowded theater include many in the blogosphere on both sides of the divide.

Perhaps this is the best way to proceed: journalists holding journalists accountable for the sake of preserving a free press, for if government ever takes the regulatory seat in this arena, a free press will cease to exist. (Someone want to remind MSNBC's Sergeant Schultz of that simple fact? While you are at it, perhaps the media generally should remind Mr. Obama and his FCC censor in waiting, Mark Lloyd.) Readers and viewers must hold journalists accountable as well.

The gristmill in the court of public opinion may grind slowly, but it grinds exceedingly fine. Eventually, clowns and charlatans are exposed and discredited, but what of the damage done in the meanwhile by people addicted to the drug of disinformation?

The most prominent examples are those planted in front of the cameras at MSNBC, especially Keith Dobermann. There is nothing redeeming about his commentary. It's not journalism, at least not classical journalism: who, what, why, where, when, and how all reported accurately, fairly, thoroughly, and with a sense of balance. He is not even a responsible, professional commentator. Dobermann simply spews his high-priced, hyper-partisan, vitriol achieving basement ratings as his reward. The trouble is he sets a terrible example for little dobermanns with access to a computer, likewise blogging vitriol. Keith just loves to pick up the lies reported by others and grind them into the minds of his viewers.

Disinformation is a political tool. It is not journalism. It is propaganda.

It has been a long time since we witnessed integrity in journalism, although a few enclaves exist. Today, lacking that integrity, we have chaos. The danger is reckless endangerment. Demagoguery, left unchecked, inevitably results in violence and physical injury or death.

Mob violence is always whipped up by some propagandist yelling fire.

Hitler did it to the Jews.

Stalin did it to capitalists and his own people.

Nero did it to the Christians.

Custer and Sheridan did it to the Native Americans.

The Klan and many others did it to the Africans.

Too many people in media and politics are doing it to anyone with the audacity to object to political correctness, those asserting devotion to traditional values. The favored way to yell fire or engage reckless endangerment is accusing someone of racism. Disinformation used to discriminate and persecute can cut both ways.

Racism is a cruel, heartless, and most often false accusation used only as a disinformation tool to force a political agenda, one of the most cynical and vicious crimes committed by one against another, yet it happens many times every hour, twenty-four-seven, in America today.

People of good will and common decency must take a stand against this great evil, or it will continue to recklessly endanger us all. In fact, race baiting only aggravates the problem of racism and racial tension, standing in the way of reconciliation and peacemaking.

In the end, rights exercised irresponsibly are soon consumed and abolished by the mob and the strongman. This experiment in self-government necessarily requires we self-regulate in order to protect the rights of everyone. And virtue is the foundation of self-regulation, as the Founding Fathers knew full well.

Rogue journalists and politicians yelling fire recklessly endanger everyone by turning the ordinary bump and grind of politics into war. Their intentional acts of disinformation are criminal, and we must police ourselves, or the government will do it for us, and on that day the conversation will be very one-sided. Rogue journalists and politicians can be just as destabilizing as suicide bombers in Baghdad. Speaking of the Founders, consider these parting shots:

> A nation of well-informed men who have been taught to know and prize the rights which God has given them cannot be enslaved. It is in the region of ignorance that tyranny begins.
>
> Only a virtuous people are capable of freedom. As nations become more corrupt and vicious, they have more need of masters.
>
> Benjamin Franklin

> Our Constitution was made only for a moral and religious people. It is wholly inadequate to the government of any other.
>
> John Adams

MONEY, POWER, AND FREEDOM: FOOD FOR THOUGHT FOR THE RIGHT AND THE LEFT

April 9, 2010

Every now and then lines intersect to reveal a truth so simple it promises to transcend mere partisanship and so-called human wisdom.

Consider this statement from Terry Miller of the Heritage Foundation:

> ...one of the prime reasons to push for economic freedom is to avoid the pernicious tendency for *government intervention that sides with the interests of big corporations and special interests* rather than with the average man or woman. The pattern we see, in the United States and around the world, is government intervention tending to support the interests of those who are already politically and economically powerful. The rhetoric may be populist, but actual government programs almost always favor the status quo. Economic freedom is the antidote, promoting competition, equal treatment for all, and the empowerment of the individual.
>
> Blog.heritage.org, April 7, 2010,
> "Who really rakes in their government largesse"

What a notion! Imagine, the problem of exploitation, of concern to both free marketers and socialists, solved by economic freedom working against powerful special interests to the benefit of average men and women.

Miller elaborates:

> ...it was in late 2008, under President Bush, that a threatened financial meltdown triggered some hasty and dangerous Washington policy decisions to bail out large firms. Unfortunately, President Obama has doubled down and more on those policies, with unprecedented levels of government spending, most favoring big finance, big auto companies, big labor unions, and now big pharma and medical insurance companies.

So while there is a lot of talk about helping the average American, the truth is it is business as usual in Washington—powerful, entrenched interests have access and influence and thereby receive special consideration.

Ask most any homeowner that was promised mortgage relief by both the banks and the government. The banks got richer. The government got more powerful. The homeowners are defaulting.

This is why Thomas Jefferson and the founders were so opposed to concentrated power at the federal level: the concentration of political power and monied interests always corrupts, to the detriment of the people and liberty itself, which serves to explain why Jefferson was also vehemently opposed to the idea of a central bank, our present-day federal reserve:

> The Central Bank is an institution of the most deadly hostility existing against the principles and form of our Constitution.... I believe that banking institutions are more dangerous to our liberties than standing armies. Already they have raised up a monied aristocracy that has set the Government at defiance. The issuing power should be taken from the banks and restored to the

people to whom it properly belongs. If the American people ever allow the banks to control the issuance of their currency, first by inflation and then by deflation, the banks and corporations that will grow up around them will deprive the people of all property until their children will wake up homeless on the continent their fathers occupied.

Perhaps it is time for all of us to rethink this whole idea of Republican versus Democratic, and capitalist versus socialist.

Perhaps we should look back at our founding principles as we look forward for the best ways to preserve freedom, knowing freedom and prosperity are intimately tied, for it is unquestionably true you cannot have one without the other.

Perhaps the free banking alternative combined with a concerted effort by the people to reduce the size of the federal government along with its ties to the power of entrenched special interests is the road away from serfdom, a road both the left and the right can agree to travel in some respects.

For additional information on the dangers of the collectivist mentality and its antagonism toward republican government and freedom, read "The Road to Serfdom," by F.A. Hayek. Here is the introduction to the latest edition:

> A classic work in political philosophy, intellectual history and economics, The Road to Serfdom has inspired and infuriated politicians and scholars for half a century. Originally published in 1944, it was seen as heretical for its passionate warning against the dangers of state control over the means of production. For Hayek, the collectivist idea of empowering government with increasing economic control would lead not to a utopia but to the horrors of Nazi Germany and Fascist Italy. This new edition includes a foreword by series editor and leading Hayek scholar Bruce Caldwell explaining the book's origins and publishing history and assessing common misinterpretations of Hayek's thought. Caldwell has also standardized and corrected Hayek's references

and added helpful new explanatory notes. Supplemented with an appendix of related materials and forewords to earlier editions by the likes of Milton Friedman, and Hayek himself, this new edition of The Road to Serfdom will be the definitive version of Friedrich Hayek's enduring masterwork.

F. A. Hayek, *The Road to Serfdom*

Further reading:

- Janice Rogers Brown—Collectivism as slavery
- Her speech "A Whiter Shade of Pale: Sense and Nonsense—The Pursuit of Perfection in Law and Politics," University of Chicago Law School, April 2000.
- "Under Obama, crony capitalism again rules the day," Washington Examiner.com, by Michael Barone, Feb. 14, 2010.
- "Crony capitalism: A Little Company Praised by President Obama," by John Stossel, Fox Business, January 14, 2010.

WITH FRIENDS LIKE AMERICA, ISRAEL'S ENEMIES FLOURISH

April 15, 2010

A dear friend, one who speaks Arabic, one who grew up in the Middle East and lived there most of his life, put it very well years ago: 'When the Palestinian says this is my land, he is right. When the Jew says this is my land, he is right too.' (They do not teach this in Islamic schools.)

It is politically correct to make Israel the bad guy and the Palestinians victims in circles frequented by Rashid Khalidi, a close friend of Barack Obama, and others emerging from the halls of academe where the narrative thrives.

As always in complex, longstanding conflicts, everyone brings measures of good and bad, but undeniable truths remain: Israel has a right to exist, and the Muslim world is hell bent on her destruction, the basis for eternal conflict. Consequently there are only three alternatives: (1) Israel and Islam continue to fight forever, (2) Islam overwhelms Israel, or (3) Islam stops attacking Israel.

Given Obama's stated policies and goals, the likely outcomes are 1 or 2 while the preferred outcome for all parties is 3. The preferred outcome can only be realized if freedom-loving people refuse to allow any encroachments by Muslim aggressors.

It is folly to conclude the goal is a separate Palestinian state leading to peaceful coexistence when over and over the stated goal from the Muslim world continues to be the complete eradication of Israel. Over and over, Israel has tried to make peace only to be met with violence.

Few people realize the Palestinians are descendants from the ancient Philistines. Moses mentioned the Philistines in Genesis 10:14 and later in 1 Chronicles 1:11–12. Most everyone is familiar with the long-running conflict between the Philistines and the Jews recorded in the book of Judges, telling the story of Samson delivering the Jews from the hand of the Philistines. And who could forget the story of David and Goliath, the giant Philistine warrior that fell by the hand of a boy with a sling? Later in life, as he fled the wrath of King Saul, David found refuge and protection thanks to the Philistine King Achish (1 Samuel 21:10–15).

Starting in the seventh century when Mohammad founded Islam, the religion was spread by the sword throughout the Middle East, North Africa, and into Iran and the Far East, its influence extending all the way to Indonesia. The cultures in and around Jerusalem, including the Philistines, were converted to Islam, Jews and Christians being the exceptions.

When a Philistine or a Palestinian says, "This is my land," he is right. But it is good to remember that Palestinians were not always Muslim and that Arab Muslims had no place in and around Jerusalem until they came by conquest in the seventh century. Arab Muslims originated in Mecca and Medina in what is now Saudi Arabia, and many came out of Africa as well. It is also worth noting the Jews migrated to the region known then as Canaan in about BC 1250, following their escape from slavery in Egypt. Two thousand years later, Muslims invaded Jerusalem and built the al-Sakhrah Mosque where the Temple of Solomon once stood.

Therefore, historically, it is simply untrue to claim the Jews stole land from Palestinians in 1948 when the state of Israel was established by the United Nations. The events following WWI are intriguing in this regard. (Resource: terrorismawareness.org)

When Jerusalem was conquered by the Caliphate or by Saladin, these are Muslim armies occupying the territory. Note, so far as we know, the very first empire to dominate the region was Egyptian long before Islam was founded. Notice also the incredible history of the region, the crossroads of the world, conquered over and over again by Persians, Hittites, Assyrians, Romans, Greeks, Turks, and many others.

Iran, Syria, Hezbollah, Saudi Arabia, Iraqi elements, Hamas, al-Qaeda, and many other Muslim nations and terror organizations have vowed to obliterate Israel. They have tried to destroy Israel and the Jews since long before 1948. Indeed, powerful Muslim forces joined the Germans before and during WWII to eradicate the Jews.

How disheartening to see an American administration turn its back on our longstanding friends and allies in Israel.

We fail to realize this central reality: our future survival is tied to the survival of Israel, for if Muslim extremism wins the day against a legitimate democracy in the Middle East and if Europe falls by immigration and disparate fertility rates, we will be even more alone in the world that we are presently.

At that point the free world will be reduced to Australia, New Zealand, Poland, South Korea, South Africa, and America.

ISLAM IS NOT A RELIGION OF PEACE: WE ARE AT WAR WITH SHARIA

April 16, 2010
Anjem Choudary: "Islam is not a religion of peace."

One of the most salient remarks at the Tea Party in McMinnville, Oregon, yesterday was, "I wish we had plain-spoken leaders again."

Someone else recalled, as an example, Reagan describing his Cold War strategy: "We win, they lose."

Recently President Obama released a report detailing his strategy in the war on terrorism, or rather, the overseas contingency operation in the effort to avert human-caused disasters. The report does not contain the words *Islam* or *jihad*.

Rather than recognizing the war for what it is and approaching it with a we-win-they-lose attitude, this president apparently believes if we backpedal, retreat, accommodate, and submit sufficiently, peace will be at hand.

This approach brings to mind a question: when, in all of human history, has an aggressive tyrant focused on world domination ever put down his weapons simply because the opposition showed weakness? Answer: never. Instead, the aggressor always sees weakness as an opportunity to escalate.

Mr. Obama may talk a good game about confronting Iran and working to keep nukes away from al-Qaeda, but our enemies know a pushover when they see one. For excellent elaboration see Charles Krauthammer, 4.16.10, 'Obama's Nuclear Posturing.'

So here we are: from the day Mr. Obama took office, the Muslim world has escalated its advance of Sharia through both overt violent jihad and by covert means, advancing Sharia-compliant financing and infiltration through immigration and other means.

For those still hypnotized by the delusion Islam is a religion of peace, take into consideration these startling statements. First, Anjem Choudary, a plain-spoken leader of another kind:

> "You can't say that Islam is a religion of peace. Because Islam does not mean peace. Islam means submission. So the Muslim is one who submits. There is a place for violence in Islam. There is a place for jihad in Islam.
>
> CBN News, March 2010,
> "UK Muslim Leader,
> Islam not a Religion of Peace."

Anjem Choudary is the leader of Islam4UK, an outfit banned in Britain as a terrorist organization. Choudary wants Sharia law to rule the United Kingdom and the world. He represents authoritative Islam as noted by foreign relations and security expert Frank Gaffney:

> Our enemy is not violent extremism, or even al-Qaeda alone. Rather, it is the millions of Muslims who - like the Muslim Brotherhood, al-Qaeda and their allies - adhere to Shariah and who, therefore, believe they must impose it on the rest of us.
>
> We are at war with such individuals and organizations. *Not because we want to be.* Not because of policies toward Israel or the Middle East or anything else we have pursued in recent years.

Rather, we are at war with them because they must wage jihad against us, pursuant to the dictates of Shariah, the same law that has guided many in Islam for some 1,200 years.

"The real reason they hate us,"
by Frank Gaffney,
American Legion Magazine,
April 9, 2010

They declared war because they must wage war according to Sharia law. Are we clear now?

In the wake of 9/11, various political leaders in the United States said one of the reasons we were so taken by surprise is we were not on a "war footing." Even in the aftermath of 9/11, people like George Bush and Tony Blair and Bill Clinton were saying Islam is a religion of peace.

Now, even Muslim clerics, if you listen, are telling us that that is a lie. A sober assessment of history would tell us most Muslims have been on a war footing since the seventh century.

Nine years after 9/11, we are still not on a war footing, and in fact, despite advances and victories during the Bush years, we are now in worse shape than we were under Clinton. Even though he didn't do much about it, at least Clinton recognized the threat.

Apparently Mr. Obama thinks he can contain the threat in a warm embrace.

For those who still think Islam is a religion of peace, please take time to view a scholarly documentary— "Islam: What the West Needs to Know."

The following are compelling statements by two featured individuals:

> The tendency of western political leaders to deny the connection between orthodox Islamic mainstream and terrorist violence is replicated in the universities and the media—wherever you look, both in western Europe and in North America. The members

of the elite class have this tendency to proclaim Islam, some "mysterious, authentic" Islam, to be peaceful, and to be tolerant, and those Muslims prone to violence are proclaimed to be non-representative fringe. Well, I would really appreciate, if people who make such claims, could then explain the continuity of violence from the earliest day of Islam, from the earliest days of the Prophet, and his immediate successors, throughout the thirteen centuries of recorded history.

Serge Trifkovic, Foreign Affairs Editor, *Chronicles: A Magazine*

The real burning question in the world today is: Does Islam, and Islamic civilization, actually sanction the violence that we are seeing being perpetrated in its name around the world? And to that, we have to answer, if we are going to be honest, an unqualified yes. The Islamic sources, the Islamic texts, starting with The Koran, but not limited to The Koran, including the Hadith, Islamic tradition, Islamic theology, Islamic law, the traditions of the interpretation of The Koran, throughout history, and Islamic history itself, all bear witness to the fact that Islam has a developed doctrine, theology and law that mandates violence against unbelievers.

Robert Spencer, author, Islam Unveiled

PARTY OF THE RICH
TOO BIG TO FAIL

April 19, 2010
So much for the new era of hope and change.
Michael Barone reported last week:

> Republicans owe no political debt to the big Wall Street firms. In the 2008 campaign cycle, according to the Center for Responsive Politics' opensecrets.org website, Goldman Sachs personnel contributed $4.5 million to Democrats and just $1.5 million to Republicans.
>
> Add in three other big Wall Street firms— Morgan Stanley, JPMorgan Chase and Citigroup— and the total take was $12.7 million to Democrats and $6.7 million to Republicans. The image of Wall Streeters as solid Republicans is as dead as J. P. Morgan himself.

News Item: The government on Friday accused Wall Street's most powerful firm of fraud, saying Goldman Sachs & Co. sold mortgage investments without telling the buyers that the securities were crafted with input from a client who was betting on them to fail.

The civil charges filed by the Securities and Exchange Commission are the government's most significant legal action related to the mortgage meltdown that ignited the financial crisis and helped plunge the country into recession.

And how did Mr. Obama benefit from Wall Street and Goldman Sachs during the 2008 campaign according to OpenSecrets.org? Look at all the nice contributions that flowed in:

Goldman Sachs	$994,795
Citigroup Inc	$701,290
JPMorgan Chase & Co	$695,132
UBS AG	$543,219
Morgan Stanley	$514,881

During the primary season he collected 7.9 million dollars from Wall Street. Do you remember the president saying something about Wall Street excesses, Wall Street bonuses, Wall Street corruption, and the need for serious reform? Also, his 2008 war chest amounted to about seven hundred fifty million dollars, twice that of any other candidate ever, much coming from unknown foreign sources. Didn't the president also say something about his concern over corporate and foreign contributions to campaigns?

We tried reaching the president for comment, but he was busy playing golf.

HUGO CHÁVEZ: STATE SPONSOR OF TERRORISM, NOT ON THE LIST

April 22, 2010

Celebrating the two hundredth anniversary of Venezuelan independence three days ago, with Russian fighters flying overhead, Venezuelan president Hugo Chávez declared, "I'm an anti-imperialist socialist!"

Political opposition leader Pablo Medina, once a Chávez ally, marked the occasion, saying, "Venezuela is headed toward a dictatorship, and the Castro brothers are helping him establish it."

Chávez hardly needs the help of the Castros when he has Iran, China, Russia, Libya, Saudi Arabia, and North Korea as allies, trade partners, and weapons suppliers.

Last year in a press release out of Tehran, Chávez is quoted saying this about the close cooperative relationship between Iran and Venezuela: "The Bolivarian and the Islamic Revolutions have a lot in common and these commonalities have consolidated the two countries' bonds" (FARS News Agency, "Iran Stresses Aid to Venezuelan Army," April 30, 2009).

Even leftists do not quibble about the dictatorial nature of both revolutions.

Almost four years ago, Iranian President Mahmoud Ahmadinejad called Venezuelan President Hugo Chávez a "brother and trench mate" (Washington Post, "Chávez's War of Words," by Jackson Diehl, August 7, 2006).

Chávez shares Ahmadinejad's hatred for America and Israel. The two leaders are trench brothers spreading hate, brothers making war using oil revenue, trench mates supporting terrorism, allies in the development of nuclear weapons to use against the United States and Israel.

Furthermore, *The Washington Times* reported yesterday:

> Iran is increasing its paramilitary Qods force operatives in Venezuela while covertly continuing supplies of weapons and explosives to Taliban and other insurgents in Afghanistan and Iraq, according to the Pentagon's first report to Congress on Tehran's military.
>
> The report on Iranian military power provides new details on the group known formally as the Islamic Revolutionary Guards Corps-Qods Force (IRGC-QF), the Islamist shock troops deployed around the world to advance Iranian interests. The unit is aligned with terrorists in Iraq, Afghanistan, Israel, North Africa and Latin America, and the report warns that U.S. forces are likely to battle the Iranian paramilitaries in the future.

A year ago the Israelis were reporting Venezuela was helping Iran skirt UN sanctions and helping Ahmadinejad acquire uranium.

Given the close relationship between Iran, the world's biggest sponsor of terrorism, and Chávez, it is good to be reminded Hezbollah and others are operating in South America thanks to Venezuelan support. This report years ago by Gustavo Coronel revealed Hezbollah operations in Venezuela. As everyone knows, both Hezbollah and Hamas terrorist organizations receive enormous support from Iran ("Hezbollah in Venezuela," by Gustavo Coronel and Venezuelatoday.net, September 1, 2006).

More reporting by Gustavo Coronel at *American Thinker*, blowing the lid off the claim Chávez is only a benevolent elected official helping the poor escape the ravages of Yankee imperialism: 'The Nation Magazine does Venezuela,' March 31, 2005.

By the way, that Yankee imperialism bit? It amounts to the United States sending Venezuela three billion dollars a year in oil royalties. It is not known how much Hollywood sends, but it is certainly more than was sent to flood victims in the Midwest.

Looks like Chávez is much more interested in Chinese and Russian imperialism, and they are very interested in buying oil and supplying weaponry to Venezuela. The Russians have sold Chávez at least a billion dollars in advanced weapons systems in the last few months. China is lending Venezuela twenty billion dollars to develop oil resources. Putin is helping build nuclear power plants. Who needs Iranian enriched uranium when you can make your own?

(Sources: Washington Post, 'Venezuela's strongman splurges on Russian weapons,' April 8, 2010, and, N.Y. Times, 'Chávez Says China to Lend Venezuela $20 Billion,' by Simon Romero, April 18, 2010.)

Additionally, according to a Spanish judge, it appears the Venezuelan government is working with terrorist groups to destabilize Columbia through assassination. (Wall Street Journal, 'Hugo Chávez and Terrorism,' March 3, 2010)

And to complete the rosy picture, according to the CIA, World FactBook online, Venezuela has long been known a center of the illegal drug trade and human sex trafficking, exploiting women and children.

Oliver Stone and Danny Glover and Sean Penn and Harry Belafonte and Barack Obama may find in Chávez a kindred spirit, but it is clear most Americans have no use for the thug dictator.

On the day Chávez receives nukes from Iran, sparking a Venezuelan missile crisis, will we have the cojones to deal with this individual once and for all? Probably not, if it happens while Obama occupies the White House.

SYRIAN MISSILES TO HEZBOLLAH: NEW WAR IN MIDDLE EAST?

April 24, 2010

Syria was added to the American list of state sponsors of terrorism in 1979. The country is run by the Ba'ath Party (visions of Saddam), and it is a military dictatorship, known to be working toward the acquisition of nuclear weapons.

Syria is also a close ally of Iran and works cooperatively with Tehran to supply Hezbollah terrorists in Lebanon, all working together toward the eradication of Israel, one of our closest allies. Hamas in Gaza, another terrorist group actively seeking Israel's destruction, receives training in Syria and support from Iran.

As a state sponsor of terrorism Syria is well known as a weapons clearing house, using commercial airliners in the past to supply terrorists in various places not just Lebanon and Gaza. Syrian support for Iraqi insurgents has resulted in many American military deaths.

Recently Israel accused Syria of supplying ballistic missiles to Hezbollah. That accusation has been confirmed by administration officials in the State Department.

As the longest standing state sponsor of terrorism on the American list, a country subject to sanctions for decades, Syria was restricted to receiving only food and humanitarian aid under the Bush administration.

In light of all this, can anyone explain why President Obama and Secretary of State Clinton are actively seeking the lifting of sanctions, allowing Syria to upgrade and maintain commercial aircraft?

Why on earth is an American president being supportive of a terrorist regime even as he denigrates Israel? Why does Obama slap Israel in the face and embrace Syria even as Syria spits in his face by sending missiles to Hezbollah?

One answer is the quest to "normalize" relations with Syria is pursued in hopes Syria will dissuade Iran from developing nukes. It is also hoped by providing aid and lifting sanctions Syria will stop meddling in Iraq. There is absolutely no reason to believe either outcome is probable.

Syria has repeatedly demonstrated the opposite intentions. Now it is feared Syrian supplies of Scud missiles to Hezbollah will spark a new war in the Middle East. So much for the new era of hope and change on the diplomatic front.

IT'S ABOUT TRUST, STUPID

April 26, 2010

A wise woman told me once, "If you want to understand someone, you can listen to what he says, but it's better to watch what he does." A human being will speak volumes, but what he actually does, that reveals true character. It is a law: the closer words match deeds, the greater the integrity.

Mr. Obama is the leader of the Democratic Party and supposedly the leader of the free world. He is supported by about half the voters, roughly sixty million people in a country of three hundred thirty million. It is arguably true he enjoys the support of most people in colleges and universities across the country. He likewise enjoys the support of most of the powerful, influential voices in the mass media. Given this kind of support, one would expect a great deal of integrity, so let's measure some of the words and their proximity to deeds, just for fun.

- During the campaign, Mr. Obama promised he would participate in public financing of campaign expenses. When it became clear he could raise much more staying private, he broke his promise.

- He says he supports the rule of law and took an oath to protect and defend the Constitution then promotes the idea of detentions based only on suspicion of future, potential violations.
- He claimed he opposes government spying on citizens and supports the rights of privacy then directed his DOJ to argue for more surveillance and complete government immunity from prosecution.
- He said he favors full disclosure of campaign contributions then accepted contributions from overseas without disclosure.
- He said he could no more disown Jeremiah Wright than he could disown his own family, and then, when Jeremiah became a political liability, Obama disowned him.
- Calling his own grandmother a "typical white person," he likewise threw her under the bus during the campaign, using her as an example of vast subliminal racism throughout America.
- He promised stimulus spending would not contain pork and it would heal the economy. It has not healed the economy and it was filled with pork, unprecedented pork (nine thousand earmarks?).
- Mr. Obama promised all healthcare deliberations would be put on television. That did not happen.
- He promised proposed legislation would be available on line for five days so people could see and review before he signed. Another broken promise.
- He promised to be a leader of all the people, working to restore American standing worldwide, then went on various world tours, apologizing for America, bowing and scraping before foreign leaders, denigrating America and holding her up to ridicule.

- He says he supports Israel then throws Israel under the bus.
- He says we must stop Iranian nuclear ambitions but does nothing substantive to accomplish this end.
- He says we must confront state-sponsored terrorism then begins the process of lifting sanctions against Syria.
- He said he would cut spending.
- He said he would not raise taxes, then through ObamaCare executes the biggest tax increases in history.
- He said he would vigorously fight terrorism and defend the country.
- He said we would prevail in Afghanistan with a new coalition of international players.
- He said he would pull out of Iraq without leaving Iraqis in the lurch.
- He said he would not force people to buy health insurance.
- He said for years before being elected he supported universal healthcare, and now he denies it.
- He said he wants to reduce the number of abortions but votes in favor of every pro-abortion bill that comes down the pike, even signing an order last year to allow taxpayer money to fund abortion overseas.
- He says he will close Gitmo then doesn't.
- He says he will prosecute KSM in civilian court in NYC then doesn't.
- He said he disagrees with recess appointments then made them.
- He called for strong border security then cut fifty million dollars from border security.
- He said he would cut waste and fraud. Both have increased.

- He said he would root out the influence of lobbyists and special interests. Both have increased.

- He said he respects the separation of powers then rigs legislation and condemns the Supreme Court.

- As a senator he opposed changing the rules to end filibuster, but now he supports changing the rules to allow a simple majority vote to end filibusters.

- He said he loves the free market then uses government to take over vast portions of the economy.

- He claims he respects states' rights then works to overrule Arizona's attempts to solve the problems associated with illegal immigration.

- He condemns Wall Street, panders to Wall Street, takes millions of dollars in campaign contributions from Wall Street, parties with Wall Street, decries bailouts, then promotes 'reform' by calling for the authority to grant unlimited bailouts.

- He promised taxpayers will not be on the hook for bailouts, and now we find we are on the hook for bailouts.

- He said the worst thing we could to during a recession is raise taxes. He is raising every tax possible, on individuals and businesses, and researching new ways of getting into our pockets, all the while and creating a two-class America where half the people pay no income tax, but the so-called rich carry the entire load.

- He decries those who play the race card, then plays the race card when it comes to immigration reform, even calling people of color to rally to him in advance of November.

- He calls for bipartisanship then kicks the hell out of Republicans at every opportunity.

- He says he supports vigorous debate and free speech then calls the Tea Party people fringe lunatics and liars.
- He calls for unity and sows divisiveness.

You may have disagreed with George W. Bush on every issue of the day. However, you cannot deny he stated what he believed forthrightly and acted accordingly, which translates to a great deal of integrity.

Given a choice, most prudent people will choose the man of integrity, even if they disagree with him, rather than support the flimflam man. Better to trust and disagree than to have no trust at all.

And the more Democrats in the House and Senate pander to the flimflam man, the more they face the wrath of the voters in November.

You just keep talking, Mr. Obama, and we'll act. Pray and vote!

THEY'RE ALL IN BED TOGETHER: NIGHTY NIGHT, AMERICA

April 28, 2010
Certain things in American life are axiomatic:

- We accept that a large number of politicians are crooks.
- We know too many big wheels in high finance are slick operators, the moneychangers in the temple.
- We know that when the big wheels and the crooks start ripping each other publicly it really means they are making new, private deals in shadowy places over cocktails.

So it came as no surprise to learn from the headlines that the big wheels at Goldman Sachs are gushing gleeful over Obama's finance reform being pushed by retiring Senator Dodd, the senate's role model for how to secure private financing at favorable rates reserved only for powerful senators with bank oversight authority.

Really? Goldman Sachs executives want federal regulation? What's the catch? Some of the more cynical among us might say the president is bought and paid for by Goldman, as are a number of other crooks, and that Dodd's finance reform is really a ploy to give the feds unlimited bailout authority.

That would mean as long as everyone is cozy in bed together, Goldman need never fear insolvency, since the American taxpayer can always be fleeced by the crooks to keep the big wheels spinning.

So when Senator Levin uses profanity to excoriate the Goldman CEO in hearings recently, that becomes the headline—not what Goldman did or did not do, not the millions shoveled to Democrats by Wall Street, not the close relationship between the president, the Fed, treasury, and Goldman and all of Wall Street, not the impotence of the SEC or the corruption systemically that led to the housing burst and the deepening recession.

The stories didn't cover the billions in bailout money that went to Goldman or the billions Goldman paid out in bonuses. (Did somebody say bribes?)

No. News coverage didn't get to the heart of the matter.

The headlines were all about counting the times Levin said shi**y in the hearing.

Meanwhile, FedHead Bernanke got on the microphone again to warn of disaster should we fail to deal with the federal deficit. Curious that Bernanke will tell us disaster looms, calling on policy makers (translation: crooks and big wheels) to do something but declining himself to make specific recommendations.

Well, Mr. Bernanke, not to be too snotty or presumptuous about it, but it's obvious we are in this mess because the feds spend too much of our money and continue doing so, and you guys at the Fed continue to play games with artificial interest rates while printing funny money, all of it just a hoax to delay the inevitable, so isn't it likewise obvious we have to do two things (?):

1. Cut federal spending radically.
2. Fire up the economy via tax cuts, increased trade, and regulatory relief.

Isn't it also obvious that this president and his Congress are doing the exact opposite of what is required, thus accelerating our speed toward hitting the wall resulting in default and bankruptcy?

So the porn watchers at the SEC prosecute Goldman to make us all believe our government is really interested in enforcement, and the Senate holds another impotent hearing which is little more than another dog and pony show, and the president meets for the umpteenth time with the big wheels, working toward re-election and more government control of the private sector while Barney Frank and Chris Dodd run interference and push the overall agenda to forward the orgy of spending, thus plunging average Americans deeper and deeper into debt and demoralization.

And if Republicans object?

Well, they're just the party of no, racist tea baggers and shills for Wall Street.

Who profits the most from Wall Street? The crooks and the big wheels and the Democrats.

Also, from the World Socialist Website, "Obama's Wall Street cabinet," April 6, 2009:

> A series of articles published over the weekend, based on financial disclosure reports released by the Obama administration last Friday concerning top White House officials. These document the extent to which the administration, in both its personnel and policies, is a political instrument of Wall Street.

Note: socialists will claim capitalism is the problem. This writer disagrees. Capitalism is not the problem. Crooks and big wheels are the problem, i.e., corruption, thanks to generalized moral decline. Perhaps we can agree on that much?

EXPLOITING ILLEGAL IMMIGRATION: THE ESSENCE OF SEDITION

April 29, 2010

Give me your tired, your poor... (legally)

The controversy over illegal immigration is not about race or class struggle or economics so much as it is about borders, boundaries, and sovereignty.

Borders define a country physically, and border integrity is critical to sovereignty, especially in an age of terrorism supported by the international drug trade.

What, then, do we make of people who have no regard for border integrity and border security? Do they care little about sovereignty? It would seem so, and here is why.

On the far left, no longer the radical fringe, there exists a huge group that actually thinks it makes sense to cede several border states to Mexico.

For them, blanket amnesty is not a matter of pragmatism; it is not even an issue of justice. Rather it is a political tool, a way to take control of border states. *They are not as interested in citizenship as they are in conquest.* Becoming American is anathema. The goal is expanding a Mexican and Latin American sphere of influence, and by any definition, that is aggression, and a threat to sovereignty. Hugo Chavez and the Castro brothers are, of course, driving forces behind this aggression.

The federal government has failed for years to enforce federal law regarding illegal immigration. The crises created by illegal immigration, especially in the border states, forced Arizona's hand. Those crises involve border violence linked to illegal human trafficking, illegal drug trafficking, and the pressure brought by illegal immigrants. Illegals consume public services without paying taxes, and legal citizens of all colors are tired of footing the bill, especially in the face of escalating violence. Illegal activity breeds illegal activity, and a lot of innocent people get caught in the crossfire, citizens and non-citizens alike.

This highlights the issue of boundaries.

In our personal lives, we draw boundaries in every aspect of life. Inappropriate touching in schools or in the workplace is not tolerated. Inappropriate behavior is policed in our public and private lives. We would never dream of allowing high school boys to mistreat the female students, and we would never tolerate employee theft in the work place, regardless of skin color.

Yet, somehow, when it comes to illegal aliens, we are expected to allow them to come here in violation of federal law. We are expected to turn a blind eye to their illegal status. We are forced to fund social services. Taxpayers are forced to finance educational services, health services, and social services, all while the government fails in its duty to enforce the law. In every other aspect of life, there are boundaries. But when it comes to illegal aliens, we have no boundaries. They are allowed to act illegally with impunity, and we are forced to subsidize illegal activity to our own detriment.

In an age of enormous government deficits at all levels, taking us to the verge of financial ruin, it makes no sense to continue the orgy of spending on any front, even if we dismiss the illegal aspects of the situation. Yet, to insist that law-abiding citizens underwrite lawlessness to their own demise, inviting violence, drug trafficking, and terrorism in the process is sheer insanity.

The president, the mayor of New York, and the radicals on the left (anymore, the majority of Democrats), insist that John Q taxpayer suffer waves of illegal immigration, and to add insult they insist we actually finance its furtherance.

Worse, they seek to dominate and manipulate the majority of citizens by playing the race card.

Come Saturday it's expected Hispanics nationwide will protest American immigration policy generally and Arizona's recent legislative move specifically. Had the federal government lived up to its constitutional responsibilities long ago, there would not be a problem or controversy, and Arizona would not have been forced to act. Failing to act today, and blaming everyone else, the federal government, as personified in the president, makes a bad situation worse by inflaming racial tensions, going so far as to encourage conflict.

Radical agitators who want to transform the Southwest into an extension of Mexico are not restrained by a concern for national security and sovereignty, nor are they restricted by any respect for common courtesy and decent free speech. They have no boundaries. They have no borders. Consequently, it is easy for them to claim Arizona's new law creates a police state, it portends Nazism, it is inherently racist, unfair, ill-advised, irresponsible, even anti-American. Thus saith the president and the secretary of Homeland Security, Janet Napolitano, a woman who sang an entirely different tune when she was governor of Arizona.

In truth, the forces that would crush the democratic process and the will of the majority in order to nullify Arizona law and force amnesty represent the real anti-American enclave. They seek the erasure of borders, they violate all civilized boundaries, and they seek the destruction of sovereignty, the essence of sedition.

I grew up in southern California and learned a bit of Spanish in high school and in the fields. In high school and during college summers, I worked on farms and ranches with Mexican men, some legal, some not. I worked hard in the hot sun, shoulder to shoulder with great individuals. I assure you, you will never out work a Mexican man.

When the white border patrol truck approached, the foreman would holler, "Andale, muchachos!" Those guys could scatter and hide like nobody's business. They worked hard for little more than minimum wage, living apart from their families most of the year, sending most of their income home every month.

And without fail, each one dreamed of full citizenship.

In those days American employers hired illegal workers, contributing to the problem, which continues to this day, and enforcement was hit and miss. So we have to take our fair share of the responsibility for creating an environment that encouraged poor and desperate people to the south to come here, break our laws, and export cash. In so doing, they were made victims twice.

Even so, the cruel reality is they are being made victims three and four times today, for they are being exploited by political radicals and by predatory employers. In my experience working with Mexicans, our employer paid them above scale. The rancher even provided free housing. But so many employers today exploit illegals mercilessly. For those who promote the idea that illegal immigration is to be ignored, they also, by default, promote the idea illegals must remain in the shadows, the objects of exploitation. Radicals use illegals as pawns, exploitive by nature, and, likewise, politicians see them as potential voters. As is usually the case, the little guy, regardless of color, is taken advantage of by every kind of insider with an agenda.

Those who argue amnesty is the solution would have us ignore the issues involving borders, boundaries, and sovereignty. Remember, we tried amnesty in the 1980s followed by a renewed effort to close the border, and what did we get? More illegal immigration on a much greater scale. Amnesty only aggravates the problem. People who promote amnesty think there is no consequence if we retreat from holding the line according to the rule of law, failing to recognize the advent of chaos and inevitable decline, the descent to racial warfare, already a fact of life in south central Los Angeles.

War is precisely what some people lust after. Not the average American taxpayer. The average American taxpayer is neither a racist nor a hard-hearted isolationist. The average American only wants to see responsible government, respect for the rule of law, and an orderly society wherein everyone can enjoy life, liberty, and the pursuit of happiness.

Illegal immigration and the accommodation of illegality threatens all that potential for everyone, including those living in the shadows.

PRESIDENT VICTIM

May 3, 2010

When a man in a leadership position says one thing then does the opposite, it can be disorienting. When he contradicts himself while delivering a speech, it's downright mind numbing; unless one understands, it is intentional double-talk, obfuscation, and redirection.

Speaking to University of Michigan graduates recently, Mr. Obama decried Washington politics, one of his campaign themes, the vitriol in public debate, the media echo chamber, incivility, and attacks on the government and the presidency.

He said it is too bad American politics are harsh, so filled with conflict, so riddled with extremist language. He appeared to be saying he is the object of unprecedented attacks, a 'garner sympathy track,' then went on to explain American politics has always been a harsh game, sometimes violent, frequently marked by hyperbole.

So which is it? Is today worse than yesterday, or is today reflective of yesterday, or, was yesterday worse than today? Well, it really doesn't matter, does it? Mr. Obama achieved his first objective: inviting graduates to believe people are mean. He is really a nice guy; isn't it too bad nice guys get attacked by extremists?

The irony is the extremist in chief is the one complaining about extremism.

Mr. Obama went on to bemoan the media echo chamber where extremism is trumpeted twenty-four-seven, where outrageous remarks are given play to attract attention (audience/ratings). He singled out one cable television outfit as the worst perpetrator of the vitriol. The White House war on Fox continues without naming Fox, because, presumably, that would be harsh and extreme. (None dare call the major networks, the largest newspapers, or MSNBC harsh or extreme…)

Odd how a president can complain about media coverage when he enjoys massive support from the vast majority of major media. What's the complaint?

The president said all this media noise and vicious politicking tend to drown out the voice of the common people, so to be sure he is in touch with common people, he reads ten letters from ordinary Americans every night.

(Millions of ordinary Americans in the streets for a year get a deaf ear and criticism from the White House, but the pulse of the people can be detected reading fifty letters a week? Millions of moms and dads and grandmothers and grandfathers objecting to this president's radicalism as reported by Fox makes the protesters fringe morons and Fox the propaganda arm of nitwits?)

Back to the president's way of keeping in touch with ordinary folks, you know, the ones he seeks to save, the heart of why he sought higher office in the first place.

He said a letter from a kindergartener gave him special pause. The youngster asked, "Are people being nice?" This is top of mind for the leader of the free world? Are people being nice?

Of course, they are not little Billy. People are mean. Subtext: people are especially mean when they read their Bibles and hug their guns, because, well, they don't like a black man sleeping in the White House. But that's okay, Billy. I'm here to change all that so that you will have hope.

Speaking of nice, in all this discussion about civility, it would be nice to hear Mr. Obama say, at least one time, that average Americans are not racists. It would help us believe he is above politics.

Once his Michigan audience was reassured he is above politics, he is playing nice, and only the mean and the misinformed would characterize him otherwise, Mr. Obama set out to tell people how they should think about the current debate over the role of government. After all, we cannot think for ourselves, you realize.

As he promotes the most expansive and intrusive government in history, he urged us not to think about big government versus small government. No. Rather we are to think about "smarter, better government." Urging us to join him in establishing smarter government, he would have us ignore the fact that, for him, smarter is bigger. (And can someone explain how an increasingly bankrupt, inefficient and corrupt government is somehow 'smarter?')

The fatal flaw in his argument came with this remark: "…the ability for us to adapt our government to the needs of the age has helped make our democracy work since its inception."

This is the great departing point. Incredibly he claims he is the catalyst for adaptation according to the will of the people, and then he ignores the will of the people.

Since our inception, the idea was that government would adapt to the consent of the governed. Mr. Obama insists the people adapt to the demands of the government: consent be damned.

Furthermore, conservatives have always argued is it the people who have made this democratic republic work. It has been the hard work, sacrifice, individual integrity, and sense of duty of the people that accounts for the greatness of the country. Government did not build America. The people built America. Yes, the government may have facilitated this or that project or reform, but free people allowed to act freely and creatively established and built the greatest country on earth, not the government.

Mr. Obama worships at the church of government while the founders' prayer focused on the consent of the governed, under God. Mr. Obama believes massive central government is the answer to all the questions, the solution to all problems. The founders believed massive central government was the root of all evil, the only question being how do we structure a system of checks and balances so as to keep the central government small so as to preserve liberty?

In his speech the president called for the preservation of liberty even as he justified his unprecedented expansion of government, expecting the people to ignore the inevitable destruction of one via the expansion of the other. The double-talk does not wash, Mr. President.

Calling for debate about the role of government, Mr. Obama dismisses debate in the same breath, insisting the times demand enormous government intervention. At the same time he invoked the words of Ben Franklin, challenging us to hold on to the idea of republic.

Remarkable. A president who tells us to preserve republic, citing Franklin, even as he deconstructs republic by contradicting the will of the people or ignoring it, even as he works against the idea of separation of powers, even as he worms his way deeper and deeper into our pockets, even as he uses his power to nullify states' rights, even after he exacts government takeover after government takeover, blending government and corporate power, the very definition of fascism.

And then he whimpers about people calling him a fascist.

His healthcare program was installed using the most devious, harsh politics imaginable. It carries with it the biggest tax increases in history. It establishes the federal government as the dictatorial power micromanaging private medical decisions. And all of it was done with no regard for the will of the majority.

Yet this president has the stones to stand there and tell us he is the kinder, gentler president, working only to form a more perfect union, according to the specifications laid down by the founders!

To convince us that government intervention can be a good thing, Obama tried this example. He said welfare reform in the 1990s (a Republican initiative leading to a balanced budget) encouraged people away from dependency, forcing them to take responsibility for their own 'upward mobility.' Yes, such intervention, reducing the reach of government and calling on people to take responsibility, is really no intervention at all, is it? It is the reduction of intervention by reducing welfare dependency, yet Mr. Obama wants to use it as an example of good government intervention?

Astounding.

From day one, this president's every move has been the furtherance of dependency. He does not believe in 'upward mobility.' He said so recently, declaring a certain level of income is sufficient, implying people should not aspire to more, even while he personally made millions last year. What is good for him is apparently bad for the rest of us. He has bluntly stated he believes in redistribution of wealth, and if his healthcare plan is not sufficient evidence of institutionalized redistribution, what could be, other than his tax plans, and the plundering of other private resources to feed the federal monster, which then doles out to his constituents, many of whom have little interest in 'upward mobility'?

Returning to the theme of civility, Mr. Obama closed his remarks by claiming vigorous debate is good, but the kind of vigor and passion that gives rise to extreme rhetoric is destructive to democracy.

Translation: just be nice and get along, and if you disagree, best to keep quiet.

People are not interested in a president preaching about how to be nice in kindergarten. People are interested in a strong leader with vision for solving problems and expanding opportunity.

The truth is this president is demonstrating weak leadership and the inability to solve problems. He is, therefore, the object of criticism, criticism he seeks to deflect by casting blame on the people and the media and the politicians. Well, Mr. President, you are one of the people, you have been the biggest beneficiary of media these last three years, and you are a politician. As you call on us to take responsibility, how about a plate full at your table as well?

Perhaps it is time for you to consider the phrase "physician, heal thyself." You call for participation, Mr. President, and when people participate in opposition, you ignore them, denigrate them, marginalize them, overpower them, then whine about power plays and denigration.

As to the so-called vitriol, Mr. President, you assumed the presidency by spewing a fair amount of your own, by spending twice the amount spent by any other candidate, much of that coming from illegal foreign sources. One day Hillary will write a book about the dirty tricks pulled during the 2008 campaign.

In office you humiliate our country by your remarks and behaviors abroad. You encroach upon individual liberties and disregard the will of the people. You challenge the traditional separation of power and seek domination of Congress and the Supreme Court. You promote social policy agendas against the will of the majority. And you are on a quest to nationalize and globalize as much as possible to the destruction of republic.

And you have the gall to blame the people for being angry, as if you are the victim?

IS OBAMA A FASCIST?

May 4, 2010

> Fascism should more appropriately be called Corporatism because it is a merger of state and corporate power. All within the state, nothing outside the state, nothing against the state.
>
> Italian fascist Benito Mussolini

> Concentrated power has always been the enemy of liberty. Government's first duty is to protect the people, not run their lives. Man is not free unless government is limited.
>
> President Ronald Reagan

How remarkable to witness in a few short years the transition from Reagan's vision of America, closely aligned with the founders, to Obama's vision, more closely aligned with Mussolini's. No doubt such a claim will rattle the cages of those who still believe Obama can do no wrong. Rather than react emotionally, let us examine the evidence and arrive at a logical conclusion.

By his deeds, is Obama creating an impenetrable state monolith, combining the joint powers of corporations and the state, and in so doing, is he actually creating a kind of fascist regime hostile to liberty?

- Exhibit one: GM-Government Motors, formerly General Motors.
- Exhibit two: nationalizing healthcare, one-sixth of the entire economy.
- Exhibit three: domination of energy via EPA, Department of Energy, cap and trade.
- Exhibit four: finance 'reform' proposals giving the feds unlimited corporate bailout authority, providing for federal domination of the entire financial system.
- Exhibit five: TARP, bailouts, the US Government holding controlling interest in Citigroup and other corporations.
- Exhibit six: the incestuous relationships between the Executive branch, the Legislative branch, Wall Street, The Fed, the banks, and Treasury.
- Exhibit seven: Fannie and Freddie, the feds controlling more than half of the home mortgage industry.

These exhibits illustrate unprecedented moves toward the blending of state and corporate power. But there is more evidence that is even more damning.

Crony Capitalism

Notice the range of cronyism occurring elsewhere. Read in this commentary how Obama wants to expand the Freddie and Fannie models to "private" financial institutions, Washington Examiner: "Under Obama Crony Capitalism again Rules the Day," by Michael Barone, Feb. 14, 2010.

"Fannie and Freddie are classic examples of crony capitalism, where government and business are in bed together. Obama wants to expand that disastrous model to the likes of JP Morgan Chase and Goldman Sachs."

Please consider this excerpt as well from Commentary: "*Obama's Economic Policy: Crony Capitalism,*" by *John Steele Gordon, April* 23, 2010:

> The so-called financial-reform bills now working their way through each house of Congress are, like the health-care-reform bill before them, not about reform at all. They do not reform anything. Instead, they make the federal government the major player in a major industry. Just as the health-care-reform bill will transform private insurance companies into the equivalent of public utilities, whose every major decision needs government approval and whose returns on capital are more or less guaranteed, these bills would do the same for big banks and other financial institutions.

Still more evidence required? Consider this analysis from the Weekly Standard:

> ...the chief characteristic of crony capitalism is favoritism for some companies or organizations (unions, for example)—in loans, grants, giveaways, and specific policies. There's another aspect. Obama isn't merely rewarding a few cronies, he's seeking more and more favored groups to reward. One way he's doing this is through his energy, health care, and other policies, which would boost certain companies and industries over others.
>
> "The Triumph of Crony Capitalism,"
> The Weekly Standard,
> by Fred Barnes, July 19, 2009

Favoritism

The 787-billion-dollar stimulus package that became the 825-billion-dollar stimulus package that was supposed to create jobs and stimulate the economy, without pork. Guess what? The lion's share of that money is going to regions of the country that supported Obama in 2008. Are you shocked that the president and his allies in Congress would so blatantly use taxpayer money for partisan purposes?

Growth of Government

Yesterday, this disquieting report headlined: 'Federal Government Outpaces Private Sector in Job Creation.'

Excerpt:

> Gallup's Job Creation Index clearly indicates that state and local governments are in the midst of significant downsizing, no doubt reflecting budgetary issues resulting from recessionary pressures on the tax (and other) revenue that funds these governments. Hiring at the federal level has apparently to date escaped these same fiscal pressures. Indeed, the federal government appears to be significantly outpacing the private sector in terms of the relative number of jobs created.
>
> "Federal Government Outpaces Private Sector in Job Creation," WSJ, by Frank Newport, May 8, 2010

Is it any wonder then people fear federal power, especially when more and more Americans are entirely dependent on the feds and while state and local governments are going belly up?

Couple this with Obama's glaring hostility toward Arizona's efforts to secure its border, and you have a prescription for increasing federal domination of the states, already a threat to republican form of government, the very life blood of liberty.

The federal government controls the money; it controls taxation; it controls the states; it controls private enterprise and increasingly; it controls the people, dictating healthcare and income levels; and soon, by proposals being floated about, the federal government will dictate what kind of car you drive, the kind of house you must maintain, the food you should eat, controlling even the ways and means of work and energy consumption, mandating the kind of light bulb you can acquire.

Mr. Obama will accomplish all of this by blending corporate and state power at the federal level, and he will fund all of it by taxing everyone but the poor: not just the rich, not just corporations, but everyone, including the middle class. Contrary to Obama's stated promises, just look at what he has done in the area of tax increases even before trying to get the Bush tax cuts to lapse.

Tax Increases

Since January of 2009, President Obama and Congressional Democrats have enacted into law gross tax increases totaling more than $670 billion, or more than $2,100 for every man, woman and child in the United States. The list of tax increases includes at least 14 violations of the President's pledge not to raise taxes on Americans earning less than $200,000 for singles and $250,000 for married couples.

"Democrats Have Increased Taxes by $670 Billion and Counting...List Includes 14 Tax Hikes Totaling Over $316 Billion on Middle Class Families," House Ways & Means Committee report, April 14, 2010

So much for Mr. Obama's promises. And we haven't even highlighted the serious discussions now being forwarded by Obama's advisors, including former SEIU officials, promoting the idea of a national sales tax. Furthermore, Obama's budget calls for 2.8 trillion dollars in tax increases in the next ten years. Increasing the power of government through taxation also enhances Obama's ability to concentrate power, reward friends, and take over larger sections of what is left of the private sector.

Meanwhile, the country is drowning in debt, and there are no clear indications the recession is turning to recovery.

As we watch Europe collapse, the president employs comedy writers to make bad jokes at the National Press Club dinner. As the champagne flows, the concentration of corporate and state power continues, ultimately to the destruction of liberty.

Conclusion

Notice how sensitive this president is to anti-government protests. He can hardly make a speech these days without joking about his disapproval ratings even as he castigates the Tea Party people, people he characterizes as uninformed, misguided, anti-American.

When a leader is opposed by the majority yet insists on pressing his agenda, we no longer have government of, by, and for the people—as articulated by Abraham Lincoln. Instead we have government "within the state, nothing outside the state, nothing against the state"—as articulated by Benito Mussolini.

REVEREND GRAHAM: OBAMA ADMINISTRATION DISENFRANCHISES CHRISTIANS

May 5, 2010

And Tony Perkins, president of the Family Research Council, says President is politicizing the military

Reverend Franklin Graham was slated to speak and pray at the Pentagon tomorrow as part of the National Day of Prayer, but he was uninvited by Pentagon officials.

While he does not blame President Obama for canceling his appearance, he does believe White House officials are responsible.

Furthermore, he believes the evangelical community has been ignored and marginalized by the Obama administration.

Two weeks ago Graham was banned from the Pentagon event due to his remarks nine years ago, remarks critical of Islam.

After 9/11 Graham called Islam a "very evil and wicked religion." Last December he said, "True Islam cannot be practiced in this country. You can't beat your wife. You cannot murder your children if you think they've committed adultery or something like that, which they do practice in these other countries."

Pentagon officials said Graham's comments contradict the policy of tolerance being promoted in the military, a policy many blame for the massacre at Fort Hood by an army major devoted to Islam.

Graham acknowledged he has been critical of Islam, saying it promotes conflict, abuses women horribly, and engages in hateful rhetoric and activities. He also asserts he is not critical of all Muslims, only a belief system that advocates violence against non-Muslims.

A recent report details the perspective of one of the largest Islamic groups in the United States, ("Ex-Muslim Defends Franklin Graham's Islam Remarks," The Christian Post, By Michelle A. Vu, April 29, 2010):

> The Council on American-Islamic Relations, a group widely accused of having ties to terrorists, urged congressional sponsors of the National Day of Prayer event on Capitol Hill to rescind their invitation to Graham as a featured speaker at the May 6 gathering. CAIR denounced Graham as an anti-Islam preacher who sends a message of religious intolerance.
>
> Franklin Graham has the right to be an Islamophobe, but he does not have the right to a taxpayer-funded public platform," said Corey Saylor, CAIR national legislative director, in the statement.

Essentially, the Pentagon bowed to CAIR. The Pentagon "submitted" to Islam.

Graham stated in a CNN interview he does not oppose Muslim prayer meetings at the Capitol or at the Pentagon, noting the double standard employed by the administration.

The Pentagon also rescinded the invitation to Tony Perkins, president of the Family Research Council, a Marine Corps veteran.

The official reason Perkins was uninvited: his stand on homosexuals serving openly in the military.

Perkins asserts the president in using the Department of Defense to oppose conservative points of view from being expressed through evangelical channels. He says it is troubling to see the administration using the military to advance its political agenda to the detriment of freedom of speech and religion.

Tomorrow is the fifty-ninth annual National Day of Prayer. Reverend Graham released this statement recently:

> As the honorary chairman for the National Day of Prayer Task Force, I want to encourage Christians to be praying for revival in our country in the coming days. On May 6, I will be leading many in prayer at the Cannon House Office Building in Washington, D.C., and I hope millions more will be joining us at prayer events throughout the nation. Let us stand together in prayer as we humble ourselves, repent of our sins, seek God's face, and ask Him to heal our land (2 Chronicles 7:14).

Graham's ministry, Samaritan's Purse, is an evangelistic outreach organization doing charitable work worldwide, including Muslim countries.

After the death, burial, and resurrection of Jesus Christ, his followers began preaching in and around Jerusalem, proclaiming Christ the Messiah, urging people to believe in him for the remission of sin. The religious rulers of the temple arrested Peter and others, demanding they stop preaching in the name of Jesus.

> Peter and the other apostles replied: "We must obey God rather than men! The God of our fathers raised Jesus from the dead—whom you had killed by hanging him on a tree. God exalted him to his own right hand as Prince and Savior that he might give repentance and forgiveness of sins to Israel. We are witnesses of

these things, and so is the Holy Spirit, whom God has given to those who obey him."

Acts 5: 29

When the religious leaders heard this, they plotted to kill Peter and the disciples.

The story gets better.

In Acts 5:34 we read:

> ...a Pharisee named Gamaliel, a teacher of the law, who was honored by all the people, stood up in the Sanhedrin and ordered that the men be put outside for a little while. Then he addressed them: 'Men of Israel, consider carefully what you intend to do to these men. Some time ago Theudas appeared, claiming to be somebody, and about four hundred men rallied to him. He was killed, all his followers were dispersed, and it all came to nothing. After him, Judas the Galilean appeared in the days of the census and led a band of people in revolt. He too was killed, and all his followers were scattered. Therefore, in the present case I advise you: Leave these men alone! Let them go! For if their purpose or activity is of human origin, it will fail. But if it is from God, you will not be able to stop these men; you will only find yourselves fighting against God.

His speech persuaded them. They called the apostles in and had them flogged. Then they ordered them not to speak in the name of Jesus, and let them go.

The apostles left the Sanhedrin, rejoicing because they had been counted worthy of suffering disgrace for the Name. Day after day, in the temple courts and from house to house, they never stopped teaching and proclaiming the good news that Jesus is the Christ.

The President and the Pentagon and the entire administration can use the full power of the government and the military and the media to stand against the one true God of love, but ultimately they will fail, as have all others who've gone before.

You can deny Reverend Graham and Tony Perkins their rights to free speech and freedom of religion. You can throw them in jail and flog them. You can persecute and marginalize Christians and promote other belief systems, giving them preferential treatment, but ultimately the sovereign Lord of the universe will prevail.

Historically, the greater the persecution, the greater the growth and influence of Christianity. This is why Peter and the disciples rejoiced when they were beaten and released. They had seen the power of God work many times, and they were seeing it again.

Fighting God is a losing battle: loving him the ultimate victory.

THE NEW INQUISITION AND THE ASSAULT ON LIBERTY

May 7, 2010

> We tell ourselves that religion and reason are incompatible, but in fact the opposite is the case. It was Christianity and the Hebrew Bible that gave us our concepts of reason, progress and an orderly world-the foundations of science and modernity.

So writes Melanie Phillips in her new book *The World Turned Upside Down: The Global Battle over God, Truth and Power*, Encounter Books, 2010.

Phillips, joining such powerhouses as C.S. Lewis, J.R.R. Tolkien, and Francis Schaeffer, argues for a return to Western religious and moral principles; otherwise we face the loss of liberty itself. She calls for a renewed intellectualism that is truly diverse and tolerant.

Intellectuals from a bygone era, when true intellectualism reigned, traced the beginnings of western civilization, and the origins of justice, liberty, reason, and human rights to the application of Judeo-Christian principles as articulated in the Old and New Testaments. Phillips enhances that intellectual tradition, showing the strength of traditional values in building a healthy society and exposing the poison of secular thinking, agreeing in large measure with Dr. Francis Schaeffer, author, teacher, lecturer, and theologian.

Schaeffer, pre-dating Phillips, had pointed things to say about the intellectual life, the relationship between reason and faith, and the trap of relying on human wisdom alone:

> Christianity is the greatest intellectual system the mind of man has ever touched.
>
> If God exists and we are made in his image we can have real meaning, and we can have real knowledge through what he has communicated to us.
>
> Christianity provides a unified answer for the whole of life.
>
> I believe that pluralistic secularism, in the long run, is a more deadly poison than straightforward persecution.

Should any teacher today stand up in a public high school and make such proclamations, however true, he would be branded a dominionist moron and a brown-shirted theocrat. He would be tarred and feathered and run out of town. Just look what happens to scientists who attempt to bring evidence challenging the theories of evolution or man-made global warming. They are hounded, ridiculed, fired, prevented from being published and denied tenure.

Another recent example of the poisoning of the democratic well, the federal government's persecution of Franklin Graham for speaking his mind about Islam. You may have noticed no one challenged his assertions. Rather they held him up for ridicule for violating the law of diversity and committing the sin of intolerance, as if tolerating evil is a virtue. Witness therefore the death of freedom of speech and infringement of the right to conscience. Witness also the government preventing the free exercise of religion, barring Graham from speaking at the Pentagon yesterday as part of the National Day of Prayer while allowing other religious traditions including Islam.

We do not have Socratic dialogue any longer. Instead, we revel in shout downs and sinister forms of persecution to silence any voice of dissent, any voice unwilling to sing in the PC choir. Those who refuse to toe the mark of political correctness are the new heretics.

Enter the totalitarianism of the secular left, the institutionalized persecution of Christians and Jews, what Melanie Phillips calls the new cultural inquisition. Consider this excerpt from a recent column she wrote titled "Welcome to the age of irrationality":

> ...since biblical religion actually underpinned reason and morality, the decline of religion means the erosion of truth and conscience. If religious totalitarianism was rule by the Church and political totalitarianism was rule by the "general will," this is cultural totalitarianism, or rule by the subjective individual.

Phillips describes the irrefutable trend historically. The Roman Church persecuted heretics during the Inquisition, the age of totalitarianism by the church (having nothing to do with Christ, by the way). That was followed by waves of atheistic fascism and communism, the age of political totalitarianism. Today we are seeing the advent of cultural totalitarianism marked by a merciless secularism that demands rigid adherence to PC tenets preached by humanism, environmentalism, socialism, communism, and so-called progressivism, all reliant on human self-sufficiency, human wisdom, human intelligence, all of it falling short for centuries, attributable to the selfish impulse of the subjective individual insisting on collectivism and rejecting any notion of moral absolutes.

Schaeffer would remind us, "...we should note this curious mark of our own age: the only absolute allowed is the absolute insistence that there is no absolute."

And one might add the only absolute floating in the sea of moral relativism is the absolute conviction that all absolutes should commit suicide and thereby submit to that relativism.

Speaking of absolutes, there is a traditional Judeo-Christian teaching reaching back thousands of years that states homosexuality is a sin, also a belief in Islam, and most other faith traditions as well. This is intolerable to the secular mind. The remedy is not the embrace of true pluralism or the Judeo-Christian response of loving the sinner while hating the sin. The "remedy" in the secular mind is the eradication of religion and anyone who stands in the way, ordinarily Christians and religious Jews. Curiously, Muslims get a pass even as they stone and hang homosexuals in various places around the world.

Relativism rules, absolutely.

Phillips' "subjective individual" determines what is right and wrong for himself and insists that determination be right or wrong for the whole of society. The radical, activist minority demands free will, denying it to others. Leftists and anarchists are justified demonstrating violently. Tea Party people demonstrate peacefully but are condemned with lies they proceed violently. As Phillips says, it is an upside-down world.

Thus you have, as reported by Phillips, a Christian pastor arrested in Great Britain recently for violating anti-discrimination laws.

He was preaching about sin and included mention of homosexuality along with a list of other sins. Because he is alleged to have caused "distress," he was arrested.

(Note: Muslims in England take to the streets regularly, promoting assassination and engaging real hate speech, but they are left alone. Let a Christian guy talk about sin and salvation, and, well, we can't have that can we?)

We have our version of such things here in America. Thanks to Obama's hate crimes agenda, you will soon see people arrested and prosecuted for causing "distress" through the teaching of historic Christianity. You will also see churches and Christian schools forced to hire practicing homosexuals, but, as with mandatory healthcare, Muslims will be granted exemptions, and the double standard will march on the PC choir raising praises to secularism, justice be damned.

Atheists and homosexual activists cheer this kind of thing, not realizing that the power of the state, once employed to nullify the freedom of one kind of person, can easily reset its sights on any kind of person, that freedom denied one can easily be denied all. Nonetheless, the cheers resound, so long as the "right kinds of people" are being arrested.

Jews, too, again?

"Certainly not," you say, "We have advanced from the dark days of the gulag and the concentration camp." Have we? Or have we only replaced those mechanisms with human rights commissions and other boards of inquisition, such as the departments of Homeland Security and Defense and Justice?

In the end, there are only two ways to organize society. One requires the force of government, the use of the bayonet, and the sheer power of the state to maintain order. The other relies of the virtue of individuals looking out for each other. It is a matter of where you place emphasis.

The force of government power to maintain order relies on human wisdom.

The virtue of the objective individual depends on divine inspiration.

The one brings tyranny, the other freedom. We must choose very soon, for we are standing at the edge of the abyss.

And Phillips makes this final compelling point:

> Of course, true prejudice and bigotry are wrong, whether towards homosexuals or anyone else. But the decent impulse to protect the rights of gay people is very different from trying to destroy the bedrock values of our society. Yet, that is precisely what it has become. As a result, Britain is turning from a liberal Christian country—whose liberalism is rooted in its religious tradition—into an illiberal, oppressive secular state with no room for religious conscience. Under the camouflage of human rights, this is the way freedom dies.

And finally, compelling thoughts on the subject of absolutes, morality and the preservation of liberty from American intellectual giants:

> To preserve the government we must also preserve morals. Morality rests on religion; if you destroy the foundation, the superstructure must fall. When the public mind becomes vitiated and corrupt, laws are a nullity and constitutions are waste paper.
>
> Daniel Webster

> We have no government armed in power capable of contending in human passions unbridled by morality and religion... Our Constitution was made only for a moral and religious people. It is wholly inadequate to the government of any other.
>
> President John Adams

> Among the most inestimable of our blessings, also, is that... of liberty to worship our Creator in the way we think most agreeable to His will; a liberty deemed in other countries incompatible with good government and yet proved by our experience to be its best support.
>
> President Thomas Jefferson, 1807

> One of the amendments to the Constitution... expressly declares that "Congress shall make no law respecting an establishment of religion, or prohibiting the free exercise thereof, or abridging the freedom of speech, or of the press," thereby guarding in the same sentence and under the same words, the freedom of religion, of speech, and of the press; insomuch that whatever violates either throws down the sanctuary which covers the others.
>
> President Thomas Jefferson, 1798

So the ACLU is, after all, anti-American, by design. It's not about separating church from state: it's about throwing down the sanctuary.

From Discoverthenetworks.org, "Roger Baldwin, founder of the ACLU":

Reflecting on his early years as the ACLU's Executive Director, Baldwin candidly revealed his original motives and objectives: 'I am for socialism, disarmament, and ultimately, for abolishing the state itself as an instrument of violence and compulsion. I seek social ownership of property, the abolition of the properties class, and sole control of those who produce wealth. Communism is the goal. It all sums up into one single purpose' the abolition of dog-eat-dog under which we live. I don't regret being part of the communist tactic. I knew what I was doing. I was not an innocent liberal. I wanted what the communists wanted and I traveled the United Front road to get it.'

BUM RUSHING LIMBAUGH

May 12, 2010

Bum Rush: To run full speed into somebody and body slam them into a brick wall. Getting forcibly ejected. Hurrying someone out of a place.

Sure, he is bombastic. Yes, he can be sarcastic. Frequently his parodies are biting. Admittedly Rush Limbaugh is a take-no-prisoners conservative commentator whose remarkable career has influenced millions of people, a man the left hates with a vengeance.

And now the vengeance is forming up in the halls of power as it has for a long while in the mainstream media.

Rush Limbaugh almost single-handedly established talk radio and alternative media. His enormous success was earned in the trenches. He contributed more than anyone to diversity in media. But now "diversity czars" in the executive branch and elsewhere ready their bouncers to bum rush Limbaugh, all in the name of fairness, of course; freedom of speech and press be damned.

First get a load of Chris Matthews on MSNBC: "If you don't challenge Rushbo and come on this show we're gonna nail you." This was his recent challenge to all Republican candidates, insisting they appear on *Hardball* to tell everyone why they disagree with Rush. During the rant Matthews accused Rush of lies, misrepresentations, and distortions. Of course, Matthews offered no details.

(Attribution? Substantiation? We don't need no stinkin' substantiation!)

It is such a glaring attempt to skewer Republicans by misrepresenting Limbaugh that it is amazing Matthews gets away with it. The only explanation is two-dimensional: the powers that be at MSNBC are Alinskyites just like Matthews, and the *Hardball* audience is brain dead.

This kind of media mosh pit is commonplace. Comically, Limbaugh's critics try to slam him, using some of his techniques, but they fall embarrassingly short every time. Rarely does the pupil exceed the master.

Annoying enough are people like Saul Matthews and the slander/ridicule machine kick started by reprobates like Bill Maher and Rachel Maddow. More troubling is the Obama headhunt to bum rush Limbaugh. Fresh from calling average American demonstrators tea baggers the chief executive recently slammed Limbaugh referencing masturbation.

The NY Post today reported:

> When President Obama was asked if he would play a round of golf with his talk-radio nemesis Rush Limbaugh, the response, relayed by a top Democrat, was: "Limbaugh can go play with himself."

Recall in early April when Obama accused Limbaugh of fomenting violence by using inflammatory rhetoric, the same tactic Bill Clinton used to attack conservatives in the 1990s in the wake of the Oklahoma City bombing. No doubt Bill and Barack have been putting their heads together. The strategy: demonize Republicans by claiming Rush is their leader. Forget that Rush has been as critical of Republicans as he has Democrats.

Still not convinced Obama has Limbaugh in his crosshairs?

Consider the president's hand-picked operative over at the FCC, the 'diversity czar,' whose ideas about freedom of speech and press exalt the likes of Hugo Chavez. Obviously, if diversity czar Mark Lloyd can stifle conservative talk radio, there's no need for congressional action on the unfairness doctrine.

Furthermore, Obama's Supreme Court nominee has similar ideas about free speech and freedom of the press. The banner headline on *Drudge* today titled 'Kagan argued for Gov't 'Redistribution of Speech,' ' is so popular, traffic shut down the server.

Essentially, Kagan has written the Supreme Court should consider first and foremost the motive behind government action limiting speech, that the effect is secondary: 'The government,' she concludes, 'may not express its disfavor with an opinion or speaker by burdening them with restrictions or prohibitions, *unless* it can show that their speech is causing *some type of public harm*." *Translation: if we determine certain speech is politically incorrect, we can justify shutting it down.*

If these people have their way, speech will not be free, it will be subject to government approval.

So the fix is in: Obama's strategy to bum rush Limbaugh marshals the power of bureaucracy legislating by decree (Lloyd at FCC), the public attack campaign Obama is coordinating with MSNBC, and a future judicial assault to be led by Kagan. As back up, perhaps Pelosi can hold on long enough to railroad the unfairness doctrine before Obama is run outta town on a rail in 2012.

Politically, Matthews and Obama believe they can rally their Alinsky base by attacking conservatives and engaging personal insult, but they fail to understand three basic realities: the voters want issue-oriented debate, they are turned off by negative campaigning, and they are weary of liberal BS, furious about irresponsible tax-and-spend policies paving the road to ruin.

No amount of bum rushing talk radio conservatives will turn the tide of the tsunami poised to break over Obama and his cronies in November. It seems apparent people have decided they want traditional American equality not European notions of fairness; they want justice and opportunity not equal outcomes through government programs to redistribute misery.

Speaking of fairness, it would be great to see Limbaugh take on Matthews and Maher and Maddow all at once. As Rush would say, it would have to be a three-to-one situation just to make it fair, but to ensure fairness, he'd engage with half his brain tied behind his back.

Limbaugh is one of the strongest leaders of the opposition, the grandfather of the Tea Party, and that's why, in Obama's mind, he must be destroyed. Matthews is glad to help, tingling all the way. Never forget Matthews declared on Morning Joe, MSNBC, Nov. 6, 2008, he considers it his job to make sure Obama is successful, causing Joe to ask, 'Aren't you a journalist?'

In the end this is a fight about the soul and future of the country, whether we will salvage freedom and our republican form of government or succumb to the collectivist, statist impulse of Alinsky's control freak flying monkeys, both in the White House and throughout government and media today.

FRIEND OF THE WORLD, ENEMY OF GOD: THE CHURCH IN AMERICA

May 20, 2010

I am a Christian, and I'm outraged by what passes for church in America. It sounds like a gross generalization, but consider the reasons. It sickens me to realize the church triumphant, once a powerful force for righteousness, goodness and justice, has become a whipped puppy, a tool of secularism and the world, a disgrace, a soiled bride, a false sanctuary, an empty promise.

The church Christ established has three jobs: evangelism and discipleship and taking a stand for righteousness.

How many people got saved in your church last Sunday? How many of your members are walking the walk? Does the power of the Holy Spirit drive your Kleenex budget through the roof? Is the carpet at the altar worn out from people hitting their knees? When was the last time you witnessed a miracle of healing or deliverance? Can you name the last time sacrificial giving put the budget in the black so much there was surplus enough to go the extra mile? When was the last time you had a voter registration drive in your church? When was the last time you heard a sermon about moral decline leading to same sex marriage, abortion, and child trafficking?

I have listened to sermons for 25 years. For the most part, I've heard seminars on how to get along with people, large counseling sessions about how to manage sin. What I needed to hear: fiery sermons about how Christ *crucifies* sin.

Oh, we talk a good game. We say we're all about passion for the Kingdom. We claim we are broken hearted for the lost. Yet we call sin a lifestyle and stand by quietly while people disease themselves and get carted off to hell, afraid to say anything according to the Word, lest we 'offend' someone, lest we be called names. Did not the Name above all names get much worse for taking a stand? Churches ordain shameless sinners and we call it enlightenment. The LORD calls it an abomination. Are we not called to take a stand?

People inside the church sin openly and no one says a word.

Welfare, once considered a reproach, is now regarded an inalienable right, even in the church: the government as robber baron called the heart of the Gospel. Government-mandated redistribution of wealth, including the destruction of self-determination in healthcare, is the new measure of spiritual authenticity: the government insisting we embrace godless Marxism in order to demonstrate godliness, the height of bizarre. And the church goes along without a whimper, stepping aside, allowing secularism to define spirituality.

Illegality is endorsed by sanctuary churches partnering with lawlessness in the promotion of illegal immigration and the stirring of racial strife calling it the heart of Christ. The president of Mexico during a recent state visit hails lawlessness and condemns Arizona to the applause of half the house and the president while the speaker insists Catholics get on board, and if anyone objects, he is condemned a racist, an anti-Christ.

Our children are overwhelmed by techno-driven depravity and perversion and the sickest practices imaginable, and all we do is click our remotes and eat junk food. High school students bully other students to suicide and we yawn and say isn't that tragic. My twelve-year-old knows the definition of "tea bagging." Until last week I was ignorant of what "hot pocket" means. My teen-aged daughter clued me in, and I almost vomited. Children use the F word in Christian schools, daily, and the adults wander around as if all is well. Government-funded promotion of homosexuality finds favor in public schools and parents can't even be bothered to question it.

Fatherlessness, divorce, broken homes, youth in rebellion and the demoralization of an entire society can be directly attributed to weakness in the church. When was the last time you heard a word about these matters from the pulpit?

We listen to a man (and his 'pastor') slander our LORD and denigrate our faith, then vote him president, or fail to vote, fearing a 'no' vote will cast us racist. Now comes word this president will leverage the EPA and enjoin churches to promote energy policy without regard for Congress, thus making the church complicit in the deconstruction of our constitutional republic.

On top of all that we are urged to go 'green' and spiritualize environmental radicalism, giving that false agenda more prominence than preaching the true Gospel. We are forced to become worldly, forced by worldliness in government, and we acquiesce, worshipping the creation, not the Creator.

Fearing their own congregations, pastors refuse to speak to the issues of the day, claiming 'political discourse' is divisive when the truth is, preaching the truth has always been divisive, the work of the courageous, not the compliant and faint-hearted. The Gospel is an offense. Did Christ come to make peace with evil, to compromise with sin, or did He come to utterly destroy them, all to set us free?

Every day in America we kill 3,700 unborn human beings. Every hour, in America, 154 unborn human beings are murdered in their mothers' wombs: 2.5 killed every minute. In a year, we murder one million three hundred fifty thousand five hundred little babies, without shedding a tear. And when our government takes our money to pay for it, we become accessories to the holocaust, raising not one word of objection. At least 50 million little souls sacrificed on the altar of worldly convenience in the last 36 years, and a nation's conscience, so seared, does not even bother to mourn. Dumpsters overflowing with little body parts ignored in the dark alleys of our emaciated souls.

What do we hear from the pulpit?

Silence.

Dr. Tiller would never have been gunned down in a church had his pastor confronted his sin. His killer might never have become a murderer had his pastor confronted him.

The fury of God's judgment will be poured out on those who murder little children, a judgment by the very One who made them, not intending they be burnt offerings to the god of this world.

The federal government resembles King George III more and more, exercising unlawful power to squander and bankrupt and tax and usurp and exploit and suppress and oppress, but Christian leaders bite their tongues, fearing the loss of tax exempt status, a faithless capitulation to tyranny: the timid and the passive causing the Founders, the saints and fallen patriots nothing but grief.

Money changers and tax collectors and false teachers overwhelm the temple and if Christ were to drive them out with a whip today he would be crucified on MSNBC to the applause of the National Council of Churches, the White House and the NEA.

Islamic radicals murder women and children and promise our annihilation, and what is our reply? We call for tolerance and submission, retreat and surrender. Where are the Christian soldiers in the ranks at home? Where are the leather-lunged preachers of old calling sin, sin, damning evil in our time? Where is the recognition that engaging self-defense is no sin, that the confrontation of evil is virtuous, even a calling?

Who first spoke out about the sin of oppression, the excesses of the Crown, the sin of slavery, the sin of economic exploitation, the sin of drunkenness and adultery, or the sin of child labor? Christ himself, and Spirit-filled pastors and apostles and evangelists and teachers, that's who!

But, you say, it is not spiritual to rock the boat. We cannot wage this kind of war and still be called peacemakers, you say. I say: why not?

Sometimes, as much as we hate it, the only way to make peace is to wage war. John the Baptist certainly understood that truth, the one Christ called the greatest among men. The Baptist called out the king for his immorality and the king chopped off his head. Abraham understood the reality that sometimes one is forced to wage war in order to make peace. He took up arms to save his family. Moses understood this reality as did Gideon and Joshua and David and Solomon and all the Prophets, as does our Lord, as did the Apostles. Our God-inspired Founding Fathers certainly understood that reality.

"Do not suppose that I have come to bring peace to the earth. I did not come to bring peace, but a sword," declares Jesus Christ in Matthew 10:34.

A literal sword? Sometimes. But for him, rather, and his ministers, the sword of the Word and of the Spirit, spoken by the Word, the Word that convicts the world of sin, leading to repentance, the Word that vanquishes evil and silences the father of lies, the Word that confronts evil, even when it is found in those considered authoritative and praiseworthy.

Pastors in America: your Lord is calling you out! He is calling you to reclaim your heritage. He is commanding you to man up, step out, and fit the battle. The Word is calling you to preach the Word without apology or compromise!

Do you want to stop the mass murder called abortion? Preach against evil.

Would you stunt the growth of radical Islam and turn the wolf from the door? Preach the Gospel.

Do you desire to save our children from perversion and depravity? Preach the Gospel.

Would you put government in its place and encourage vibrant American citizenship based on the Founders' vision? Preach the Gospel, the very Gospel that breathed life into that vision!

Are you concerned about economic deprivation that hits the poor most cruelly? Preach the Gospel.

Is your shepherd's heart desire the healing of families and marriages? Preach the Gospel.

If you want to see people saved and sanctified, preach the Gospel, for God's sake, preach the Gospel!

In many respects compromise is the worse of sins for it denies the power of God and encourages others to sin.

May God forgive us for our sin, and may He bless those pastors who have stayed the course without compromise all these years, for they have borne the burden. They have the stripes to show for it, and in that, they have suffered with Christ as few ever have, or ever will.

Therefore, great is their reward, and great our shame if we fail to follow the One inspiring them to love and good deeds.

* Horatius Bonar, 19th Century Scottish pastor and poet, often wrote against the worldliness that he perceived was creeping into the church. If he was concerned about it in his day, how much more should we be alarmed today when the difference between the Church and the world is hardly noticeable. It is important for those who profess a love for Christ to understand that friendship with the world is enmity with God. Bonar published this little piece in The Christian Treasury as a help for his readers to remember the importance of our fight against the world and to remain diligent in our watch for worldliness.

Love Not the World — Why?

Because the gain of it is the loss of the soul.—Matthew 16:25.
Because its friendship is enmity to God.—James 4:4.
Because it did not know Christ.—John 1:10; 17:25.
Because it hates Christ.—John 7:7; 15:18.

Because the Holy Spirit has forbidden us.—1 John 2:15.
Because Christ did not pray for it.—John 17:9.
Because Christ's people do not belong to it.—John 17:16.
Because it will not receive the Spirit.—John 14:27.
Because its Prince is Satan.—John 13:31; 16:11.
Because Christ's kingdom is not of it.—John 18:36.
Because its wisdom is foolishness.—1 Corinthians 1:20.
Because its wisdom is ignorance.—1 Corinthians 1:21.
Because Christ does not belong to it.—John 8:23.
Because it is condemned.—1 Corinthians 11:32.
Because the fashion of it passeth away.—1 Corinthians 7:31.
Because it slew Christ.—James 5:6; Matthew 21:39.
Because it is crucified to us.—Galatians 6:14.
Because we are crucified to it.—Galatians 6:14.
Because it is the seat of wickedness.—2 Peter 1:4; 1 John 5:19.
Because its God is the evil one.—2 Corinthians 4:4.
'Love not the world! It cannot be your home,
Thy fatherland must be the world to come;
There lay up treasures for eternity;
And where thy treasure is thy heart shall be.'

—H.B.

MEMORIAL DAY MEMORIES

May 28, 2010

> Greater love has no one than this: that he lay down his life for his friends.
>
> John 15:13

I was just a high school kid when the news came Pacheco had been killed in Vietnam. My dad, a WWII vet, took me to the memorial service. We said a prayer when the news came Tibbits had also been killed over there.

Dad never said much about WWII. When he did talk about it, he only talked about all the fine young boys who lost their lives, his dear friends. Then he would tear up and excuse himself.

My best friend's dad served with honor in the South Pacific where so many died. Roger Jamieson is at rest with all his fallen comrades, including his cousin, so many young men who never got a chance to enjoy life to the fullest.

When my son marched off to Iraq, my heart melted. There is no experience quite like fearing for your son's life, praying at three in the morning, knowing he is facing death in a hellhole thousands of miles away.

We were fortunate. Ian came home, wounded, but in one piece.

The Glimpse family, however, mourned the loss of Marcus. The Jones family mourned the loss of Derek. The Higgins family mourned the loss of James. Others came home seriously wounded, and the Crabtree and the Jones families rallied with others in the community to come along side their sons, to honor the service of brave young men and women willing to serve the rest of us and protect us.

Americans have always been on the front lines, fighting for freedom and justice, always in defense of country, always in defense of goodness and virtue. And when the fighting was done, we have always felt it our duty to reach out to former enemies in the spirit of reconciliation, forgiveness and love, working to help them rebuild even as we welcomed their refugees as new American citizens.

This Memorial Day, each of us should take time with friends and family to think long and hard about the blessings of liberty delivered to us by those willing to die on our behalf.

Think about the 2.2 million Americans who've been killed and wounded in freedom's cause. Think about the millions of friends and relatives, wives and husbands, and little kids who've lost loved ones during the last 234 years.

And give thanks.

> With malice toward none, with charity for all,... let us strive on to finish the work we are in,... to do all which may achieve and cherish a just and lasting peace among ourselves and with all nations.
>
> Abraham Lincoln, Second Inaugural Address,
> Mar. 4, 1865 Sixteenth president of
> United States (1809–1865)

OBAMACARE: ADD SENIOR CITIZENS TO ENDANGERED SPECIES LIST

June 8, 2010

> But we have to pass the bill so that you can find out what is in it, away from the fog of the controversy.
>
> House Speaker Nancy Pelosi

Well, it passed and we are starting to see what's in it and what it means for the country, especially for senior citizens. Obamacare is only the acknowledged first step in nationalizing the entire healthcare industry, but already financial experts don't see a way to stop the bleeding. Costs will soar. Quality care will diminish. Access will shrink.

The 940-billion-dollar patchwork plan supposedly designed to cover about eight million people without health insurance will probably drive that many seniors out of the system according to one analysis. And the 940-billion-dollar figure is only the beginning.

In the first decade, try on upwards of three trillion dollars for size, according to the Congressional Budget office cited in this Weekly Standard story, March 18, 2010, by Jeffrey H. Anderson:

Based on earlier incarnations of the proposed overhaul, the total costs would be about a third higher (the exact number can't be gleaned from the CBO's analysis, which is only preliminary and is not a full scoring)—making the total price-tag between $2.5 and $3 trillion over the bill's real first decade.

How would we pay for all of this? According to the CBO, by diverting $1.1 trillion away from already barely-solvent Medicare and spending it on Obamacare, and by increasing taxes on the American people by over $1 trillion.

Remember all those people who expressed worry about *rationed care,* translation: *death panels?* What fools they were, we were told. What lunatics to even suggest the US government led by the benevolent one would seriously consider restricting care to anyone for any reason! Obama's own actuary points the accusing finger:

> In Medicare, the results of the new law will be disastrous. Obamacare will cut payments to the private insurance component of the program (called Medicare Advantage, or MA) by nearly $200 billion over ten years. The chief actuary of the program says this cut will eventually drive 7 million seniors' many with low-incomes' out of the plan they would prefer to enroll in. And it will mean thousands of dollars in benefit reductions for every MA enrollee, beginning next year. These seniors won't be silenced with patronizing and one-time checks. In addition, the new law imposes arbitrary price cutting for all manner of Medicare services, which the chief actuary says will harm access to care by forcing scores of institutions to stop taking Medicare beneficiaries.
>
> James Capretta, ObamaCareWatch,
> June 6, 2010, Politicio

Don't believe only one source?

President Obama's nominee to head Medicare and Medicaid under Obamacare is an open advocate of the British National Health Services'

NICE (National Institute of Clinical Excellence) and its methods of rationing care.

The left is furious with Obama and the Dems for failing to get the public option and for failing to put private insurers out of business. The right is furious with Obama and the Dems for wasting tax dollars on a boondoggle that will increase costs, lessen care, and drive doctors out of the profession. And the voters are furious with Obama and the Dems for running up debt and forcing a bureaucrat between patient and doctor.

November should be quite a spectacle. Meanwhile, many forces are hard at work to get Obamacare repealed or ruled unconstitutional before the patient bleeds out red ink.

THE POWER OF POSITIVE POLITICS

June 11, 2010

It is difficult to be positive in an increasingly negative world driven darker by instant access to news. On the other hand, the more negative the environment, the more attractive become those who promote a positive outlook.

This was the genius of Franklin D. Roosevelt and Ronald Reagan. When it comes to thinking about glowing examples of the power of positive politics, these two shine incomparably.

They knew a precious secret: one is either driven under by circumstances, or one takes the lead and drives circumstances in new directions; one is either enslaved by situations, or one takes the situation in hand and masters it.

How is this for one of the most powerful, positive statements by any politician, ever?

> I know in my heart that man is good. That what is right will always eventually triumph. And there's purpose and worth to each and every life.
>
> Ronald Reagan

If this man truly believed this, and those closest to him confirm it, then this has to be one of the greatest set of core values guiding any successful politician, that is, if the greatest good for the greatest number is the goal.

Here is another Reagan gem:

> Life is one grand, sweet song, so start the music.

Consider these statements by President Franklin D. Roosevelt:

> Happiness lies in the joy of achievement and the thrill of creative effort.

> Human kindness has never weakened the stamina or softened the fiber of a free people. A nation does not have to be cruel to be tough.

Both men possessed a glittering sense of humor as well.

> No matter what time it is, wake me, even if it's in the middle of a Cabinet meeting.

> Politics is supposed to be the second oldest profession. I have come to realize that it bears a very close resemblance to the first.
>
> Reagan

> I'm not the smartest fellow in the world, but I can sure pick smart colleagues.

> Remember you are just an extra in everyone else's play.
>
> Roosevelt

Both leaders shared generous portions of positivity and humor. And they shared a common faith that engendered those qualities.

Wouldn't it be great if we had more of these characteristics in abundance in the political class today?

Parting shot, great advice:

Be interesting, be enthusiastic... and don't talk too much.

Norman Vincent Peale

GOVERNANCE BY BAYONET

June 17, 2010
What people feared most is unfolding before our eyes at a pace no one imagined. Americans are increasingly anxious about the future for their children and grandchildren, viewing the implosion in Europe a foretaste of America's future. The vast majority think the president is upside down when it comes to the economy and energy. In every category the president's numbers are horrendous.

The chief executive is operating outside the rule of law in opposition to majority sentiment. And just how is the president operating outside the rule of law?

Without congressional action or a court ruling, forcing BP to establish a fund for spill reparations and damages initiated and managed solely by the executive branch, an unprecedented, illegal action defying the rule of law, using the threat of criminal prosecution by DOJ to acquire 'voluntary' compliance. What's that, you say? Obama has received more campaign contributions from BP than any other politician in history? Read all about it: 'Obama biggest recipient of BP cash,' Politico, by Erika Lovley, May 5, 2010)

Another example of the tendency to operate outside the rule of law: skirting Congress using the EPA to institute cap-and-trade regulations. And the connection to BP in view of pending cap and trade legislation?

"It's been widely reported that a major part of the Kerry-Lieberman bill was essentially written by BP," said Senate Minority Leader Mitch McConnell (Repbulican, Kentucky) in a floor speech late last week. "This is clearly an inconvenient fact: An administration that seems to spend most of its time coming up with new ways to show how angry it is with BP is pushing a proposal that BP helped write."

We all know how Obamacare passed by hook and crook. Mitt Romney in March said Obama has betrayed his oath.

Even Rachel Maddow accuses the president of an unconstitutional power grab, referencing his intention to use indefinite detentions in the war on terror, the fear being the government might eventually use such detentions against American citizens.

Pass the bayonets, please, and ignore the rabble.

DEPTHS OF MORAL AND FINANCIAL BANKRUPTCY

June 28, 2010

The rapidity of change combined with false assumptions and an errant worldview spell moral and financial bankruptcy thanks to the 'leadership' of Barack Obama.

When it comes to economics, Obots have fallen from the heights in very short order. Not long ago they were heralded visionaries; the enlightened new guard, bringing fairness and greenish egalitarianism to an exploited world, an egalitarianism they believed provided them the moral high ground to install socialism even at the point of a bayonet. Flying full in the face of human nature and denying the absolute connection between God and any altruistic impulse, Obots inevitably resort to the bayonet, for no one in his right mind willingly submits to slavery, and no one without God can conjure real altruism.

The proof came with the unavoidable results of Obamanomics: debt, currency crisis, recession leading to depression, high unemployment, enormous growth of government, demoralization, despair.

For many decades American youth were brainwashed in college to believe capitalism was inherently unfair, even vicious, the very capitalism that established the universities and prosperity enabling them to access 'higher' education, a post-Christian education that taught them to hate everything good about their own country. The university served up a worldview detached from the realities of life, bathed in the utopian dreams of Marx, Lenin, and Engels. During those same decades, foreign infiltration and propaganda partnered with the work of radicals on campus, and still it wasn't enough to thoroughly destroy Lady Liberty.

America won the Cold War, Eastern Europe was liberated, conservatism enjoyed resurgence in America, and China and the Soviet Union acknowledged the limitations of collectivism, the down side of mass murder, and the blessings of free markets.

The Europeans have come to realize BHO is a schoolboy without credibility, and they too have turned from the abyss of massive public debt and run away entitlements, their cherished soft socialism proven bankrupt, for a time sustained by American productivity.

Still, a reactionary remnant continues the collectivist chant, finding a favorite son in Barack Obama and his Obots, all still stuck in the past.

Combining communism and environmentalism to convince people they are most benevolent, Obots peddle an agenda of hope and change, nothing more than a repackaging of every other godless, anti-American, tyrannical movement that has gone before, seducing people into believing they can trust raw, unchecked power in the hands of wild-eyed ideologues spouting soft and pleasing platitudes about delivering the down trodden and halting the rape of Mother Nature.

It was, and always is, a picture painted of utopia, a utopia possible by sheer human will, perfection achieved only by destroying traditional Americanism deemed the root of all evil when in truth Americanism remains the root of all that is good in the world, the only force in the world sufficient to withstand the combined evils of Nazi Germany, Imperial Japan, Maoist China, Stalinist Russia and assorted other, lesser henchmen, including Mugabe, Castro, Chavez, Ahmadinejad, and Kim Jung Il.

Do not hold out hope for change in Congress or the White House or the halls of the UN. Facts and developments, proof and persuasion do not influence these ideologues. Obots claim an exclusive romance with the scientific method and routinely cheat on her. Despite monumental failures by BHO and his minions in almost every department imaginable in only eighteen months, this president and his pals are hell bent on driving the final nails in the coffin of Americanism, even if it means a return to the gulag and the concentration camp and their own destruction, the very definition of fanaticism.

This then is their blind fanaticism combined with rank inexperience and a prideful hatred of tradition, traditions proven worthy of respect for centuries: Republican government based on the idea rights are God-given and all are created equal.

Denying God and proven methods of self-governance, Obots everywhere prove daily the proverb: "There is a way that seems right to a man, but in the end it leads to death" (Prov. 14:12).

The trouble is Obots are dragging us all down to new depths of moral and financial bankruptcy unless we intervene. We have four months to work, argue, persuade, and then vote, for it has been said rightly this election is the most important in all of human history. On its results depend the future of freedom and goodness.

BARACK'S BIG BLUFF: PLAYING POKER WITH THE AMERICAN PEOPLE

June 29, 2010

Professional wrestlers don't complain about the methods they use to draw crowds. Box office is the thing.

Hookers don't complain about their professional tactics. Johns are the thing.

Why then does Obama complain about politics? Voters are the thing, as he well knows, unless, of course, elections can be manipulated, and then, citizens become sheep.

BHO, a hybrid political operative groomed since adolescence, has about as much right to complain about politics as wrestlers and hookers do their professions, for he has much in common: he is in the game, and the game is all about seduction, manipulation, and putting up false fronts.

Obama's recent remarks at the G20 in Toronto reveal his deep alienation from the American people, his growing combative posture driven by that disconnect, and his hypocritical whining about political opposition. How can such a smart man miss the writing on the wall, actually participating in his own demise?

Promising to escalate his unpopular activism after the November elections, he said in Toronto,

...when I start presenting some very difficult choices to the country, I hope some of these folks who are hollering about deficits and debt step up because I'm calling their bluff. And we'll see how much of that- how much of the political arguments they're making right now are real and how much of it was just politics. All right?

Obviously, Obama is thinking about certain Republicans and Tea Party people when he sneeringly refers to "these folks." Condescendingly, he dismisses legitimate concerns about deficits and debt, actually hoping we believe protesters are only "bluffing." What disdain he displays for the majority of people, refusing to acknowledge that many in the opposition reside in his own party!

"...when I start presenting some very difficult choices..."

The man does not present choices. Rather, he dictates "solutions," and a clear majority of people believe his "solutions" actually aggravate problems intentionally.

Furthermore, he oozes arrogance. Is it presidential to attack your own people on the world stage? Of course not. Yet that is Obama's well-established pattern. However, on one point he is right: we shall see just how fed up the people have become.

We'll see in November who is all bluff and who actually holds the winning hand. My bet is on the native intelligence and common sense of the people. They know Washington and this administration are so corrupt the power brokers will do most anything to keep the ball rolling, so they are watching, very carefully, and preparing to run the crooks out of town.

The president as quintessential politician decries politics. The big bluffer accuses others of bluffing, then bluffs some more, fearing November.

For your information, Mr. Obama, the majority of Americans are deeply alarmed you have taken us down to a place of horrendous debt. It took 232 years—from 1776 to 2008—for us to run up five trillion dollars in debt. You have tripled that in eighteen months, yet you have the gall to talk about the concerns of average, hard-working Americans as bluff?

Be assured the people will "step up."

And for anyone interested, it's not only Tea Party people crying foul. World leaders and all the finance chiefs at the G20 agree: public debt is as toxic as oil in the gulf. Obama appears unwilling to stem either tide. The more dispersant he sprays, the higher the toxicity.

"Never let a good crisis go to waste," echoes the voice of Saul Alinsky in Obama's inner ear, an ear attuned only to the voices of other Alinskyites: Emanuel, Pelosi, Clinton, Reid.

"Pride goes before destruction, a haughty spirit before a fall" (Prov. 16:18).

WHY DO THEY SAY OBAMA IS ANTI-AMERICAN?

July 2, 2010

> ... *a tyrant... unfit to be a ruler of a free people.*
> Declaration of Independence,
> referencing King George III

Before anyone can make evaluations about what is or is not American, a definition of Americanism must be agreed upon, restricting the discussion to the American form of government for our purposes here.

As far as the founders were concerned, our constitutional republic was established to limit the size and power of government so as to protect the rights and freedoms of the people. America is not a democracy: it is a republic. Anyone who works to dismantle the republic is by definition anti-American.

The Constitution was designed to limit government through an ingenious system of checks and balances. Any proposed law must be passed by both houses of Congress and then be signed by the president to become law. If the president vetoes a proposed law, Congress can override him. And in any case, judicial review is in place to determine if laws are 'constitutional,' meaning, essentially, do they pass the test of being put in place according to the terms of the Constitution defining the limitations of government, that is, its proper role again, a matter of protecting rights and freedoms.

Americanism then has been defined by limited government reflecting the will of the people carried faithfully to the legislative table by elected representatives operating faithfully according to their oath to protect and defend the Constitution. Notice the oath taken by elected representatives does not call on them to promise to protect and defend the country but rather the Constitution, upon which the survival of the country depends.

Three other essential realities in the definition of Americanism must be taken into account: (1) according to the Declaration, we have always held that God grants rights and government is established to secure and protect those rights, (2) the individual and his/her right to pursue life, liberty, and happiness must never be subjugated to the group or the masses or some dictator's notion of collective pre-eminence, and (3) the notion of rights and freedoms individually held necessarily demands economic freedom, for the only alternative is government-run economics, which violates the rights of the individual and the concept of limited government.

Therefore, anyone working against the Constitution or diluting its power to protect the rights and freedoms of the people can rightly be identified anti-American. Anyone suggesting that government has the power to take away rights is, by definition, un-American. Anyone who says man is the giver of rights must logically believe that man can take away rights, an anti-American point of view. Anyone who denies the rights of the individual and the pre-eminence of the individual, pushing the notion of collectivism and government control of the economy, is, by definition, anti-American.

It should also be noted that the founders sought to balance power between the states, the people, and the central government, that, indeed, should there be questions of where the emphasis should reside, preference was given the states and the people by the Tenth

Amendment: 'The powers not delegated to the United States by the Constitution, nor prohibited by it to the States, are reserved to the States respectively, or to the people.'

Thomas Jefferson said, "The Tenth Amendment is the foundation of the Constitution."

Obviously, the founders' intent has been turned upside down. We have federal supremacy at every turn. Obama is working feverishly to continue the trend. Take his treatment of and attitude toward the state of Arizona concerning border security as a prime example.

American patriots fought off the British king, contradicting his claim under the doctrine of the 'divine right of kings,' substituting the American idea of the "divine right of individuals." The present regime in Washington would have us return to the divine right of kings.

So how exactly is Mr. Obama anti-American?

Healthcare

There is nothing whatsoever in the Constitution, stated explicitly or by inference, giving the federal government the power to take over entire industries or parts of industries and nothing ever intended by the founders allowing the central government to require individuals to purchase anything, much less health insurance. There is no power granted the government to intervene between doctor and patient, yet all this and more, including expanded taxing authority, is contained in Obamacare. Mr. Obama's penchant for unilaterally taking control of other industries banking, finance, investment houses, automobile, energy' has nothing to do with the office and duties of president, is glaringly unconstitutional, and, therefore, anti-American.

BP Escrow Account

The rule of law requires individuals and companies be governed by law, and if laws are broken, there are legal remedies in place for redress and holding law breakers accountable. Nowhere does the Constitution give the president authority to act outside the law no matter his alleged altruistic or benevolent motives. Indeed, the president's duty is to protect and defend the Constitution and enforce the law, not circumvent it or dilute the rule of law by the raw exercise of unrestrained executive power. Of course BP was glad to set up a twenty-billion-dollar damages fund and pay out immediately—all done without court action or Congressional approval—under threat of Obama's justice department. Kings behave this way, not presidents. (For more, see Ben Stein's column, "Our Caudillo President," American Spectator, June 16, 2010.)

Finance Reform
(Updated December 20, 2010)

This newly passed set of regulations gives the federal government unlimited bailout authority, and it essentially puts the federal government in charge of all banking and investment activity, another unconstitutional exercise of federal power violating the Constitution, on its face anti-American, much like the Federal Reserve system, the central bank that Thomas Jefferson identified as the greatest threat to liberty. Finance reform gives the Federal Reserve even greater powers to oversee lending and regulate other financial transactions.

Immigration Reform

Given Obama's eagerness to exercise raw executive power on many fronts, it should come as no surprise he is actually considering the use of an executive order to provide amnesty to illegal aliens resident in the United States. Should this occur, there will no doubt be many who view it a political move. How better to immediately recruit twelve to twenty million new Democrat voters with the stroke of a pen? Such a maneuver by Obama would obviously be anti-American and unconstitutional, but it would take years to deal with it in the courts or in Congress. Meanwhile, he would achieve his goal of rigging elections

One could go on and on with regard to this administration's stated interest in controlling media and the internet, its willingness to engage preventive detention and even more expansion of entitlements, pursuing gun control and the extra-legislative strategy of using the EPA through administration rules to establish terms of proposed Cap 'n Trade regulations.

When a person becomes president, he takes an oath to protect and defend the Constitution.

Can anyone honestly say this president is holding true to his oath?

THE PEOPLE VERSUS THE POWERFUL

October 1, 2010

The gulf between the people and the powerful widens daily. Developments bring to mind Proverb 28:15: "Like a roaring lion or a charging bear is a wicked ruler over poor people."

"Buck up!" they roar. "You're complainers," they charge. "It would be inexcusable for Democrats to sit out November second," roars the lion, excusing himself from all responsibility of course.

This president and his party, and many who have enabled them, can no longer escape the scrutiny and disdain of the people. The powerful have been found corrupt or complacent, self-serving and scandalous, fatuous failures. The rage of the people has therefore been kindled, a rage building for many months, soon to be poured out.

The people said no to profligate spending and multi-generational debt. The powerful roared and broke the bank, running up more debt in eighteen months than all previous presidents combined.

The people said no to more and more taxation to feed the spending addiction in Washington, and the powerful charged and slashed back at the people, calling them selfish, unpatriotic, even racist, all the while raising taxes more than six hundred billion dollars then claiming no tax was raised, no longer caring they've been found liars time and again.

The people said no to more government power and control. The powerful sneered, curled the lip, and seized more and more control. The lion nationalized the banks and other private industries. The bear took over the healthcare industry and the financial sector and sought control of energy and more control of education.

The people said no to increasing encroachment by the lion and the bear who only charged forward to invade every aspect of private lives even as they squandered our resources, destroyed our relationships around the world, and bowed to tyrants and terrorists, turning their backs on our own men and women in uniform.

And when confronted by the people time and again, the powerful turned and roared ridicule, calling them stupid, ignorant, moronic, swayed by slogans, mesmerized by media, hypnotized by hypocrites, led astray by liars. No longer able to conceal their blatant wickedness, the lion and the bear tried to devour the people, making them poor and forcing their children into deeper poverty.

Yet in America, the people still have the final word. No matter the depths of depravity plumbed by the powerful, no matter the roaring of the lion or the charge of the bear, come November 2, the people will prevail, so long as the powerful are prevented from roaring and charging against free and fair elections.

For if the powerful ever gain control over elections, thus preempting the right of the people to self-governance, the only remedy then will be the right to bear arms, and we ain't lion.

CHRISTIANS: WE ARE TO BLAME!

October 5th, 2010

Christians, who have committed themselves to doing God's will, bear a higher level of responsibility for injustices in America. Much has been given to us, and much will be expected. If we choose not to vote, if we isolate ourselves in a Christian subculture and ignore the injustices around us, if we do not encourage the oppressed, help orphans and widows, or work for a just society, then we will bear a significant measure of the blame for the evils that surround us.

"Voting: Civic Duty *and* Christian Duty?"
by Ken Connor, Human Events, Oct. 11, 2006

Does evil surround us today? The evils of government power run amok and generalized moral decline are evidenced everywhere.

Public money is diverted to fund the murder of babies. Public money is used to promote sexual deviancy. Public money is spent to promote Islam even as it is spent to suppress all things Judeo-Christian.

Public money is spent to convince students they are not created by divine power but rather the accidental result of evolved rodents mating indiscriminately. Public money is spent to convince all of us that the handicapped and the elderly deserve medical care only so long as the government deems it fiscally responsible. Public money is spent urging us to worship the creation rather than the Creator.

Public money is being spent to promote immorality, which creates moral decline, requiring that order be maintained by the bayonet not individual self-control fueled by an embrace of virtue. Thus, the government funds the demise of virtue.

Public money is spent to convince us that dependency on government and the entitlement mentality are preferred to the biblical principle of "don't work, don't eat." In other words, public money is being spent to promote socialism and to destroy capitalism, which means our tax money is being spent to diminish freedom, the bedrock principle of the republic the founders' envisioned.

Public money is spent and public debt is such; we are being driven into bankruptcy while our enemies sharpen their knives, and our friends forsake us. And it's all because Christians decided not to vote in 2006 and 2008 (see Afterword).

If Christians stay away from the polls this November and in 2012, shame on us. We'll have no one to blame but ourselves when the inevitable transpires.

TUESDAY IS NOT ABOUT DIFFERENT OPINIONS ON THE ISSUES

October 31, 2010

The election Tuesday is not just another election.

It is not about Democrats versus Republicans.

It is not about differing opinions on the issues.

It is not about Americans debating different ideas about how to "form a more perfect union."

This election is about much, much more than political parties, opinions, issues, or the collective interest in furthering this experiment in self-government.

Obama and the Democrats want people to believe we are all Americans, believing in the same essential values. They want you to believe this because they are in the business of deceiving people about their real intentions.

During the campaign two years ago, Obama went so far as to say there are no red or blue Americans, just Americans. *He does not believe that*, but he will tell you he believes it so that you will continue to believe the fantasy he is a unifying force. He wants you to believe he is not a radical Marxist. He wants people to believe he really cares about protecting and defending the Constitution even though he denies the very heart of the Constitution and its purpose: to limit government and protect the people from the excesses of government.

The reason Obama and the Dems have fallen so far so fast is the truth has been revealed: they do not believe in the people or the Constitution. Rather, they believe in expanded government power and influence driven by their own narrow ideological agenda to the exclusion of all other considerations, *despotism by any definition.*

They can never sell this stuff up front, so they cloak themselves in patriotism and sow the seeds of socialist domination behind the veneer of patriotism, all in the name of benevolence, of course. Anyone who stands opposed is a racist, an ignoramus, or a divisive Republican obstructionist. That is the cruel and deceitful methodology Alinsky taught Obama. Even as he attacks his opponents with the most underhanded methods, Obama paints himself the great post-racial, post-partisan president, the height of political theatre, smoke and mirrors at its best.

Listen to his words. He is no unifier. He is more than willing to pit white against black to further his own political career and his agenda. He is glad to become the hyper partisan, all the while claiming an embrace of bipartisanship at the same time accusing his opponents of hyper partisanship. (How can Republicans be the party of "no" when they're outgunned on every front?)

Obama leads a party of Democrats who don't have one ounce of integrity simply because they constantly say one thing, and do the opposite.

Examples?

He said during the campaign that tax increases and increased government spending would be the worst thing to do in a recession; then he went right ahead and increased spending and debt to record levels even while he was slipping in tax increases left and right under the radar.

He said they would never allow public money to fund abortions, but that is happening now both at home and abroad.

He said transparency would be his hallmark. Obviously he had no intention of keeping that promise.

He said he would confront special interests and not make backroom deals then did exactly those things to get healthcare passed.

He said he would end the war and scale back domestic surveillance then escalated on both fronts.

What is it called when you say one thing and do another?

What is it called when you claim to embrace Americanism then work to undermine it?

Obama and most Democrats do not believe in our founding principles. They talk about being true Americans, but, in truth, they are anti-American.

If we compare their words and actions to the definition of true Americanism, we see the truth. We can best do that by comparing what they believe to a straightforward definition of Americanism provided by Dennis Prager. (Prageru.com: "Give us five minutes, we'll give you a semester.")

Reach into your pocket. Take out a coin. Read what it says. Every American coin displays the three pillars Americanism. (Prager's three points below with my elaboration.)

1. *E Pluribus Unum:* "from the many, one." People from all over the world have come here to become Americans, not to import their language and customs to this land but to become Americans, to live free and better their lot according to our way of life. Coming here to crowbar one's language and culture violates E Pluribus Unum. It may be the way of multiculturalism, but it is not Americanism. Thus, the Obama/Democrat agenda to multiculturalize this land is anti-American.

2. *Liberty.* We believe in liberty not equality. Americanism has always meant we embrace the idea that government is established to protect liberty and that the government that governs least governs best. (T. Jefferson) At least that is

what the Declaration says and what the Constitution was designed to achieve. It is the uniquely American idea there is an inverse relationship between government and freedom: the less government, the more freedom; the greater the government, the less freedom. Europeans and others believe government should level the playing field, that government should intervene in private lives to engineer equal outcomes. That is the notion of equality provided cradle to grave, a notion promoted by the French revolution and Karl Marx, not the American Revolution and Ben Franklin, as Prager notes. Obamacrats support the idea of equality, not liberty, and, therefore, they are anti-American. We all believe that all people are created equal, but after that, their own success or failure is up to them, not government. Liberty is far superior to the idea of equality because it demands limited government, providing the greatest good for the greatest number.

3. *In God We Trust.* Many years before the American Revolution, colonists believed God had a divine plan to spread the good news of his love throughout the world and that America had a special role to play in that divine plan. However, couched within that early Christian foundation was the idea of grace, that all are welcome at the table, that all should be allowed to follow the dictates of conscience as they thought best, again, the concept of liberty. Therefore, the Judeo-Christian foundation of the nation provided for the most widespread tolerance and acceptance ever known to any human civilization. We have trusted God to promote that freedom and tolerance based on the idea that the Creator is the one who bestows human rights, and, therefore, no human being or human institution can compromise, mute, or destroy those God-given rights. Obamacrats talk a good game about God, but they do not mean the Judeo-Christian God the founders embraced, the God of love and liberty.

The Obamacrat god is a god of works and control, not grace. Tolerance is a nice word, but it is not found operative in application. If you cross an Obamacrat, you will find out just how much grace and tolerance exists: none. Furthermore, notice how control is central to their theology. What have Obamacrats done since 2006? Every move has been made to acquire more power and control over the private lives of Americans. Obamacrats seek control. They trust in themselves and no other. Obamacrats do not trust in God; they trust in themselves, and that is the essential groundwork of tyranny. All autocratic regimes begin with the powerful elite seizing power under the banner of "we know better than you do, and we will act on your behalf, according to our human wisdom to the exclusion of all other considerations." It is a distinctly anti-American point of view. It is also dangerous, lethal to the very foundation of Americanism envisioned by the founders.

To sum up: Americanism asserts E Pluribus Unum; Obamacrats promote the opposite-multiculturalism.

Americanism promotes liberty; Obamacrats insist on control, forcing equality via government intervention, always a prescription for tyranny, just as the founders warned.

Americanism confidently proclaims trust in God; Obamacrats are their own gods, a distinctly anti-American point of view.

Therefore, this election is not about issues or political parties or competing visions of how to form a more perfect union.

Rather, it is about the survival of Americanism itself.

FACT-DRIVEN VOTERS CONFRONT ARROGANCE-DRIVEN ADMINISTRATION

November 2, 2010

Bill Clinton said yesterday this is not a fact-based election. Once again, Mr. Clinton is wrong, on purpose. Let's keep in mind the only reason Mr. Clinton is on the stump is he wants to present the appearance of party loyalty so he can help position his wife to run against Obama in a few months, at least that is one interpretation.

How about a few fact-based reasons the voters are turning out in waves to wash away the stain of liberalism run amok?

The great news of the day is Americans are engaged in the process of self government once again, something liberals hate because it takes them out of the driver's seat. Average citizens from various walks of life are coming together to agree on certain core American values, values not supported by the present administration. Those core American values include:

- limited government
- financial responsibility
- liberty
- strong national defense

- border security
- economic freedom

The present regime is made up of any number of radicals in the judiciary, and the legislative and executive branches, people who believe in opposing "values":

- expanding, intrusive, pervasive government
- increased taxation, spending, and debt
- control
- cowering national defense posture
- lip service to border security and amnesty
- socialism

Those in power are thoroughly out of sync with the majority of the people. That spells b-a-c-k-1 -a-s-h. Thank God the people have a remedy: the secret ballot.

Money issues are driving this election, but there are other considerations.

The people were concerned about spending at the federal level during the Bush years, but in the last two years, concern became alarm then outrage. Looking out a few decades, we see total debt at 118.8 trillion dollars, documented by Dr. David Jeremiah in his new book *The Coming Economic Armageddon*.

Sure, the near-term debt is bad enough, thanks to Obama and the Democrats: twelve trillion dollars. But considering the promises made with regard to Medicare, Social Security, and the Prescription Drug Program (launched under Bush), we are looking at a debt load of 118.8 trillion dollars overall.

That means every single American living today, regardless of age, is in three hundred eighty-three thousand dollars of debt—far more than the cost of an average home. We have effectively saddled our children and grandchildren with insurmountable debt, leaving them in a hopeless situation.

We have a population of 311 million people, about 139 million in the workforce, with high unemployed and 44 million on food stamps. Less than half the population feeds the rest, and Mr. Obama wants to raise taxes on them? (Until recently, Mr. Obama was all about raising taxes and has done so on the middle class, largely through healthcare "reform.") Meanwhile, real unemployment is 19 percent. It is clearly unsustainable. And all of it traceable to liberal policies rammed down the throats of Americans for years: skyrocketing entitlement spending, tax increases and the creation of crushing debt.

Obama and company have already raised taxes about six hundred billion dollars, most of it hidden within the healthcare laws enacted by hook and crook against the will of the people. Obama's proposed tax increases will be horrendous, effectively destroying any chance of economic recovery, as many Democrats readily admit, fearing their party will implode behind this administration's ill-advised policies.

Common sense Americans are wise to the game, furious about the deception from on high, and fired up to put a stop to it.

Bestselling author and radio talk show host Michael Medved said recently it will take at least ten years to repair the damage done to this country by Democrats during the last four years. Obama's healthcare measure is an absolute financial disaster, as we are already seeing. Never mind it will also mean shrinkage both in terms of access and quality, even as costs soar and private insurers are driven out of business while government power and control increases enormously. And that is only one of the areas needing repair.

Conservatives hold the key. This republic has always thrived when the government gets out of the way, allowing the people to work and create and build and advance. It has been proven time and again that prosperity comes from tax cuts and reduced regulation. Once the economic engine is fired up by these means, tax revenue flows in abundance, revenue we must direct at the debt even as we cut government programs left and right. The federal government has become a monster, sucking the lifeblood out of the country. It must be harnessed, contained, and chopped down to size if we are to survive as a world power.

Tea Party people hold the key. When Angle of Nevada and others insist we should cut the departments of Energy and Education, both Jimmy Carter epic failures, they are absolutely correct. Those federal departments waste fifty billion dollars a year, at least, and contribute nothing substantive.

Did you know the largest employer in America is government? Again, Dr. Jeremiah gives us the facts.

- State and local government employees increased from 6.4 million to 15.2 million between 1960 and 1990.
- As of December 2009, there were almost two million federal employees. That number will increase 15.6 percent this year, thanks to Obama. The annual federal payroll is 15.5 billion dollars. About 19 percent of federal employees make more than one hundred thousand dollars per year.

Some will say military spending is also a problem. It is, but it pales in the face of government entitlement spending. There are some who claim it is a hopeless situation. Entire nations are going bankrupt. The United States is essentially bankrupt. Printing funny money to cover our obligations is only applying a Band-Aid to a gaping wound. It may stop the bleeding for a moment, but without surgical intervention, the patient will bleed out eventually.

Americans cannot afford to vote for conservatives who promise financial responsibility and then go back to their inattentive ways. The moment these new public servants are sworn in, we must watch them like hawks, making sure they deliver on their promises, even as we work to elect a true conservative to the White House in two years.

Mr. Obama and his people moved quickly to railroad a blizzard of legislative initiatives and administrative rules most Americans oppose. The arrogance-driven Obama administration refused to stop or even slow down when it became clear the people were opposed. Consequently, in addition to the outrage over taxation, spending, and debt, the people smell a tyrant, and, true to form, Americans always deal with tyrants.

Those are the facts, Mr. Clinton, facts that motivate the majority of responsible citizens to repudiate your party at the polls today.

ELECTION OBSERVATIONS

November 3, 2010
Nancy Pelosi—Speaker No More

The very best news of the day: Obama is now immobilized, neutralized, contained, and rendered a lame duck. After twenty-two months of his radicalism driving the country to its knees, the opposition takes substantial power, at least allowing for a check on the out of control executive branch. After twenty-two months of spitting in Republican faces, the president now calls for bipartisanship and cooperation and so on.

Publicly, Republican leaders will be gracious. Privately, they no doubt have plans to right the ship of state whatever it takes, not to exact revenge but to serve the people, knowing this is their last chance, for if Republicans fail as in the past, a third party will likely emerge from the smoke and take over, and the party of Lincoln will be no more.

Elections are great entertainment. We love our elections in America. They are real-time dramas, displaying all the diversity of the nation, allowing for the full exposure of loons from both sides of the aisle. Carl Paladino with his baseball bat promising to keep us entertained was one highlight last night. Also it was wonderful to see Floridians run Grayson out of town on a rail, replaced by a real statesman and man of integrity, Daniel Webster.

However, some loons kept their jobs or got hired on to continue squandering our resources: Boxer, Governor Moonbeam, Reid, Schumer, Barney the Frank, and so on.

The most hilarious development yesterday was hearing Nancy Pelosi insist Democrats would retain a majority in the House. She cheerfully predicted a huge last-minute Democrat turnout would save the day. She thereby took wishful thinking to psycho-land. Time to adjust the medication.

The most hilarious scene last night, once it was apparent the anti-Obama backlash would mean huge Republican victories across the nation, was watching the Grisly Gang of Ghouls at MSNBC thrash around, desperately spinning explanations, spewing hate, and interrogating the victors as if they were criminals.

Imagine Rachel and Chris and Keith and Lawrence actually trying to save face, asserting the Republicans failed because the tsunami wasn't big enough! That's right, the Grisly Gang actually wanted viewers to rejoice that Republican successes were not successful enough, and, therefore, the huge success was actually a failure! Only the freeze-dried pretzel logic of a liberal meltdown could produce such analysis!

Never mind that Republicans set records for sweeping the House, winning the majority of governors' races, and placing upward of six hundred people in state legislative seats! One can only conclude the Gang was forced to join Pelosi at the pharmacy to up the dosage.

(However, to be fair, you have to give Chris Matthews some credit. He actually blamed Obama for being a do-nothing President, incapable of governing. By the way, does that make Chris a racist?)

Russ Feingold, an Obama Democrat serving in the Senate since 1992, fell hard last night to Republican Ron Johnson in that Wisconsin contest. Defiant to the end, Feingold vowed to fight on, yelling "forward!" in Howard Dean fashion, presumably into the Valley of Death.

Generally what viewers observed on television last night: a huge group of Republicans, conservatives, and Tea Party candidates humbly thanking voters for trusting them to serve, aware they will be held tightly accountable, and a large group of Democrats, liberals, and Marxists, seething and snarling and continuing the chant about moron Tea Party people, fear-driven voters, an uniformed electorate, and a misunderstood president. In other words, those prevailing were tracking with reality as statesmen, and those losing were distinctly otherwise.

John Boehner is a class act. He will be the new Speaker of the House. Pelosi is dethroned, hallelujah. A real public servant takes up the gavel with humility and heart. First order of business: cut spending, balance the budget, repeal portions of Obamacare, and extend the Bush tax cuts to avoid a tax increase, which would be devastating. One hopes and prays conservatives will fight hard, fight fair, and fight to win for the next two years. The fate of the nation hangs in the balance.

Harry Reid won in Nevada. Did he really? Harry Reid has been in the Senate since the last dinosaur fertilized the desert outside Elko. Harry 'This War Is Lost' Reid was challenged by a largely unknown Tea Party grandmother, and she almost pinned him to the mat. Without the help of millions upon millions of dollars from out of state and a last minute hysterical push from corrupt unions, casinos, and other model citizens, Harry would be out on his ear. The vast majority of Americans hold Harry in contempt, yet he has the audacity to claim victory with pride, vowing to fight on! For what? What will you fight for now, Harry, another chance to embarrass yourself? Harry won? Not really. No man as corrupt and disrespected as Harry Reid can be called a winner unless you consider George Armstrong Custer and Benedict Arnold winners.

In the end, the Republicans set a record by picking up sixty-three seats in the House, almost achieving parity in the Senate, moving to substantially control redistricting in the states, setting the stage for more gains in two years. Meanwhile, the people have spoken: cut wasteful spending, get this economy back on track, aggressively protect America, and cut the Marxist crap.

The returns demonstrated that representative government is alive and well in America, that the people, when energized and attentive, will move against elitists with fierce intent, that the powerful are still accountable to the people, as it should be, and must always remain.

Now let us see if those elected actually deliver.

SHARIA LAW IS NO BIG DEAL

November 9, 2010

Assuredly, 70 percent of Oklahoma voters revealed irrational paranoia, passing a ban on Sharia Law, the legal foundation of the religion of peace. Don't those Okies know the rest of us want to embrace other ways of life, blend our Constitution with the traditions of others, and achieve true multicultural, cosmopolitan status?

In the long history of Islam, dating back to the middle of the seventh century, other cultures have had nothing to fear from Muslims. So long as people willingly submitted to invasion, domination, and conversion, there was peace. This is how Muslim influence was exported from Mecca and spread from Spain to Indonesia, only through peaceful means, invitation, and introduction of Sharia law, all in the name of peace and order. Resorting to violence was always the fault of those refusing the invitation.

Things have worked out well for centuries for the billions of people throughout the 10/40 window. Why would the Okies be concerned about Sharia law at all? Besides, there are only thirty thousand Muslims living there, for heaven's sake! What's the big deal?

Perhaps the Okies aren't in favor of marital rape, allowed under Sharia.

Maybe Okies don't like the idea of cutting off the hand of a thief, called for under Sharia.

Can it be people in Oklahoma really do not support the idea of killing women—moms, sisters, daughters—just for being accused of impropriety, provided for under Sharia?

Apparently, wife beating is anathema to Okies, another tenet of Sharia.

And then there are the little matters such as the ban on insurance, the prohibition against charging interest and complete changes in both family and finance law, not to mention no provision for appealing decisions, no trial by a jury of one's peers, the imposition of dietary and wardrobe rules, and segregated public swimming facilities.

Perhaps the good folks in Oklahoma aren't so misguided? Maybe they have read the news reports about the spread of Sharia in Britain?

National security experts (1) with the Center for Security Policy have long asserted Sharia poses a serious threat.

They write:

> Though it certainly has spiritual elements, it would be a mistake to think of sharia as a 'religious' code in the Western sense because it seeks to regulate all manner of behavior... economic, social, military, legal and political. Our leaders have failed to perceive—let alone respond effectively to—the real progress being made by the Muslim Brotherhood in insinuating sharia into the very heartland of America through stealthy means.

Maybe those Okies are on to something! What does that say about the president, the multicultural left, and the federal bench?

PS: The fruit of sharia:

Headline: "Christian Woman Sentenced to Death in Pakistan for 'Blasphemy'"

- Distinguished contributors to the report include:
  Team Leaders:
    • Lieutenant General William G. "Jerry" Boykin, US Army

(Ret.); former deputy undersecretary, Defense for Intelligence
• Lieutenant General Harry Edward Soyster, US Army (Ret.), former director, Defense Intelligence agency
Associates:
• Ambassador Henry Cooper, former chief negotiator, Defense and Space Talks; former director, Strategic Defense Initiative
• Stephen C. Coughlin, Esq., Major (Res.) USA, former Senior Consultant, Office of the Joint Chiefs of Staff
• Michael Del Rosso, Senior Fellow, Claremont Institute and Center for Security Policy
• Frank J. Gaffney, Jr., former assistant secretary of defense, International Security Policy (Acting); president, Center for Security Policy
• John Guandolo, former special agent, Counter-Terrorism Division, Federal Bureau of Investigation
• Admiral James A. "Ace" Lyons, US Navy (Ret.), former commander in Chief, Pacific Fleet
• Brian Kennedy, president, Claremont Institute
• Clare M. Lopez, senior fellow, Center for Security Policy
• Andrew C. McCarthy, former chief assistant US attorney; senior fellow, National Review Institute; contributing editor, National Review
• Patrick Poole, consultant to the military and law enforcement on anti-terrorism issues
• Joseph E. Schmitz, former inspector general, Department of Defense
• Tom Trento, executive director, Florida Security Council
• J. Michael Waller, Annenberg Professor of international communication, Institute of World Politics, and vice president for Information Operations, Center for Security Policy
• Diana West, author and columnist
• R. James Woolsey, former Director of Central Intelligence
• David Yerushalmi, Esq., General Counsel to the Center for Security Policy

THROWING ISRAEL TO THE WOLVES

November 10, 2010
Item:

> (AP) U.S. Secretary of State Hillary Rodham Clinton announced Wednesday that $150 million dollars in direct aid was being transferred to the Palestinian Authority. The latest U.S. aid brings the amount of direct funding for 2010 to $225 million and total assistance to the Palestinian Authority including that through third parties to $600 million, Clinton said.

So let's see. The president is globetrotting again, and from somewhere in the Far East, presumably in his spare time between defining "jihad" and visiting mosques, he finds time to condemn Israel for building apartments in east Jerusalem, blaming Israel for fouling up the eternal peace process.

Israel, one of America's closest friends until the age of Barack, is to blame once again, according to the intellectuals. We are urged to believe the Palestinians and their extremist friends in the dark world of international terrorism are the aggrieved, exploited, and abused minority, only trying to establish their own nation.

Let's keep in mind Israel has never forfeited a right to build in east Jerusalem, acquired after victory in the 1967 war. Israel has always worked for a unified Jerusalem. Jerusalem is not, in their view, an occupied territory. Even Barack said he supported the notion of a unified Jerusalem during the campaign, but as we all now know, we weren't supposed to believe anything he said during the campaign, by his own admission on 60 Minutes last Sunday.

The insistence by the Palestinian Authority that Israel forfeit rights in the West Bank is just another setup to walk away from peace talks, condemn Israel, and pursue the forever agenda: the annihilation of the state of Israel.

Now the United States is giving the PA one hundred fifty million dollars on top of millions and millions and millions given them and the PLO in Gaza. Early in his term, Obama approved eight hundred million dollars for Abbas, and, likely, most of that went to purchase arms for Hamas to attack Israeli civilians.

And the insanity marches on. Our own government has spent us into oblivion, and now we are supporting the teetering PA?

Mindless.

More than a billion dollars in less than two years funneled from American taxpayers to violent extremists in the Middle East, money that would have gone a long way toward helping widows and orphans in this country, but one supposes this administration is more interested in aiding adversaries and alienating allies, to the detriment of everyone except the bad guys.

Meanwhile, the masses, the little people, both Israeli and Palestinian, shed their blood in the crossfire.

Ah, leadership.

(The Truth about the Middle East Prager University—Google it!)

Parting shot: Report on total US aid to Palestinians in recent years:

> Since the signing of the Oslo Accord in 1993 and the establishment of limited Palestinian self rule in the West Bank and Gaza Strip in 1994, the U.S. government has committed over $3.5

billion in bilateral assistance to the Palestinians. Since the death of Yasser Arafat in November 2004, U.S. assistance to the Palestinians has been averaging about $400 million a year. During the 1990s, U.S. foreign aid to the Palestinians averaged approximately $75 million per year. Despite more robust levels of assistance this decade, Israeli-Palestinian conflict and Hamas's heightened role in Palestinian politics have made it more difficult to implement effective and lasting aid projects that serve U.S. interests.

> "U.S. Foreign Aid to the Palestinians," by Jim Zanotti,
> Analyst in Middle Eastern Affairs,
> Congressional Research Service
> August 12, 2010

POWERFUL DEMS TELL OBAMA NOT TO SEEK RE-ELECTION

November 16, 2010

It is deeply regrettable watching the country's first black president trip, stumble, and fall, and there appears no remedy. Obviously the election was devastating. This Asian tour, conducted at obscene cost, is a bust. Democrats are jumping ship at an accelerated rate. No word is heard from Oprah or Colin Powell, silent indictments perhaps. Powerful Democrat critics are even telling the president he should announce he is not running for re-election.

All this against a grim backdrop: terrorists escalate, American standing plummets; the economy is adrift in the doldrums.

Any number of disillusioned pundits, radical leftists, and liberals attempt blaming conservatives in media and politics for the demise of the Obama White House, but that is no remedy, nor is it an explanation. In the end, the man has no one to blame but himself.

The reasons are obvious.

He campaigned as a left-of-center liberal, willing to moderate in the name of unifying the country, calling for a new culture in Washington, promising a post-racial, post-partisan utopia. Once in office, he immediately moved to govern from the far left, jolting the people with serial doses of radicalism. Perhaps no president in history has been as disconnected from the people he governs.

More than anyone else, he gave birth to the Tea Party movement by putting his radicalism into hyper-drive then turning and calling his own people Astroturf morons and enemies. When they were called racists, his silence endorsed the smear. He has tried many times pitting conservative against liberal, white against black, black against white, white against brown, brown against white, and for what?

Personal political ambition and advantage: utopia lost.

Now you have Bobby Jindal, the governor of Louisiana, pulling back the veil further, describing a president "managing" the Gulf oil disaster with only his political future in mind. Jindal's book details Obama's overt focus on political fallout and public perception, even to the exclusion of granting aid to those displaced by the disaster, never mind the environmental impact.

Even more damaging: a recent column by two Democratic powerhouse consultants, both urging the president not to run for reelection. Douglas Schoen (Clinton WH) and Patrick Caddell (Carter WH), writing an opinion in the November 14 *Washington Post,* conclude:

> We are convinced that if Obama immediately declares his intention not to run for reelection, he will be able to unite the country, provide national and international leadership, escape the hold of the left, isolate the right and achieve results that would be otherwise unachievable.

Translation: Get out of the way so we can try to salvage this thing.

Even worse, in a November 9 Politico article by Mike Allen and Jim Vandehei headed 'President Obama isolated ahead of 2012,' the president is shown alienated from most all the power players in his own party. It is reported most cabinet members have turned their backs as well. Never has a president seen such an outflow of staff in such short order.

Worse yet, blogger Ulster Man, claiming an inside WH source, has been writing about an administration in chaos, the president's emotional outbursts over trivial matters, erratic behavior, listlessness during crucial meetings about the war in Afghanistan, depression, and even alleged use of medication. Reportedly, staffers have been stunned by the vast difference between the public and private faces of the president.

It is rumored therefore, an enormous scandal is about to break out of the White House, about the time Robert Gibbs is expected to resign, or shortly thereafter, once the House changes hands. In other words, things are going from very bad to much worse.

Walter Williams wrote two and a half years ago he hoped our first black president would be an extraordinary breakthrough personality, someone as valuable to the national political conscience as Jackie Robinson was to our sense of sportsmanship, character and citizenship. Williams lamented then, hoping he was wrong about Obama, knowing, however, the man does not have the right stuff.

No one should have supported Obama just because of charisma or skin color or rhetorical ability, and no one should oppose him for those reasons either.

Rather, we oppose him today, just as we did three years ago, for two outstanding reasons: radicalism which is anti-American, and inexperience.

Now, those chickens have come home to roost. We can only hope black youth and others will not be discouraged. Rather, we pray they redouble their efforts to join all of us in rebuilding the nation—work neglected for decades—work that must focus on common sense, traditional Americanism and a restored sense of the importance of morality and individual virtue.

GIVING THANKS FOR OUR MEN AND WOMEN IN UNIFORM

November 25, 2010

Far from home on this Thanksgiving Day, there are more than 350,000 American men and women serving in the military to protect and defend us. They serve in more than 135 countries. Many have served multiple deployments. The highest concentrations are in Iraq and Afghanistan, Europe and east Asia.

Recent reports indicate the situation in Afghanistan is deteriorating: the government is corrupt and increasingly critical of US and NATO efforts to stabilize the situation; violence is escalating to record levels; coalition casualties are on the rise; and the Taliban insurgency has become more sophisticated. All this as election results from September have finally been released, leaving many with no confidence in the Afghan system.

President Bush ordered the invasion of Afghanistan shortly after 9/11, the purpose being to root out and destroy responsible al-Qaeda and Taliban forces. No doubt an unspoken dimension of the strategy was also the containment of Iran, especially in the wake of the US invasion of Iraq. The Bush doctrine—democratizing Iraq and Afghanistan as the best way to turn the tide of Islamic radicalism—

appears to be making some progress in Iraq, although the threat of a Shi'ite theocracy remains high.

Afghanistan is extremely complex, given the drug trade and the involvement of traditional war lords plus the inclusion of Taliban, al-Qaeda, and other elements such as terrorist influences within Pakistani intelligence and the constant flow of weapons and fighters sponsored by Iran.

The man most familiar with the complexities and challenges of Afghanistan is no longer the US military commander in the region. General Stanley McChrystal was relieved of duty by President Obama last summer. McChrystal was highly critical of the president's handling of the war.

Many observers recall the many months of indecision early in the Obama administration when it came to Afghan war policy. Indecisiveness was seen as weakness, and, no doubt, in traditional fashion, Muslim fighters escalated as a result.

Obama has assigned General David Petraeus to replace McChrystal who reportedly had a good relationship with Afghan President Hamid Karzai. Ever since, the relationship between Obama and Karzai has deteriorated to the point of public argument.

Meanwhile the anti-war left in America continues to express criticism of Obama, accusing him of not following through on campaign promises to end the wars in both Iraq and Afghanistan, claiming he is acting just like Bush in the war on terror. Critics from the right criticize the president for poor leadership, lack of vision, serial failures, telegraphing the end game, and for sending confusing messages as to strategy and mission. At the same time, most Americans have grown weary of the war, and few seem to understand why American troops remain. Isn't leadership supposed to address these circumstances effectively?

Making matters worse, American media does not even bother reporting on Afghanistan in any meaningful way.

Caught in the eye of the storm, handicapped by restrictive and lethal rules of engagement, stands the American soldier, fighting bravely for an ill-defined cause, led by incompetence in the civilian sector, criticized by the international community, and ignored by American media.

Dear American soldier, we remember you. We, the majority of Americans, appreciate you. We pray for you. And we look forward to welcoming you home one day soon. Despite all the crap you have to put up with, Happy Thanksgiving anyway...

Happy Thanksgiving to the brave men and women from Canada, Great Britain, Romania, Spain, Australia, Turkey, Italy, France, and Germany who also fight and sacrifice in Afghanistan for all freedom-loving people in the world.

NEW WORLD ORDER: MANY ARE THE PLANS OF MAN

November 26, 2010

Politicians think they have the answer. Economists think they hold the key. Religious people believe they know the secret path to peace. Military men believe they will be the last ones standing. Others believe technology will be our salvation.

Chinese Premier, Wen Jiabao, has a plan. Russian Prime Minister, Vladimir Putin, has a plan. Iranian President, Mahmoud Ahmadinejad, has a plan. Obama and Castro and Chavez and Kim Jung Il and many others have plans. And all those plans are ego-driven strategies designed to acquire power and control others. Pride and presumption have always paved the path to war goaded by the lust for world domination.

Presidents have spoken of a New World Order. Walter Cronkite and many others, including the Rockefellers, have all pointed to the ultimate need for a world government, a global authority, if mankind has any hope of survival.

Whether it is soft or hard despotism, it boils down to the same thing in the end: a small group of powerful elite suppose they know best, giving themselves permission to rule the rest of us. They tell us such a global government is the only way to avoid nuclear annihilation or the demise of the human race brought by other weapons of mass destruction, by pandemics, or environmental disasters. (No one yet knows how to deal with a massive asteroid careening toward Earth, but we are working on it!)

For many years we have heard about secret societies and shadowy groups, power players behind the scenes, all scheming to take over the world: the Bilderbergers, the Trilaterial Commission, the Council on Foreign Relations, the Illuminati, Freemasons, Bohemian Grove, the worldwide Communist conspiracy, the worldwide Capitalist conspiracy, the United Nations, or the European Union, and a global banking conspiracy.

The deeper the world drops into crisis, the more we think about fear, and the more some welcome the strongman, one who will take away all the chaos and conflict, the one who will usher in a new world, a new order, a time of peaceful prosperity.

For Wen Jiabao and Putin and Castro and Chavez and Obama, the "one" is a system, a man-made government that will determine all matters of justice, the concentrated human power of secular government intervening to save the world.

For Muslims it will be the Twelfth Imam (Shiite) or the Muntazar (Sunni). Most everyone has a messiah. Native Americans, the Japanese, Buddhists, the ancient Aztecs and Mayans, Hindus, even Eskimos all have a savior in mind, all yearn for deliverance, all claim to know the one who will deliver the human race from mass suicide.

Intriguing: the universal impulse to worship a creator and the universal sense that a central authority figure (or man-made system) will intervene to prevent the end of the world.

Yet throughout human history, only one has actually demonstrated sufficient power over life and death to prove his claim of being the "one." Only One walked among us, clearly showing he possesses the power to command the wind and the waves. Only One claimed ultimate authority, saying he was and is the One true God. And only One has influenced the world for good like no other.

To know the One who has all power is to know the end of the story. It is to know the "happily ever after" truth that lies ahead. It is to know that the One true God is the very embodiment of everything loving, everything true, and everything good. Knowing all this is to know the One who drives away all fear.

One world order? Most assuredly it is coming. But it will not be fashioned by the hands of man, nor will it be ushered forward by the wild imaginings of fearful mystics. Rather, it will be established forever by the One who originated everything, the One who takes responsibility for everything, the One who now sits at the right hand of God and who is God, the One who will "wipe every tear from their eyes," the One who will establish his kingdom forever, where "there shall be no more death, nor sorrow, nor crying; and there shall be no more pain, for the former things (will) have passed away."

Read all about it, starting in Revelation 19:11 to the end of the book.

MAN UNTO HIMSELF: THE DEATH OF COMMON SENSE

November 30, 2010

It is no coincidence that illusory thinking emerged from the death of common sense. If it is true that illusory thinking now impairs huge numbers of Americans, it may be logical to assert that one contributing factor is the death of common sense. It is likewise probable the embrace of illusory thinking perfected in American universities was fatal to common sense as well.

How does one know common sense is largely dead in America?

The contemporary intellectual class (CIC) in leadership today tells us Islam is a religion of peace, but the clear evidence says otherwise.

The CIC insists more government spending and higher levels of debt will turn the economy, but that has never happened; it only makes matters worse. (Hit the road, Maynard Keynes! Welcome, Milton Friedman!)

The CIC claims being nice to dictators, murderers, and terrorists will turn them into puppy dogs, but all we see are growing packs of snarling Dobermans.

The CIC says we can convert from a petroleum-based economy to a green economy overnight and unless we do so we face environmental catastrophe, but the science is not supportive, and the green push turns out to be a myth built on a lie promoted by snake oil salesmen.

The CIC says violence on TV, in movies, and in popular music does not encourage youth to act out; licentiousness does not unleash the AIDS pandemic; sloth does not create poverty; the government is better than Mom and Dad at raising kids; monogamy is quaint but unrealistic; having wealth is a crime; abortion improves a woman's health; the recent election was not a referendum on Obama's policies; and Grandma at a Tea Party is a racist.

A Muslim terrorist is prevented from killing thousands in Portland, but his murderous impulse is the fault of Americans or Israelis or Zionists or the FBI.

Profiling air passengers is racist and groping Grandpa is security.

The very ones who've promoted incivility now decry it and blame it on the civil.

Indeed, common sense is largely dead. How did it die?

Every viable society has a book of wisdom, written or orally shared, a code for living, a social contract, a blueprint for encouraging healthy, productive human interaction. In the West, that blueprint was for centuries the Judeo-Christian traditions derived from both the Old and New Testaments, summed up best by Christ:

> Love the LORD your God with all your heart and with all your soul and with all your mind. This is the first and greatest commandment. And the second is like it: Love your neighbor as yourself. All the Law and the Prophets hang on these two commandments.
>
> Matthew 22:37–40

(Note that loving God is like loving your fellow man, that you cannot love God and hate your brother.)

There is demonstrable linkage between the act of loving God and the prominence of common sense in the mind of the one taking

Christ's advice seriously. There is also a connection between rejecting the God of love and the tendency to practice illusory thinking.

For example, people like Bill Maher and Christopher Hitchens and Richard Dawkins tell us atheism is the only reasonable belief for intelligent people. Further, they claim people of faith are destructive to the general welfare. Consequently, the eradication of religious faith and the embrace of atheism is the path to human salvation.

None of these assertions are supported by evidence or logical argument. All are presuppositions emanating from the biased mind that rejects God out of hand. Promoting atheism simply insists people deny the existence of God. There is no proof that God does not exist. There is ample evidence he does. Yet we are encouraged to deny existent evidence and embrace non-existent evidence, and we are thereby encouraged to arrive at errant conclusions, the essence of illusory thinking.

Atheism and its cousin secular humanism are rooted in the belief that humans are gods unto themselves, that humans are intellectually and morally self-sufficient, and that humans alone can determine what is right versus wrong, what will work versus what will not work. This too is illusory thinking if one takes the time to look at the track record. The last century provides an excellent testing ground.

Humans—apart from the mind-renewing influence of a loving God, with access to modern technology, unrestrained by transcendent moral authority—managed to murder almost one hundred million people in the last century, a period of time noted as the pinnacle of human learning and "understanding."

If Maher and Dawkins and Hitchens (the MDH trinity) are correct, we should expect the twentieth century to have been a glowing example of the efficacy of human self-sufficiency, human self-reliance, a shining demonstration of our ability to deliver ourselves quite apart from any God. After all, the twentieth century was not only a time of ultimate human learning and achievement, it was also marked by the greatest turning away from God yet witnessed in recorded history.

Therefore, the observable laboratory for proving the theses of the MDH trinity existed substantially in the twentieth century.

And did we achieve salvation in that one hundred years by the sheer force of human will and intellect?

Quite the opposite. Do we need more time, perhaps millions of years, to evolve? Shall we look for evidence in other epochs? Perhaps there is a different explanation?

The MDH trinity will tell us wars and mass murder and genocide are the result of religious belief driving conflicts that arise between adherents. No doubt this is true to an extent. It is easy to document the impact of a belief system that encourages believers to kill non-believers. More than nine million dead Christians at the hands of Muslims during the course of fourteen hundred years is sufficient evidence of belief playing out in behavior. That behavior has nothing to do with "love your neighbor as yourself," of course, a belief that yields altogether different results such as the greatest global outpouring of benevolence and charity ever witnessed in history.

Still we cling to the illusion that Islam is a religion of peace and Christianity is the religion of war: another illusion that is the fruit of an unregenerate intellect, one separated from divine renewal, hostile to the essence of love.

Further, the sin of faith asserted by the MDH trinity cannot be found in the hearts of Stalin, Hitler, Mao, Ho Chi Minh, Pol Pot, Lenin, Hirohito, Mussolini, Wilhelm II, Tojo, or Franco, taken together, men responsible for almost one hundred million deaths in only a few decades, all of them driven only by the religion of political power, self-serving on its face, most of them inspired by atheistic Marxism, beliefs deriving from the illusion humans are sufficient unto themselves to manage things toward healthy outcomes. Obviously not so.

Common sense shows that belief ultimately leads to behavior. Cognitive psychology is not the alpha and omega explanation of brain function, personality, intelligence, and behavior, but it does cover most ground.

Obviously, the mass murderers of the last century acted according to their beliefs.

Timothy McVeigh believed certain things, and those beliefs drove him to act.

Osama bin Laden believes certain things, beliefs he shares with at least twenty million jihadists who've launched sixteen thousand deadly attacks against the West since 9/11.

Mohamed Osman Mohamud believed certain things during the course of the last four years, beliefs which drove him to attempt mass murder in Portland last Friday.

Mother Teresa and Billy Graham believe certain things driving their behavior. The lady ringing the bell by the little red pot at the grocery store this Christmas acts according to her beliefs, as do those with the Red Cross, Operation Blessing, Samaritan's Purse, and World Vision.

Christ acted, saving the world from sin and death.

When the greatest, most influential person in all of human history speaks, the wise heed. When he declares our sorry, death-like state apart from God, urging us to love God, knowing it will lead us to love one another, the wise heed, especially when the evidence is clear that it works.

And when the wise heed, common sense resurrects, dispelling illusions, ushering forward the greatest good for the greatest number, God's plan ever since the rebellion in the garden.

In the garden: bliss.

Our first act outside: murder.

The MDH trinity insists we remain outside the garden.

The real trinity invites us in.

THE LOW POINT FOR LIBERALISM: SELF-RIDICULE

December 2, 2010

> What Democrats call "nuanced," most people refer to as "stupidity."
>
> Evan Sayet, actor, writer, comedian

Politicians like Harry Reid and Nancy Pelosi should realize their day is done when they become the subjects of ridicule from the left, from the right, and most people in between. Remaining oblivious to this reality reveals they're oblivious in most things.

Imagine in this day and age expecting to be taken seriously, advancing amnesty and tax increases right in the middle of economic chaos and escalating violence thanks to illegal immigration. Lame ducks indeed. What will it take to get their attention? Do we have to pull a *Wizard of Oz* and drop a house on them?

Examples of the ridicule, some of it starting months ago:

All year long, the Democrats were telling people to "get out and vote." Then people told the Democrats, "We voted, now get out!"

                 Jay Leno

They say Nancy Pelosi was aware, as far back as 2003 that we tortured and didn't raise any questions about it. Which raises the big question: what did Nancy Pelosi know, and when was she going to tell her face?

                 Bill Maher

It's time to take off the pink tutu and put on the boxing gloves because it's time to fight for the people.

        Michael Moore addressing President Obama

Saturday Night Live rips Pelosi even before the recent two-year, three-ring circus.

And the very best Democrat joke of the year: Al Franken.

Evan Sayet, like so many others (Michael Medved, Charles Krauthammer, P.J. O'Rouke, Jon Voight, David Horowitz), changed from being a leftist to embracing conservatism, realizing the left just doesn't make sense, and, further, many on the left actually hate America.

This is reminiscent of the classic Reagan quote: "The trouble with our liberal friends is not that they're ignorant; it's just that they know so much that isn't so."

One does not have to travel far to detect the inherent confusion bound up in the heart of a leftist, the belief that:

- government can perfect imperfect man, like believing you can use a marshmallow to drive a railroad spike into granite.
- racial reconciliation is achieved by discriminating against 80 percent, patronizing 20 percent, and infuriating everybody.

- prosperity comes from stealing the means of production from productive people, and simultaneously subsidizing sloth, otherwise known as "The New Deal," or "The Great Society." (Trillions spent. Results? Epic failure.)
- war can be won by phased surrender.
- it is best to convince your own people they are inferior to their enemies just to avoid a hassle.
- when attacked, write a check.
- success is failure.
- gun control will control crime.
- abortion should be funded by taxpayers to solve the non-existent problem of global warming.
- universal health care is a constitutional right, just like the enumerated rights to housing, clothing, food, space shuttle rides, and tickets to Disney World.
- poverty is noble.
- real hatred can be justified if it's for a noble cause
- benevolence is offering the poor a bad cup of coffee and a short ride in your limousine.
- partisanship is evil only when the other side indulges.
- fiscal responsibility is for suckers.
- doing what does not work, time and again, is enlightened.

Boiling this down to a conclusion, there are three kinds of leftists:

1. The soft, misguided, bleeding heart do-gooder who never contributes to anything but Planned Parenthood, all the while demanding the rest of us pay higher taxes to fund food stamps to feed a growing population of people born out-of-wedlock

2. The hippie-turned-corporate pin stripper, working both sides of the room, lining his pockets and demanding we save the spotted owl unless the owl interferes with the wind farm he has in mind, then screw the spotted owl
3. The hate-America Alinskyites hired by Soros to stuff ballot boxes, break kneecaps, finance Bill Ayers, and bank roll MSNBC

It was one thing having to put up with Carter, Mondale, and McGovern, the soft liberals leading an army of hippies in transition. That was at least tolerable.

It is quite another thing being dominated by a federal government infiltrated by Alinskyites all the way from the local post office to White House, watching them wreck our economy and hand the keys to the Chinese.

But let forty-two Republican senators write the president yesterday, telling him they'll dig in their heels until he agrees to prevent taxes increases so as to save the country; well, then the Alinskyites go berserk, claiming fascist Republicans are trying to destroy Obama, not actually save the country from Obama: the former a gross fiction; the later, truth.

Parting shot:

The mystery of government is not how Washington works but how to make it stop.

P. J. O'Rourke

THE CORPSE THAT IS LIBERALISM

December 6, 2010

> You don't raise taxes in a recession.
>
> President Obama, summer 2009,
> interview with NBC's Chuck Todd

Knee-high rubber boots must be sold out in DC, given all the BS floating around lately with regard to extending the Bush Tax Cuts. Keep in mind that letting those tax cuts lapse would amount to the largest tax increase in history right in the middle of a deep recession, the worst thing we could do at this intersection, as Obama has always acknowledged.

For one thing, the country just saw new unemployment figures. The government says we now have higher unemployment at 9.8 percent with real unemployment hovering around 18 percent, and 40 percent of those without work remaining idle six months or more while fully 10 percent of the population is on food stamps, a record.

All this in the context of a stalled and declining economy overall with fears raging over bankruptcy, hyperinflation, and general collapse worldwide.

Few if any dispute the fact a huge part of the problem stems from government spending, government regulation, and government taxation, whether at home or in Europe, especially in view of the chaos created by entitlement spending in Portugal, Spain, Greece, Ireland, and Italy. If we are to believe reports, the Europeans are scared spitless over the prospect of general financial collapse even as Americans read about increasing US bank failures, a declining housing market, and other signs we are in deep trouble.

It has been reported that delay on extending the Bush tax cuts could feasibly cause a stock market crash, and should the Chinese dump their dollars on the market (currency they have acquired and held to help the US artificially avoid inflation so that Americans will keep buying Chinese goods), hyperinflation will hit like a tsunami.

So, against this rather disturbing backdrop, what do we hear from lame-duck Democrats?

Republicans are terrorists for wanting to hold the line on spending and for wanting to keep the Bush tax cuts in place. That's right. Bringing real, proven solutions to address dire economic problems is being a terrorist, according to Sen. Robert Menendez (Democrat, New Jersey). He accused Republicans of holding the tax cut issue hostage on Friday: "Do you allow yourself to be held hostage and get something done for the sake of getting something done, when in fact it might be perverse in its ultimate results? It's almost like the question of do you negotiate with terrorists?"

When challenged for making this outrageous comparison, the good senator said,

> Not surprisingly, Republicans would take a comment out of context in order to change the subject from their millionaires-first tax plan. The critical point for middle class Americans remains that Republicans have chosen to jeopardize tax cuts for every middle-class family in order to guarantee an average tax cut of $104,000 for each millionaire.

Sorry, Bob, your arrogant tongue spoke clearly, revealing your heart and mind, both more interested in sparking class warfare than solving economic problems, the trademark of a Democrat party hijacked by radicals.

By the way, Bob, Pelosi says the best way to stimulate the economy is unemployment payouts. If that is a good way to stimulate the economy, then why is it anathema to let the rich keep more of their money, which they will spend, thus stimulating the economy? (Never mind that Pelosi is once again in la-la land when it comes to economic development and unemployment payments. When the unemployed spend a few dollars, it is only for subsistence, and there is no growth in the economy at all. When the rich spend money and invest, it is much more likely jobs will be created and thereby influence economic growth. Simple logic and Econ 101 supply all the justification required.)

Furthermore, remember the Democrats are constantly whining about the lack of bipartisanship, even as they liken Republicans to terrorists and Scrooge. What a great basis for encouraging cooperation on the hill.

Lame Duck Chuck Schumer, quacking before the cameras this weekend, cynically returned to the old canard that Republicans love the rich, hate the poor, and wish to punish the unemployed right before Christmas.

Missouri Democrat Senator Claire McCaskill says Democrat failure to stop Republican efforts to extend the Bush tax cuts should cause people to riot. Now there's statesmanship for ya.

Please understand this central point: leftists hate the rich but only the conservative and corporate rich. They believe the rich to be a criminal class. They believe the only way to acquire wealth is to behave in some nefarious, exploitive way. (But remember leftists with fortunes like Soros, Michael Moore, the Clintons, John Edwards, and John Kerry, well, that's another matter...) There is little or no evidence for this position, but in order to attack the rich and tax them into oblivion, one must first demonize them.

The rich and middle class already carry a far greater proportionate share of the tax burden, as reported by the Tax Foundation in 2007 in a paper titled, 'Who Pays America's Tax Burden, and Who Gets the Most Government Spending?' In another report by Tom Murse in U.S. Government Info published on line August 10, 2010 we read: 'The top 25 percent: Americans who earned at least $66,532 paid 86.6 percent of the nation's income taxes, up from 86.3 percent a year earlier.' (Hey, Bob, how do you propose saving the middle class that you've already destroyed by taxing it to death?)

Half the wage earners in this country pay no federal income tax whatsoever.

So instead of working across the aisle to solve economic problems by keeping taxes low, a proven method for reversing recession, the Democrats are once again playing politics, posturing for the 2012 elections, demonizing the rich and Republicans, claiming a special affection for the middle class, stirring up racial strife, and escalating class warfare.

In an age when the people cry out for leadership, statesmanship, and courageous government action to save the day, we are shackled to the decaying corpse of liberalism, which is the worldview that got us into this mess in the first place.

There is no justification for discriminating against the rich, just as there is no justification for discriminating against anyone, although there is plenty of justification for rejecting the likes of Menendez, Schumer, Pelosi, and McCaskill and their entire political philosophy.

It is time to stop dragging the corpse around. It is time to bury it.

We started the job in this last election. Let's finish it in the next.

ISLAM VERSUS CHRISTIANITY: THE STARK HYPOCRISY OF THE LEFT

December 9, 2010

Have you noticed how our friends on the left and the far left and the moderate left never complain about separation of church and state when it comes to Islam?

Perhaps it's because they know for fourteen hundred years, Islam has operated as a complete system all rolled into one, combining religion, politics, government, law, culture, society, the arts, education, family life, diet, medicine, wardrobe, economics, and the military. Islam is not so much a religion as it is an entire system of life, cradle to grave. There is no separation of anything, much less church and state. Islam is both church and state and everything else, the most comprehensive and pervasive theocracy ever known. (For those who might be tempted to level the same accusation against Judaism or Christianity, a few questions: is America a theocracy; is Israel a theocracy; are there any Christian theocracies anywhere?)

Knowing the Muslim tendency toward despotism, those on the left likely decline criticism, deciding (1) what Muslims do remains their business, (2) any criticism would immediately be branded bigoted and Islam-o-phobic, and (3) it is paramount to preserve and promote multicultural political correctness at all costs. Any in depth evaluation of Islam would certainly attract the PC police, interfere in other people's private business, and risk the bigot label, so, by all means, the only option is stuffing one's head in the sand, hoping against hope the religion of peace will stop waging war.

Consequently, the left gives a pass to a system of belief that clearly advocates and participates in violence perpetrated against anyone outside the confines of its theocracy. No matter tons of evidence to the contrary; in the mind of a leftist, Islam is a religion of peace and should be allowed free reign. Heaven forbid we should ever discuss the issue of separation of church and state in a Muslim context.

However, when it comes to Christianity in America or Europe and anywhere else, it is an entirely different story. In this context the gloves come off and fists fly. The left has no problem condemning Christian America with a seething virulence. The true religion of peace, founded and led by the Prince of peace, is anathema to the leftist mind, a mind insisting that Christians are the agents of theocracy despite the fact none exists anywhere in the world, despite the fact that Christians were the authors of the First Amendment to the US Constitution: "Congress shall make no law respecting an establishment of religion, or prohibiting the free exercise thereof…"

It is truly remarkable the ability of the left to so contort themselves as to arrive at torturous conclusions as far removed from reality as can be: a warring theocracy routinely yielding brutal dictatorships is to be tolerated and even embraced; a peace-loving, love-based tradition delivering world-class charity and democratic republicanism, freedom, and prosperity, that tradition is to be condemned, attacked, and destroyed.

For the left it matters not their attacks on Christians remain unwarranted interference in the lives of private citizens fully within their rights to freely exercise their faith without state interference. The left would use the state to destroy Christianity, and, indeed, it works twenty-four-seven with those means and ends in mind. The documented linkage between Christian faith and the founders' vision drawing the best from those principles without violating the Establishment Clause is a nuance beyond leftist comprehension.

For the left it is perfectly okay to discriminate against Christians because, after all, the direction of the PC flow of traffic when it comes to the bigot violation is a one-way street. Translation: it's impossible to be a Christ-o-phobic bigot because Christ is fair game because, well, you know, wars and stuff and the Native Americans, and stuff.

For the left, nourished by the traditions of atheism, agnosticism, and secular humanism, any notion of God within Western culture is so repugnant, so anti-PC, so contrary and obstructionist to their utopian designs that God and his followers deserve whatever they get. So fervent is this leftist belief it blinds them to their inner Nero, making them comfortable with their Muslim alliance even though such an alliance requires they turn a blind eye to the grim treatment of women and children.

The founders knew all about the dangers of combining church and state. They knew from bitter experience in Europe that allowing government the duties of the church led to despotism, and they knew as well that giving the church the power of government likewise worked against the interests of republican government and against liberty itself. The founders also knew liberty was God-given and only a moral and virtuous people would proceed as individuals to protect and defend liberty at its foundation, the consent of the governed working to prevent the excesses of government. Therefore, the First Amendment was put in place to keep government out of the business of the church and to prohibit the church from taking over government, for neither is suited to the work of the other. However, the founders never intended that godly principles should be expunged from the public square, as the left so gleefully, and errantly, asserts.

Even a casual reading of the Federalist Papers and the writings of the founders concerning the First Amendment bears all this out. For comprehensive studies, consult these most recent scholarly works, edited by Daniel Dreisbach, Jeffry Morrison, and Mark David Hall: "The Founders on God and Government" and "The Forgotten Founders on Religion and Public Life."

Finally, one need not look far to see the fruit of our folly.

- The newborn Prince of peace is loathed and assaulted by secularists at Christmas, the same people who promote a mosque at Ground Zero, a mosque to be dedicated on 9/11. (Can you say 'victory mosque?')

- Billy cannot pray in school or read his Bible or wear a T-shirt that says anything about Christ, according to the ACLU.

- Hakeem must have halal food available at the school cafeteria, and he must be allowed to wash in segregated facilities, and he must be provided several prayer times daily.

- A cross honoring those who died defending liberty is removed from public view, even as Sharia law is promoted and embraced by American politicians.

- Terrorists, by their own admission, are rightly identified as Muslim enemy combatants, but they are treated as if they are American citizens.

- Christian-American citizens are treated like enemy combatants—slandered, insulted, and marginalized, the objects of increasing pressure to deny them their basic constitutional rights.

- A president saying he is a Christian while he does everything possible to stifle Christianity even as he helps fund mosque renovations worldwide after bowing to the Saudi king and sending billions in aid to Muslim states with direct ties to terrorist organizations.

- So much for progress and progressivism.

MARINE LOSES LEG, RETURNS TO COMBAT

December 10, 2010

During the last nine years, first in Afghanistan and later in Iraq, the all-volunteer American military has fought bravely and successfully against a ruthless enemy willing to commit suicide, kill women and children, use roadside bombs, booby traps, and civilian snipers.

The cost has been high in blood and treasure.

The number of American wounded totals 41,583, according to the Department of Defense.

Total KIA: 5,844.

One wounded warrior and his fellow Marines exemplify the finest in honor, courage, and duty, demonstrating that catastrophic injuries need not be the end of the story.

Garrett Jones, a veteran of hundreds of combat operations, was on foot patrol in July 2007 in Iraq with Company E, 2d Battalion, 7th Marine Regiment, when a blast from an improvised explosive device almost killed him.

Thanks to the quick work of his fellow Marines, Garrett's life was saved, but his left leg had to be amputated. After the blasts, in order to radio a chopper for evacuation, three Marines ran back to the command post under fire while others tended to Garrett, who only had moments before he would have bled out. Rob Pofahl is the man who came to Garrett's aid to apply the tourniquet. His quick response saved Garrett's life. Garrett's dad, retired police officer Scott Jones, says he loves Nathan Handville and Pofahl like sons and provides additional information:

> Nathan is now out of the Marines—also medically retired. He lost partial use of his right hand, and he gradually lost his vision in his right eye. He is blind in that eye now. He is married and has a baby, living in his home state of Florida. Nathan was the squad leader when they got blown up. He refused any pain meds until after he knew Garrett was evacuated and taken care of.

What happened afterward is remarkable, even astounding.

After surgery in Germany, Garrett was taken to a naval medical facility in Bethesda, then the NMC in San Diego for more treatment. He lost forty pounds during the course of bed rest and seventeen follow up surgeries to deal with burns, infections, and shrapnel. Garrett was well enough to welcome his fellow 2/7 Marines upon their return home, an emotional reunion for everyone.

Despite his injuries, Garrett wanted to return to duty with this fellow Marines, those men who'd saved his life, especially when news came the 2/7 was being deployed to Afghanistan.

Within a few months of the blast, he was fitted with several prosthetic devices, all for walking, and one specially designed for him to see about returning to a long-held passion: snowboarding.

Remarkably, only one month back on his feet, by December 2007, only five months since the blast, he was snowboarding in Colorado with fellow wounded warriors, a recreational outlet that strengthened him physically and psychologically, leading him to believe that, indeed, one day he could rejoin his unit.

In early 2008 Garrett had the opportunity to meet the commandant of the Marine Corps, General James Conway. He asked the general for permission to return to his unit. Soon, Garrett was back with the 2/7, serving in intelligence, helping the battalion gather and disseminate information vital to operations in Afghanistan. Thus,

Garrett Jones became the fastest amputee to return to combat duty and one of the few to do so. And, by the way, it was not a walk-on role. He had to go through all the pre-deployment training endured by his fellow Marines.

Again, Garrett's dad fills us in:

> In Afghanistan, he did spend most of his time working in the intelligence shop. But the warrior spirit dies hard, and he begged his way into being allowed to go spend a week with his beloved Echo Co out on a FOB. He actually saw action out there, participated in an ambush of some Taliban fighters, killing them. The senior NCO out there asked Garrett if he wanted to be written up for another Combat Action Ribbon, and he refused, saying that Echo (2/7) had been out there fighting and sacrificing for the whole deployment, and he hadn't, so it just didn't feel right to him.

Garrett, a devout Christian, went on to work with and encourage other amputees, urging them to set new goals and strive to achieve them. Now retired from the Corps, Garrett continues snowboarding competition and runs a shooting review website: http://shooterreviews.com/garrett_jones.

He is also attending university fulltime in Oregon, preparing for post-graduate work in prosthetics or a career in intelligence.

(Update: Garrett is now married. He and his wife are expecting their first child, summer 2011.)

"PROGRESSIVES" SAY OBAMA FOUND WANTING

December 13, 2010

> Never kick a cow chip on a hot day.
>
> Will Rogers

> Like a dog that returns to his vomit is a fool who repeats his folly.
>
> Proverbs 26:11

We don't seem to learn from our mistakes, do we? Let's take a peek at some of the chip kickers of the day as they insist bipartisanship and civility are the keys to our economic salvation.

First, the first lady. She tells us obesity is a major national security issue. Therefore, the government must intervene to manage school lunch programs. Step aside, Mom and Dad. Michelle Obama has recipes ready to force feed your children. Somehow, carrots will stop Iranian missiles launched from Venezuela. Perhaps someone on her enormous one million-dollar-per-year revolving staff will remind her it is unconstitutional to force Mom and Dad to buy wheat grass juice and tofu.

Not to be outdone, the president, eternally health conscious (between cigarettes), agrees to a tax deal with Republicans, the ones he calls hostage takers, violating the no-negotiations-with-terrorists policy. One Dem congressman from Boston, infuriated with the president for negotiating with Republicans, called them 'blackmailers.' Senator Menendez called Republicans terrorists, noting their plans to fly planes into buildings unless the president extends tax cuts to the rich. After all, what kind of government allows people to keep their belongings?

Meanwhile, some Republicans and Tea Party folks were screaming bloody murder because the deal extends unemployment benefits, resulting in a ton of new spending. The deal provides certain energy credits as well, all to help Obama stomach humble pie.

Oh, and by the way, the tax deal is not even in writing yet, so members are being asked to vote on a fill-in-the-blanks measure subject to manipulation in secret before, during, and after the vote. More chip kicking, reminiscent of the health bill, portions now found unconstitutional, at least by a lower court.

So on Friday Pelosi caught the first flight to Norway for a little Nobel hobnobbing to stand shoulder-to-shoulder with Chinese human rights activists, a rebound from her no-show at the Cancun climate change summit that bombed as badly as Keith Olbermann's surprise birthday party.

Speaking of the Drollberman and his fellow chip kickers, did you get a load of his recent raging rant against Obama? The Doberman castigated Obama, calling him no better that the "treacherous and traitorous" Republicans he capitulated to on taxes. Keith, demonstrating why he will never earn a Ph.D in economics, is livid, livid I tell you, that Obama has turned his back on Keynes and all the little people, only to feed the "insatiable maw of capitalism" by subsidizing the "idle and corporate rich" who never created a job in their lives.

Lighten up, Francis.

Forgive the impertinence, but, with a thirty million-dollar MSNBC contract, has Dobermann created even one job, or is he speaking from direct experience when he describes the "idle rich?"

Oobermann the Pompous goes on to eviscerate Obama for a failure to negotiate claiming Obama is in a position of strength. A position of strength? Should we conclude Obama draws strength from being thoroughly repudiated by a huge majority of the American people?

To be fair, we really cannot blame "progressives."

It's their pattern: self-deception, epic failure, demonization of the opposition, followed by devouring their own. It is observable history repeating itself. Only Jimmy Carter has lived long enough to be regurgitated more than once.

Dobermann would have us believe he is no enemy of progressivism, no traitor to the cause, no Obama assassin by denouncing the president so viciously. No!

Dobermann insists he is a man of principle, loyal only to the many millions who've been on unemployment forever, all the while claiming he cares about deficits created by the very progressives he worships, insisting the solution to the economic Armageddon they caused is tax the rich and continue this orgy of spending! Now how's that for principle-driven politics!

(Rest easy, Maynard, you still have friends in the asylum.)

The generalized meltdown on the left sounds like chip kickin' to the average moms and dads who hit the streets almost two years ago to confront the insanity of tax and spend socialism, those common-sense patriots attacked by Pelosi and Dobermann and others as Astroturf-driven, hate monger racists.

Somebody ought to tell progressives squealing "Wee, wee, wee" all the way home that thanks to a measure of certainty provided by extending the tax cuts, business people are now saying they look forward to investments in job-creating enterprises, and thus the economic picture has improved markedly for 2011 in just a short time, at least in terms of perception and optimism, no thanks to Obots.

Lost on Droolbermann and his meandering minions, raising taxes at this juncture would crash the market and tank the economy, but never mind all that; there's chips to kick!

At least Obama recognizes the folly of fanaticism.

Bonus features:

Maybe the best chip kicker of the day is dethroned congressman Alan Grayson from Florida. He ran into a number of peace-loving progressives on MSNBC lately. After claiming the tax deal amounts to the biggest corporate giveaway in history, Grayson was filleted, fried, and serve up as an appetizer by the other panelists who apparently agreed with Florida voters that Grayson should be kept as far from the House as possible.

And, fresh from his victory in Nevada, here is chip kicker Harry Reid's contribution? According to MSNBC:

> Two big Las Vegas casino companies that pumped more than $650,000 into Nevada Sen. Harry Reid's re-election would benefit from a controversial Internet gambling measure that the Senate majority leader is attempting to tuck into the massive tax cut bill, according to lobbyists and Senate staff members familiar with the measure.

Parting shot:

Progressives! Remember Keith and the Gang insisted you elect Obama and company, giving him endorsements galore, forwarding the messianic vision. Now they would have you tar and feather the man. Please think thrice before taking Keith Olbermann's advice about anything ever again.

THE PERFECT
LAW THAT
GIVES FREEDOM

January 13, 2011

Once again Sarah Palin is the lightning rod for the wrath of the Left, her only crime, upholding traditional American values. No one in modern times, other than George W. Bush, has received more threats, condemnation, criticism, false accusations, outright slander and vicious verbal assault, and as the perpetrators continue, in the same breath, they complain about hate speech.

In truth she is the prime example of what happens to anyone in this country who contradicts the religion of the Left practiced by zealots in power, media, entertainment and education.

Still, traditionalists promote the perfect law that gives freedom, turning the other cheek.

One psychotic murders innocent people in Tucson and the talking heads go on a rampage of blame, recrimination, political attack and accusation—-decrying vitriol even as they promote it: the lynch mob complaining about vigilantes.

Even so, people of good will work to restrain the tongue and still make their views known.

Politicians call for more laws to restrict the free exercise of citizen rights, provoking widespread anger already kindled by government action, politicians who then turn and blame The People for the anger and sense of alienation. Usually the problem and rarely part of the solution, legislators grab more power, causing furious dissent, making problems worse.

The People demonstrate peacefully as they give voice to their objections, sometimes loudly, yet the politicians call them "evil mongers," "anti-American," "ignorant," and "delusional." Common courtesy is cast aside along with any sense of public service.

A memorial service for the Tucson victims last night turns into a pep rally for college kids. Did anybody tell these kids a memorial service is supposed to be a somber event?

Common folks promote common courtesy since little is witnessed.

One of the most divisive and deceptive presidents in history stands up calling for civility and unity, expecting everyone to ignore his contributions to the generalized sense of anger and alienation, and there remains a nagging sense too many are trying to derive advantage from the tragedy, compounding it.

All the while, there is a growing awareness we need a return to first principles coupled with a renewed respect for seasoned speech. In Psalm 15 we read:

> [1] LORD, who may dwell in your sacred tent? Who may live on your holy mountain? [2] The one whose walk is blameless, who does what is righteous, who speaks the truth from their heart; [3] whose tongue utters no slander, who does no wrong to a neighbor, and casts no slur on others; [4] who despises a vile person but honors those who fear the LORD; who keeps an oath even when it hurts, and does not change their mind; [5] who lends money to the poor without interest; who does not accept a bribe against the innocent. Whoever does these things will never be shaken.

In James chapter 1 we read:

> 19 My dear brothers and sisters, take note of this: Everyone should be quick to listen, slow to speak and slow to become angry, 20 because human anger does not produce the righteousness that God desires. 21 Therefore, get rid of all moral filth and the evil that is so prevalent and humbly accept the word planted in you, which can save you. 22 Do not merely listen to the word, and so deceive yourselves. Do what it says. 23 Anyone who listens to the word but does not do what it says is like someone who looks at his face in a mirror 24 and, after looking at himself, goes away and immediately forgets what he looks like. 25 *But whoever looks intently into the perfect law that gives freedom, and continues in it—not forgetting what they have heard, but doing it—they will be blessed in what they do.* 26 Those who consider themselves religious and yet do not keep a tight rein on their tongues deceive themselves, and their religion is worthless. 27 Religion that God our Father accepts as pure and faultless is this: to look after orphans and widows in their distress and to keep oneself from being polluted by the world.

Our Founders, informed by the Scripture, knew our country would only survive and thrive if her citizens remained self-regulating, and that virtue is the lifeblood of self-regulation. They knew this experiment in self-government would fail without a virtuous and self-regulating citizenry.

We are in danger of losing our freedom because we ignore the perfect law giving liberty its life.

REAGAN: COURAGEOUS, CONSISTENT, COMPASSIONATE, COURTEOUS

February 1, 2011

As we approach the 100th birthday celebration of Ronald Reagan, our 40th president (1981–1989), we would do well to remember his legacy, his encouragement, and his greatness. Three quotes highlight his greatness:

> "Freedom is never more than one generation away from extinction. We didn't pass it to our children in the bloodstream. It must be fought for, protected, and handed on for them to do the same."

> "If we ever forget that we are One Nation Under God, then we will be a nation gone under."

> "Let us be sure that those who come after will say of us in our time, that in our time we did everything that could be done. We finished the race; we kept them free; we kept the faith."

Reagan loved America with a burning passion. He loved freedom and justice for all. He viewed our country as a "shining city on a hill" beckoning all people from all corners of the earth. As much as Roosevelt and Churchill he was a great liberator, one of the giants of the 20th century. He was consistent, courageous, compassionate and uncommonly cheerful and optimistic, the epitome of greatness.

Ronald Reagan personified the best in the American character:

- He boldly proclaimed American exceptionalism with a humility that contradicted the ugly American stereotype.
- He respected the native intelligence and goodness of the American people, and we trusted him because he earned that trust by being straight with us.
- He genuinely connected with the majority of Americans, naturally promoting goodness.
- He sought friendships and alliances at every turn without capitulating to tyrants or ignoring core values.
- He promoted economic freedom, demonstrating prosperity comes when government steps out of the way, allowing the energy, creativity and work ethic of the American spirit to flow abundantly.
- He stood for the underdog and boldly defended the rights of the unborn despite criticism from his own political allies.
- Coordinating with Margaret Thatcher and Pope John Paul II he confronted the Soviet empire, helping bring it to an end, without firing a shot.
- He made no apology for the link between faith and freedom urging all Americans to work for the betterment of the next generation.
- More than most any President he sought inspiration from the Founders, quoting them often, and freely.

- He restored American pride at home and our reputation abroad, all with a smile and incomparable kindness.
- He believed anything was possible in America, and proved it in the way he conducted himself.

No story reveals the true character of this great man better than the real life account shared by John Barletta, U.S. Secret Service agent, the man who guarded the President for ten years, traveling with him everywhere, and serving as his riding partner at the ranch and at Camp David.

In his book "Riding with Reagan," Citadel Press, 2005, Barletta shares the story of how the President's Alzheimer's disease was first diagnosed, and what happened afterward. Keep in mind Mr. Reagan was an expert horseman. He loved his ranch, his horses, and riding, almost as much as he loved our country.

John Barletta writes, on page 208:

> I had known the president for more than a decade. During that time, his memory had been incredible. He could remember the names of friends that he had not seen in forty years, and he could tell stories down to the smallest detail…
>
> In late 1993, President Reagan flew to Chicago to deliver a speech. Mrs. Reagan was with him, and once they got to their hotel, he seemed confused. Turning to Mrs. Reagan, he said, "I'm afraid I don't know where I am."
>
> In early 1994, I sensed that his memory was faltering… He was forgetting things more often, and when we went out riding, he would make mistakes—-the sort of mistakes that not even a rookie rider would make.
>
> [Subsequently, an examination, and the diagnosis.]
>
> I was amazed at how courageous and gracious Mrs. Reagan was in both confronting her husband's disease and dealing with all the challenges.

For the President, it was a particularly troubling diagnosis. Not so much for what he feared it might do to him, but instead for what it would mean for the people around him. His mother Nelle had been afflicted with the disease, as had his younger brother Neil. He had watched both of them descend into a world in which they did not recognize those who loved them, and they could no longer care for themselves. I think he was most concerned about what this would mean to Nancy. He often said that his life began when he met Nancy. They had cared for each other deeply, and now she would also be his caregiver.

In this final letter to the country he loved, the President wrote, "Unfortunately, as Alzheimer's disease progresses, the family often bears a heavy burden. I only wish there was some way I could spare Nancy from this painful experience."

(At the ranch) I'd go to him and he'd be staring at something. 'John, I know I'm supposed to do something with this, but I can't think of it. Would you help me?' He was having difficulty remembering how to buckle the cinch, which is what goes around the horse's girth that holds the saddle in place. Sure enough, he had it on wrong. From the time that started happening, I would have my horse already saddled when he came up, so I could watch him tack up his horse. Often, he would put something in his hand and then hesitate. That would tell me he was having trouble. I would just take his hand and move it to the right position. A big smile would come over his face, 'That's what I was trying to do.'

Those tough times drew us even closer.

One morning Mrs. Reagan called me at the command post, "John, will you come down here, Ronnie's having a problem." So I rushed down to the house and asked, "What's the matter?"

"Will you tell my husband that you're ready to go riding? He won't leave." Mrs. Reagan had a technique she used if she wanted the President to get going. She would use the line: "You need to go, because people are waiting."

He would never ever want to keep people waiting. It was so impolite.

...things began to deteriorate. I went to Mrs. Reagan and said, "Mrs. Reagan, he's making too many mistakes up there. I can't protect him from himself. He's making rookie mistakes, and he's been riding for fifty-five years. I don't think he should ride anymore. It's getting that dangerous."

"Then you have to tell him, John."

"I don't want to tell him that, Mrs. Reagan. You need to tell him that."

"No," she said with tears in her eyes. "I can't. John, you've got to talk to him and tell him, because he'll understand, and he'll take it better if you tell him."

I walked down to the house, knocked on the door, and went inside. He was sitting by the fireplace, reading. He was an avid reader. He'd go to sleep with a book on his chest just about every night.

"Mr. President," I said, "we had a lot of trouble out there this morning, didn't we?"

"Yeah, I did."

Even in the bad times, he was still polite.

"It's just at the point where this riding isn't working out. Sir, I don't think you should ride anymore."

Knowing him like I did and understanding what horseback riding meant to him, I felt like I was telling someone I don't think he should breathe anymore. I was now practically in tears.

He got up and put his hands on my shoulders and said, "It's okay, John. I know."

That was it. We never rode again. We never talked about it.

He could see how upset I was, and he was trying to make me feel okay.

That was the kind of guy he was.

A WEINER NAMED ANTHONY

March 4, 2011
A well-orchestrated mob, burning Crosses in the night
UnCommon Cause, Van Jones and "the politics of hatred"

Congressman Anthony Weiner (Dem.-N.Y.) is the leader of a mob looking to destroy Supreme Court Justice Clarence Thomas and his wife, Ginni.

In a recent appearance on Fox, Weiner made this outlandish statement: "We learned recently that Ginni Thomas, the spouse of Justice Thomas, has received more than $700,000 from organizations whose existence is based on making sure the healthcare law is ruled unconstitutional."

This is a flat-out lie.

Weiner knows he is lying, but hey, any slander works in the effort to prevent ObamaCare from being heard by the full court. Knocking out Thomas increases the odds of survivability you see.

Fact Mr. Weiner: IRS records indicate Ginni Thomas was paid $686,000 by ONE organization, the Heritage Foundation, over the course of five years—2003 through 2007—about $140,000 a year, comparable to salaries paid by the very "best" Leftist think tanks everywhere.

Fact: Notice the inclusive dates—-her work for Heritage occurred long before Obama was elected, long before the passage of ObamaCare.

Fact: The Heritage Foundation has existed since 1973. Its existence is not 'based on making sure the healthcare law is ruled unconstitutional.' It is a conservative research and education outfit. It does not profit from the healthcare industry. It is a non-profit organization. Does Heritage receive contributions from doctors and others in the healthcare industry? Of course, and so does a full range of left-wing think tanks.

Mr. Weiner, Ginni Thomas's work had nothing to do with ObamaCare and the continuing existence of the Heritage Foundation has nothing to do with the survivability of ObamaCare.

You are a liar, Mr. Weiner, and you know it. You are a propagandist liar and a fraud.

Supreme Court experts, even on the Left, see nothing in these circumstances warranting recusal.

Weiner and friends know that nailing Thomas increases the odds this healthcare monster will survive judicial review. They are grasping at straws to try and minimize the will of the people being expressed through House representatives these days. They are trying to overcome lower court rulings ObamaCare is unconstitutional. Isn't that obvious?

This is also a fully orchestrated attack on all things conservative, including the Tea Party, given Ginni Thomas's alignment with both.

And as John Fund reminded Bill Maher and Weiner recently, nobody cried 'conflict of interest' when Hillary carried the healthcare water for Billy and the boys.

Watch Fund destroy Maher and Weiner single-handedly on YouTube: "John Fund Battles Bill Maher and Rep. Weiner on Glenn Beck, Sarah Palin and Clarence Thomas." Great entertainment.

Trouble is Weiner, like Obama, is glad to trash the Constitution and destroy the separation of powers simply to forward social and political agendas. That's how reprehensible these people remain. Rude and sarcastic just doesn't carry the day, Weiner. Most people see you for what you are.

The effort to destroy Justice Thomas goes back years to the Anita Hill * accusations leveled during his confirmation hearings, but they've flared up in recent months given his apparent oversight in not properly filing paperwork to report his wife's income.

Some would say the flare ups have much to do with Obama's decline and the November election results as well.

Others say the flare ups have intensified as judges rule ObamaCare unconstitutional, pushing it rapidly up the ladder to the SCOTUS.

Everybody is getting into the flare up act. The mob is gleefully burning Crosses in the night.

Colbert spent a great deal of time recently ridiculing Justice Thomas.

Reporter and columnist Christian Hartsock taped Common Cause zombies led by Van Jones at their convention recently, leftists saying the vilest things, now the subject of a congressional investigation. (YouTube: "Progressive" Ralliers Call for Lynching of Clarence Thomas.")

Hartsock asked several Common Causers: "After we impeach Clarence Thomas what should we do with him?"

First Answer: "Put him back in the fields."

Another Causer: "Cut off his toes one by one and feed them to him."

Another Causer: "Torture."

Another Causer: "String 'em up!"

Obviously, Justice Thomas is top of mind for the Causers. Do you suppose they'd just received marching orders?

Indeed, Common Cause was one of many organizations that started beating the drum calling for the head of Justice Thomas, accusing his wife of malfeasance, and leveling the charge of conflict of interest. Weiner is just one of the duller tools in the Common Cause shed.

Many other Leftwing mobsters and vigilantes are swarming the blogosphere burning Crosses outside the Thomas's house. They certainly do know how to communally organize and orchestrate a mob, as we've seen in Madison, thanks to Obama's inner Alinksy.

Over on Capitol Hill, 74 Democrat legislators have signed a letter condemning Justice Thomas. No question these 74 are only acting in the public interest.

Finally: why the frequent reference to burning Crosses?

Well, you see, the Thomas's are devout Christians, and we just can't have that on the Supreme Court now, can we?

And finally, since Justice Ginsburg emerged from the bowels of the ACLU, should she have recused herself from every case brought by them and every issue central to their advocacy? After all, it wasn't her husband doing anything political, it was her, directly.

And how about Elena Kagan? She did a ton to forward ObamaCare. Judicial Watch is investigating. Where is the Weiner called Anthony alleging a gross violation of judicial ethics by Kagan?

Parting shot: recall Kagan saying speech could be limited by government if it was shown harmful. Should Kagan therefore encourage Eric Holder to prosecute Van Jones and his Common Cause night riders?

THIS COLUMN IS RACIST

March 16, 2011

"I have a dream that my four little children will one day live in a nation where they will not be judged by the color of their skin, but by the content of their character."

—Rev. Dr. Martin Luther King, Jr.

An NFL player says team owners treat players like slaves. The player, a Black man, will make $10 million this year. He could not be reached for clarification. He is touring Africa on a goodwill trip.

A little good will goes a long way.

According to Obama, the Cambridge Police "acted stupidly" trying to protect a homeowner's property. When the homeowner showed up, a Black professor, he turned on the police, refused to obey orders, then insulted them. Acting strictly according to procedure, they arrested the guy, but the President said they acted stupidly. Once Obama finally obtained the facts, he seemed to back down, but never apologized.

According to the President and his friends, Jeremiah Wright and Louis Farrakhan are heroes, but George Bush and his kind are criminals. Just ask Percy Sutton, attorney for Malcolm X, and big Obama cheerleader. Just ask Khalid al-Mansour, mentor to Black Panthers,

Jew hater, Christian hater, so-called professor who encourages Muslims to attack and maim white people, and big Obama cheerleader, one who helped Obama get into Harvard, a real boy scout. (Jihadwatch.org, "The Obama-Mansour Connection.")

Jesse Jackson calls for war in Madison, Wisconsin, after fomenting racial tensions in Portland, Oregon last year, but it's all about the colors of the rainbow.

A black "professor" out of North Carolina actually says the only solution is killing all white people. No kidding. (WND.com, "Professor: exterminate the white people," Oct. 22, 2005)

Al Sharpton says school choice is racist. Of course. You can't be allowing people the freedom to use their own tax money to educate their own children as they see fit. How blatantly un-American can you be to suggest such a thing? Obviously racist. (The latest in Sharpton shooting blanks.)

Speaking of Sharpton and Jackson, who could forget a few years back the Duke University lacrosse players accused of rape and racism and raked over the coals by the mainstream media for at least a year, only to be exonerated by DNA evidence in the end? (American Thinker.com, "Racism 101 at Duke," April 12, 2006)

Remember this gem: Black Panthers standing outside a polling place during the 2008 presidential election in Philadelphia. One has a truncheon. Its only purpose is cracking skulls. The Panthers taunt voters. One says: "That's why you're gonna be ruled by a black man, Cracka!" (BigGovernment.com, "New Black Panther Party President admits to Philadelphia voter intimidation," July 9, 2010)

The Panthers were convicted. Obama's AG Eric Holder declined to follow through with the penalty phase. Holder says enforcing the law without regard to race, his sworn duty, would demean "his people," in this case, and, he says, it's a lie his Justice Department is racially motivated. Really?

A civil rights lawyer weighs in decrying the incident and criticizing Holder and the Obama administration. He must be a racist. Anyone who highlights the incident is a racist, a mere political opportunist. (Fox video on YouTube, "Eric Holder Drops Charges on Black Panthers for Voter Intimidation.")

Notice, the civil rights attorney identifies the Black Panther Party as a hate organization, so designated by the Anti-Defamation League and the Southern Poverty Law Center. The Black Panther Party, dating from the 1960s, has always been a Marxist group promoting violent overthrow of the U.S. government. Saying so makes you a racist.

In the wake of Katrina a Black singer said, "Bush doesn't care about black people," accusing Bush of being a racist.

If you opposed the power of public employee unions and their unholy alliance with radical leftists using tax revenue to finance political activism, well, you are obviously a racist according to Charles Rangel. (TheHill.com, "Rangle Abolishing collective bargaining akin to slavery," March 1, 2011)

If you want to hold hearings to determine the threat level posed by radical Islam domestically, you're a racist, according to Black legislators weighing in at the hearings recently.

If you suggest government affirmative action housing programs interfering with the private mortgage industry led to the financial meltdown, you are a racist.

If you suggest universal healthcare is not a constitutional right: racist.

If you think turning a blind eye toward illegal immigration is not such a great idea: racist.

If you suggest we must reform welfare and entitlement spending if the nation is to survive: racist.

If you don't swing with the green agenda promoted by Van Jones: racist.

If you suggest affirmative action actually works against the best interests of Black Americans: racist.

Anyone who levels legitimate criticism of President Obama is a racist.

Anyone who hits the streets to protest government spending, waste, fraud and mismanagement is a racist.

Write a column like this: racist.

You know, it is difficult to extend the hand of friendship when it keeps getting chopped off.

Haven't we learned by now that playing the race card indiscriminately only stirs up violence and resentment, the exact opposite of what Dr. King would have us do?

So then, who is the real racist?

Bonus material: a real solution from a black man who experienced real slavery, Frederick Douglass: 'I have one great political idea...the best expression of it I have found in the Bible. It is in substance, 'Righteousness exalteth a nation; sin is a reproach to any people' [Proverbs 14.34]. This constitutes my politics' the negative and positive of my politics, and the whole of my politics.'

Parting shot: So-called 'progressives' attending a recent Common Cause event said Justice Clarence Thomas should be 'sent back to the fields,' or should be 'strung up.' Now, now. These were not racist comments. They weren't even reported in the MSM. No. These were merely the statements of frustration uttered by enlightened citizens concerned about social justice and the plight of all oppressed people. (Christian Hartsock, *"Progressive Ralliers Call for Lynching of Clarence Thomas," YouTube video, Feb. 2, 2011)*

Ask these people about the vicious, insulting treatment they've received, not so much for being black as for being black and Conservative:

Larry Elder
Janice Rogers Brown
Walter Williams
Alphonso Rachel
Condoleezza Rice

Thomas Sowell
Anne Wortham
Ken Blackwell
Lt. Col. Allen West
Michael Steele
Herman Cain
Shelby Steele
J.C. Watts
Armstrong Williams
Star Parker

IRAN DECLARES WAR ON ISRAEL, AGAIN

March 19, 2011
Obama: transparently indecisive
To dither: 'to be nervously irresolute'
While Obama dithers over Libya, Iran and Hamas and Hezbollah are escalating violence against Israel. At least Obama is transparently and decidedly anti-Israel while he remains decidedly undecided about most everything else.

Boy, it sure is a good thing the 'freedom revolution' happened in Egypt, eh?

Amazing how we've heard very little from Cairo lately. Did the paradise of Sharia flower overnight? Well, we know this much: Christians have been slaughtered, and the new Egypt allowed Iran to ship weapons through the Suez Canal.

Ah, progress!

Fortunately, the Israelis intercepted the Iranian ship, thus preventing that shipment of weapons to Hamas, but that didn't prevent Hamas from shooting 50 rockets at Israel this morning.

Standing virtually alone in the fight against Jihad, Israel cannot rely on American protection given the current administration. Consequently, terrorists escalate, Obama capitulates, increasing the chances of all out war.

Perhaps it is time for Hillary to issue a statement decrying Hamas rocket launches, but we'll have to wait many days. It will likely contain words like "unacceptable," and "inappropriate," and "international community," and "U.N. resolution," and "construction in the West Bank," and "separate state." Maybe they'll push harder for a divided Jerusalem, making matters much worse.

Writing just days ago, Alan Dershowitz states Israel has the right to attack Iran right now, citing the shipment of weapons, again, an act of war by Iran:

> The recent attempt to ship arms to Hamas in Gaza is an act of war committed by the Iranian government against the Israeli government. The Israeli Navy seized the ship, loaded with weapons designed to kill Israeli civilians, and traced the weapons back to Iran. Nor is this the first act of war that would justify a military response by Israel under international law. Iran has sent other boatloads of anti personnel weapons to Hamas and Hezbollah. In addition, back in 1992, the Iranian leaders planned and authorized a deadly attack on Israel's embassy in Argentina. That bombing, which was carried out by Iranian agents, constituted a direct armed attack on the state of Israel, since its embassy is part of its sovereign territory. Moreover, the Iranian government has publicly declared war on Israel by calling for it "to be wiped off the map."

Imagine the howls from the international media should Israel launch an attack against Iran, however justified. 'Justice' demands Israel just stand there and take it, don't you see.

Dershowitz continues:

> Under international law, these acts of war' known as Casus Belli' fully justify an Israeli armed response. Even the UN Charter authorizes a unilateral response to an armed attack. Providing weapons to a declared enemy in the face of an embargo has historically been deemed an armed attack under the law of war,

especially when those providing the weapons intend for them to be used against the enemy's civilians. So too is the bombing of an embassy.

So too was the taking of the U.S. Embassy in Tehran in 1979 with Americans held hostage for 444 days. Carter let them get away with it, dithering all the way, and we are still paying for that cowardly retreat, compounded today by the new Dithering Idiot in Chief.

REVISED DECLARATION OF INDEPENDENCE FOR 2011

April 22, 2011

Every now and then as things develop it's necessary to cut political connections between one group and another, and, for good cause, establish separate operations according to the laws of Nature and God. Good manners require the initiating party explain the reasons for declaring independence.

First, some background about what we believe and how those beliefs require us to exact severance.

It is obvious that every person is created equal, including babies still preparing to enter the world. All human beings are precious, sacred, created by a loving God. This God endows each one of us with ironclad, inseparable civil rights, to name a few, the right to Life, Liberty and the opportunity to work toward Happiness in this world.

Government exists to secure all civil rights provided by God. Government can only do its job if it first gets permission from The People. Government is therefore placed under the control of The People and exists to serve the interests of The People. The traditional moral precepts of the majority of the people, dearly held for millennia, make up the foundational moral code of the society, and government, if rightly securing the rights of The People, will exemplify a respect for that foundational code.

When any government begins to run rough shod over The People, or when government behaves in a way that contradicts the will of The People, or when government actually destroys the civil rights of The People, then The People have an overriding Right and Duty to change their government and make it behave, or, failing that, they have a Right to abolish that abusive government and craft a replacement as they see fit. Simply put: in America we do not suffer tyrants.

Obviously, the wise and prudent will not run about recklessly demanding government be abolished on a whim or for shallow, temporal reasons. Historically, most people would rather endure government abuse hoping matters will change as opposed to engaging the very painful and dangerous work of revolution.

However, when abusive government refuses to change, refuses to listen to The Will of The People, and indeed, when such government insists on escalating its abuses against The People, demonstrating a clear intention of moving toward central control, even Despotism, then it is not only the Right of The People but their Duty to throw off such a government and appoint others devoted to serve as protectors of liberty, life and the pursuit of happiness.

For decades, and especially since 2006, the American people have suffered patiently under the dictatorial rule of government officials and bureaucrats in Washington, D.C., officials who have abused their authority, trampling upon the rights and liberties of The People. So grievous have these abuses become, especially in the last two years, The People have concluded the usurpations of the federal government exceed those of the King of Great Britain during the 18th century, abuses and deprivations causing the issuance of the first American Declaration of Independence, sparking the American Revolution.

The injuries inflicted upon The People of these United States by elitist politicians in Washington, and by the current occupant of the White House, are so numerous and so outrageous as to warrant a recounting of their history, demonstrating the clear intention of this government to exert complete control over most aspects of American life, to the destruction of our Constitution, our freedoms and our God-given civil rights.

Let the facts speak for themselves. This President and his allies have:

Systematically promoted a globalist agenda, contrary to the notion of American sovereignty;

Fraudulently installed a national healthcare system against The Will of the People, on its face an example of illegal wealth redistribution, exacting the largest tax increases in history without the consent of those being taxed, going so far as to force individuals to purchase insurance, a clear violation of the Constitution, even insisting government control all medical decisions from cradle to grave;

Squandered the nation's resources creating insurmountable debt and bankrupting the country, leaving our posterity with little hope of economic recovery, for decades, perhaps forever. Making matters worse, in their efforts to 'fundamentally transform America,' public officials in the Senate and the White House have refused to enact the most basic common sense measures to avoid economic catastrophe;

Installed so-called finance reform that effectively concentrated more unconstitutional power in the federal government, giving that government virtually unlimited bailout authority and control over financial institutions. This, in addition to other power plays allowing the government to take over private industries in other sectors without any authority whatsoever;

Mismanaged government control of half of the residential mortgage industry, control seized, in itself unconstitutional, causing the greatest financial crisis since the Great Depression, all in the name of redistributing wealth by fraudulently providing homeownership to unqualified buyers;

Failed to adequately provide for the national defense by releasing secret Justice Department documents advising the CIA on intelligence gathering, acting against the combined advice of several former CIA directors, and in so doing, seriously damaged the ability of the United States to provide for the common defense, helping our enemies, demoralizing our military and intelligence professionals;

By executive order allowed taxpayer money to be spent overseas provisioning abortions, a move in complete contradiction to the will of The People;

Contrary to the rule of law, due process, and the presumption of innocence, promoted the idea of detentions based only on suspicion of future, potential criminal violations;

Argued for more surveillance of private citizens without a warrant, insisting complete government immunity from prosecution;

Refused to fulfill obligations enforcing the law in the instance of Black Panthers threatening voters in 2008 in Philadelphia;

Declared the EPA a lead agency to begin enacting provisions of Cap 'n Trade legislation without such legislation being passed by Congress, effectively using the EPA for executive action outside the provisions of the Constitution, including attendant taxation, without representation;

Ignored the 10th Amendment at every turn, seeking to punish states whenever they are perceived acting contrary to federal will, as in the case of Arizona's immigration law;

Promoted on every front the same-sex relationship agenda, again, against the Will of the Majority;

Refused to defend in court settled law in the Defense of Marriage Act, arbitrarily declaring DOMA unconstitutional, an act usurping the powers and responsibilities of the Supreme Court, another violation of the Constitution, and the oath of office;

Vowed to override the Supreme Court on the matter of free speech and campaign finance involving unions and corporations, even using the State of the Union Address to essentially declare war on the Justices;

Accepted campaign contributions from foreign sources over the internet in violation of the law, thus corrupting the American electoral process;

Virtually ignored border security and illegal immigration and reduced funding intended to secure the southern border;

Engaged several world tours to apologize for America, bowing to foreign tyrants, accommodating enemies of the United States, denigrating friends and allies, and rendering foreign relations and foreign policy impotent, and in disarray.

Appointed any number of extra-constitutional executive czars working to effect substantial change in society without the consent of The People, the Congress, or the Courts, as in the case of appointing a same-sex activist to promote homosexuality in the public schools, going so far as to encourage normalization of aberrant behavior even in the minds of young children, all to the exclusion of parental involvement and consent;

Aggravated racial tensions and promoted class warfare by pitting one group against another;

Denied our Judeo-Christian heritage, proclaiming we are an emerging Muslim nation, working in various ways to deny Christians their civil rights;

Involved the U.S. in an illegal Libyan adventure, without any strategic purpose, with no perceivable national security interest, placing American military personnel under the command of NATO, a war costing taxpayers $2M per day;

Completely neglected domestic energy development having everything to do with national security and economic recovery;

Systematically sought to infringe 1st and 2nd Amendment rights;

Deployed resources to destroy private citizens, most notably, Sarah Palin.

Time and again The People have sought redress, through free and reasonable expression. Over and over by ballot, letters, emails, phone calls, peaceful demonstrations and petitions, The People have asked the federal government to balance the books, clear the debt, get out of the way so The People can accomplish economic revival, and relent from power grabs to centralize and concentrate power.

Time and again The People have been ignored. And when The People began protesting in the streets two years ago, as is their Right as free people under the Constitution and the laws of God, government officials, including this President, denigrated those good citizens, calling them racists, hate mongers, tea baggers, tools of corporations, puppets of partisans. Even when those good people voted in November 2010, sending a clear "STOP" message to the President and Congress, those good people were either maligned or ignored.

The character of a President and a Congress is thus marked by every act which may define a tyrant, and, they are, therefore, unfit to be the rulers of free people.

We The People, therefore, appealing to the Supreme Judge of the world, solemnly declare our full intention, by any rightful means available, to remove from office all those politicians and office holders who have been complicit in the above delineated offenses, and to severe ourselves from them, refusing to recognize their authority. We declare, by the Rights afforded us by our Creator, that we are Absolved from all Allegiance to the present abusive and lawless regime in the Executive Branch and in the U.S. Senate.

And for the support of this Declaration, with a firm reliance on the protection of Divine Providence, we mutually pledge to each other our Lives, our Fortunes, and our sacred Honor.

DEATH OF OSAMA: CAUSE CÉLÈBRE?

May 2, 2011

A lot of people give Barack Obama credit for killing master terrorist Osama bin Laden, among them, Dick Cheney and George Bush, two individuals Osama condemned and Obama denigrated. Ah well, there's no accounting for class in some people. On the other hand, how do you account for the classless, self-aggrandizing, two-faced deceivers in the White House?

Last night Obama said a number of things when he announced Osama's demise. If you listened carefully, you heard a lot of "Me," and "I" in those remarks.

Oh, he gave our military and CIA the obligatory nod. However, any objective observer must acknowledge Obama wanted everyone to know, he is the man. He used this development, as he uses every opportunity, to advance his own cause, which, at the moment, is re-election.

If Obama could sell socialized medicine by the blood of Osama, he'd do it.

One of Obama's remarks was especially irritating.

"The death of bin Laden marks the most significant achievement to date in our nation's effort to defeat Al Qaeda."

Translation: 'I got Osama and therefore I am responsible for our greatest achievement.' Really Mr. Obama? Seriously?

A question, please, Mr. Obama. Does your achievement eclipse the efforts of others to:

- capture and incarcerate hundreds of terrorists,
- kill thousands of terrorists on the battlefield,
- defeat the Taliban in Afghanistan (until two years ago),
- liberate 25 million Iraqis and remove the mad man Saddam,
- forward the dream of Iraqi freedom bought by the blood of thousands of Americans, (a dream now at serious risk),
- decimate Al Qaeda leadership, eradicate of most of bin Laden's networks, bases of operation and resources, and prevent further terror attacks on our soil, that is, until you took office?

Seems to a lot of people that Mr. Bush and his administration, loved by the military throughout, were and are responsible for several "most significant" achievements for many long years after 9/11, with no help from Democrats, the Left, or Mr. Obama at any time during those long and difficult years. Indeed, Mr. Bush's job, and the work of the military and intelligence services were made more difficult by the words and actions of Mr. Obama and Co. What is "most significant" was Mr. Bush's ability to fight and win at home and abroad versus an array of adversaries.

Another of Mr. Obama's troubling remarks was: "Our war is not against Islam. Bin Laden was not a Muslim leader." (To his credit he used the word *war* at least.)

Perhaps Mr. Obama's affection for Muslims and his embrace of Islam dims his view of history, or perhaps he simply cannot stomach the clear lessons of history, choosing to ignore centuries of Muslim aggression perpetrated against the West.

To be sure many modern Muslims want peace and swear off violence, but that still leaves many millions armed to the teeth, worshipping the martyr bin Laden. In truth, bin Laden was the leader of millions of Muslims practicing a form of Islam, a fundamental branch of the warrior code brought by Mohammed in the first place. We'd be better off knowing our enemy, seeing him with a clear eye, and being led by someone who speaks the truth without equivocation.

Speculation has it the killing of bin Laden was ordered, that *he was not to be taken prisoner.* Who knows? Reports conflict. There is no clarification from the WH yet. Perhaps Eric Holder had trouble deciding where to try bin Laden had he been taken into custody. Maybe the administration was fearful of taking bin Laden alive, fearing reprisals or a PR challenge. (They couldn't very well send him to Gitmo.) It seems to others bin Laden possessed a wealth of information, intelligence that could have saved many American lives.

We do know the Saudi king hated bin Laden's guts. We do know Obama behaves as if the Saudi king is his monarch. Can we then conclude Osama's assassination was as much an act of war as a service to the king?

Mr. Obama also said in his prepared remarks he will relentlessly defend Americans and our friends in the days to come. For some, that kind of talk reveals the deceiver.

We can only imagine how the Israelis feel after Obama turned his back on them, giving their enemies quarter, even encouragement, first promising a united Jerusalem, then working to divide the city.

Career CIA personnel must be biting their tongues in view of Obama's release of top secret intelligence documents which made their work much more difficult and dangerous. President Obama, as commander in chief, commands a military he despises. Never forget he joined the howling mob condemning our soldiers as thugs killing civilians. Never forget he decried enhanced interrogation, methods leading Navy Seals to bin Laden's door. Never forget Obama stood by and didn't lift a finger as Seals and Marines were prosecuted for no reason, then found not guilty. Never forget how Obama publically criticized our military for Gitmo, in reality a model prison, and for Abu Ghraib, an anomaly. Never forget Obama joined the leftist screed that cast the Seals a Cheney death squad.

Military personnel, operating under impossible rules of engagement, must be shaking their heads like Justice Alito, amazed at the brazenness of a chief executive operating beyond accountability, military people now being forced to pretend same-sex behavior has a place in the barracks and on the battlefield causing no injury to military readiness. So much for Mr. Obama's sense of relentless defense.

By Mr. Obama's logic, if Gitmo was a recruiting tool for terrorists, then battalion La Cage aux Folles ought to rebuild Al Qaeda in a heartbeat. Remember that Muslims go a bit crazy about homosexuality. Imagine the fate awaiting a homosexual American as a prisoner in the hands of a Muslim terrorist.

Finally, in his prepared remarks, Mr. Obama urged us to remember the sense of unity we felt right after 9/11, a unity utterly destroyed in short order by Leftist political operatives, including Mr. Obama, people who put personal ambition ahead of country.

They can wrap themselves in the flag and urge unity today, but those words sound hollow when it is clear the agenda remains the "fundamental transformation of America," according to a President who talks about the greatness of American values, then works to replacement them with a set of values the Founders would find horrifying, chief among them, ultimate dictatorial power in Washington, and the necessary death of individual liberty to make way for global collectivism.

So, bin Laden is dead, but his minions press on to achieve his vision of global collective theocracy, while Obama moves forward with his parallel vision, global secular socialism.

And all this is cause for celebration?

PINBALL PRESIDENT

May 29, 2011
After ambushing Netanyahu and kissing the boots of Hamas, our Pinball President bounced off the schooling he received from the Israeli prime minister to shoot out across the seas.

Have you noticed this guy's pattern? At most every controversial turn he hops on Air Force One for another expensive, ineffectual junket to hobnob with elites overseas.

Obama went on to fumble the toast to the Queen, then bored the Parliament to tears before squeezing the Europeans for $40 billion in aid to the illusory Arab spring movement, even as Hamas leaders were saying they'd never recognize Israel, essentially telling Obama to go to H-E-double hockey sticks.

Pin. Ball. Wizard. Not.

Back home inflation is eating Americans alive, the debt crisis intensifies, and all Obama's allies can do is demonize Paul Ryan, sharpen their knives for another round of carving at Palin's table, and dig dirt on every other viable GOP candidate, relishing a replay of 2008 when Obama's flying monkeys managed to snooker the public and assassinate Clinton and McCain all with foreign money and millions of new starry-eyed voters now buried under mountains of crushing debt.

Bang. Flash. Buzz. Ding, ding, ding.

The slaughter goes on in Syria, Libyan civilians are being roasted, unopposed Venezuela continues to arm and seek nuclear weapons, and freedom lovers in Iran are ignored. At the same time, Obama is making nice with the Taliban in Afghanistan, Shi'ites are on the verge of taking over in Iraq while the Pinball President takes time to play ping pong, flip burgers and assure the stricken in Missouri he'll soon be there, as if his presence will somehow soothe and reassure.

The financial Titanic steams full on, oblivious to the massive iceberg dead ahead, its razor edges about to rip the guts out of the global economy. The Pinball President at the helm orders "stay the course" as his crew below decks dismantles our last defense against tyranny, thereby squeezing the last breath out of liberty.

Tomorrow Obama will urge us to honor our war dead, those 2.2 million who gave their lives that liberty might live. He honors their sacrifice by dismantling the republic they died to preserve.

Tilt.

KRUGMAN, THE ANTI-AMERICAN LEFT, AND 9/11

September 11, 2011

Paul Krugman, the so-called economist, the genius who claims Obama's stimulus was insufficient (arguing the President should have wasted much more of our money,) this 'intellect' writes today in the N.Y. Times online:
"What happened after 9/11 — and I think even people on the right know this, whether they admit it or not — was deeply shameful. The atrocity should have been a unifying event, but instead it became a wedge issue. Fake heroes like Bernie Kerik, Rudy Giuliani, and, yes, George W. Bush raced to cash in on the horror. And then the attack was used to justify an unrelated war the neocons wanted to fight, for all the wrong reasons. The memory of 9/11 has been irrevocably poisoned; it has become an occasion for shame. And in its heart, the nation knows it."

I agree with Krugman. What happened after 9/11 was shameful.

People like Krugman jumped to conclusions and immediately started demonizing our President, even as they made excuses for radical Islam. Krugman and the anti-American Left used the invasion of Iraq to cause division at home. Why? Only to advance their narrow ideological agenda, a distinctly anti-American agenda. "United

We Stand," lasted only a few months, thanks to people like Krugman and the cruel and cynical Left.

Krugman and his kind ignored the Authorization to Use Force passed by Congress, giving the President a green light in Iraq. They ignored the Bush administrations many efforts to get the U.N. on board, as well as the work done to form the coalition.

They ignored intelligence reports from a variety of nations indicating Saddam had WMD, intended using WMD, was developing WMD, had used WMD against the Iranians and his own people, and was deeply supportive of Al Qaeda and other terrorist organizations.

They ignored substantial intelligence indicating Saddam had renewed his nuclear weapons program.

Krugman and Co. ignored the Gulf War cease fire agreement .

They ignored the fact renewed hostility, rather than being primarily a matter of preemption, was instead a legal resumption of the Gulf War due to Saddam's serial violations of the cease fire agreement.

Subsequently, when evidence of WMD weapons programs was discovered, they ignored the news and denied the reality that the invasion of Iraq in 2003 was fully justified for any number of reasons.

And when the surge resulted in victory and success and when the Iraqis established their own constitution, Krugman and his Leftist traitors ignored the desire of the Iraqi people to embrace freedom.

When America helped rebuild and restore Iraq and helped the Iraqis profit from their own oil resources, Krugman and the anti-American Left continued the chant 'no war for oil,' even though it was clearly proven a lie.

When the Iraqis embraced elections and demonstrated incredible courage to face down terror in league with our military, Krugman and his cowardly allies stood silent instead of admitting their mistake and applauding the Iraqis.

And when our young men and women fought and died and came home wounded all to defend the idea of liberty and help the Iraqis achieve it, for however long, Krugman and the anti-American Left denigrated their sacrifice and gave aid and comfort to our enemies.

Now, on this 10th anniversary of the horrors of 9/11, perpetrated by radical Islamic terrorists still operational in the world, and within our own borders, Krugman has the classless affrontery to attack good men who acted on our behalf, giving their full measure of devotion, a devotion lost on the dark heart of people like Krugman who've no conscience, no sense, and no vestige of patriotism existent in their withered souls.

The shame is all yours Krugman.

The rest of us honor the fallen and our military and patriotic leaders today and we encourage one another in faith and love of country.

AFTERWORD

"Preparing for the Future and the 2012 Elections"
By David Crowe
Founder and Director of Restore America
www.restoreamerica.org
December 14, 2010

Without God we can't, but without us, He won't.

Dr. Lloyd Ogilvie,
former chaplain, United States Senate

Two days ago Congressman Paul Ryan said, 'The decisions made by the new Congress in the next year and by the American people in the next election will determine whether we embrace *bold ideas* to restore the American dream, or accept the status quo as our 'new normal' and merely try to manage America's decline."

I went on to say, 'If we fail in the next 23 months to awaken the Body of Christ to its responsibility at the ballot box, we are, as Paul Ryan stated, simply accepting' faithlessly' the satanically-inspired status quo as our 'new normal,' and marching' by choice' back into the harsh realities of the contemporary 'wilderness' and away from the blessing of God.'

Of the 52 million evangelical Christians who are eligible to vote, 20 million did not vote in the November 2008 general election! Worse, 30 million did not vote in the 2010 election!

Is this the "new normal" for Christians in America?

If America is to be restored to the vision, values, and wisdom of the Founders, Christians must take their 'salt and light' citizenship responsibility far more seriously and vote in much greater numbers in the 2012 Election!

It is necessary that Christians embrace the *'bold idea'* that we should get our citizenship house in order to avoid our own and the nation's fiscal, moral, and spiritual bankruptcy. Honoring the One we claim is Emanuel, 'God with us,' and all who have sacrificed life and limb to preserve our country, is a good work, pleasing to our LORD.

(Printed with permission.)

EPILOGUE

Boomers were given every advantage. We were raised in a time of relative peace and tremendous prosperity. We enjoyed security, good education, and the comforts. We were told we could do anything, that we were wonderful. After college, we took affluence for granted and ran up a lot of debt. Overall, we were spoiled rotten. Discussing our generation with a friend lately—how we did preserving liberty and passing on the blessings to the next generation—his assessment was: "We blew it."

Perhaps it's time to make up for that.